Dodger Stadium

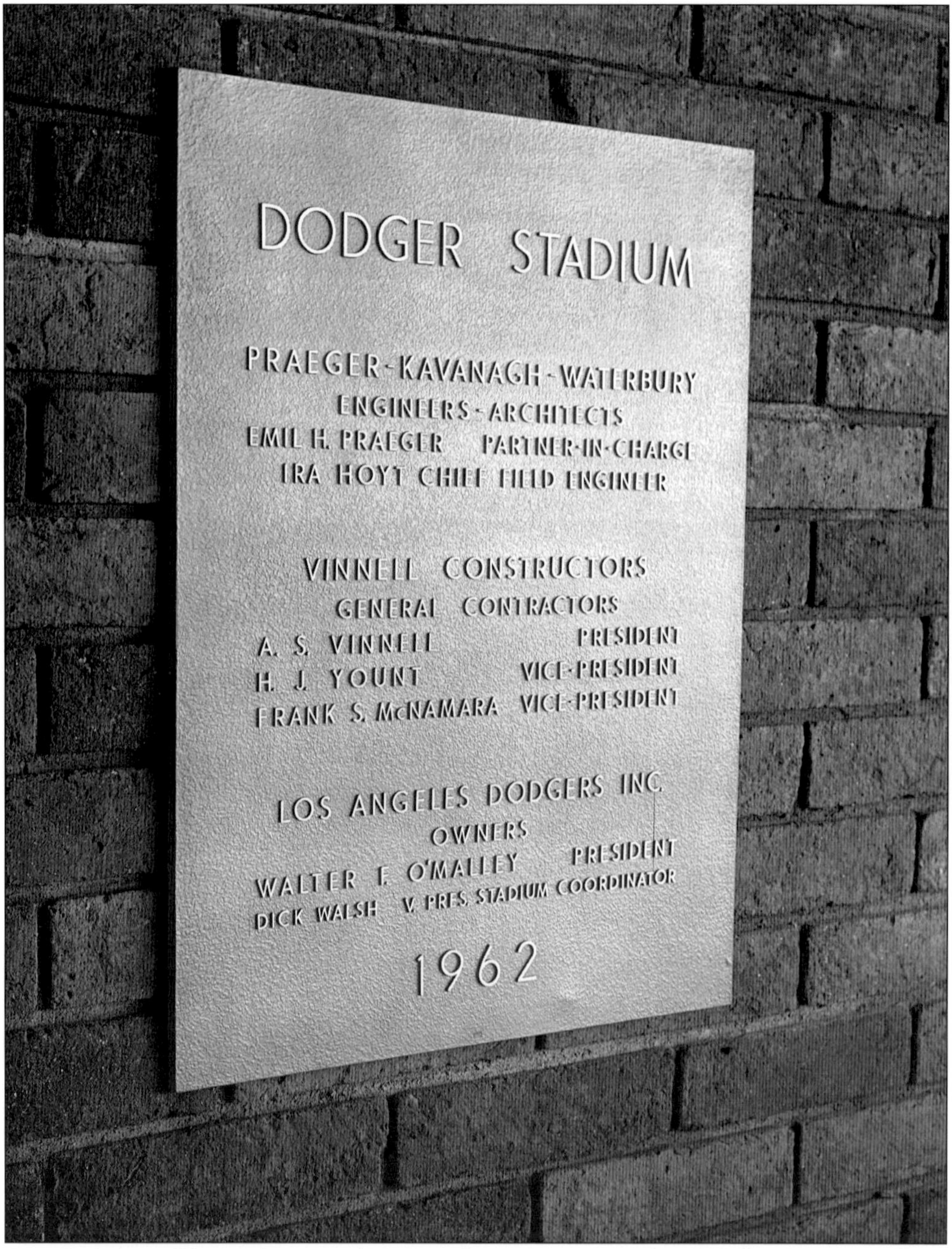

THE BUILDERS. Those who contributed to the construction of Dodger Stadium are saluted on a plaque that remains in place on the top deck of the ballpark behind home plate. Those attending a dedication ceremony in April 1962 included the family of Dodger President Walter O'Malley, along with engineer Emil Praeger.

Dodger Stadium

Mark Langill

Arcadia Publishing

ISBN 978-0-7385-2868-7

Published by Arcadia Publishing
Charleston, South Carolina

Printed in the United States of America

Library of Congress Catalog Card Number: 2003114524

For all general information contact Arcadia Publishing at:
Telephone 843-853-2070
Fax 843-853-0044
E-Mail sales@arcadiapublishing.com
For customer service and orders:
Toll-Free 1-888-313-2665

Visit us on the Internet at www.arcadiapublishing.com

For Diane Langill, the All-Star mom who let her son have fun at the ballpark.

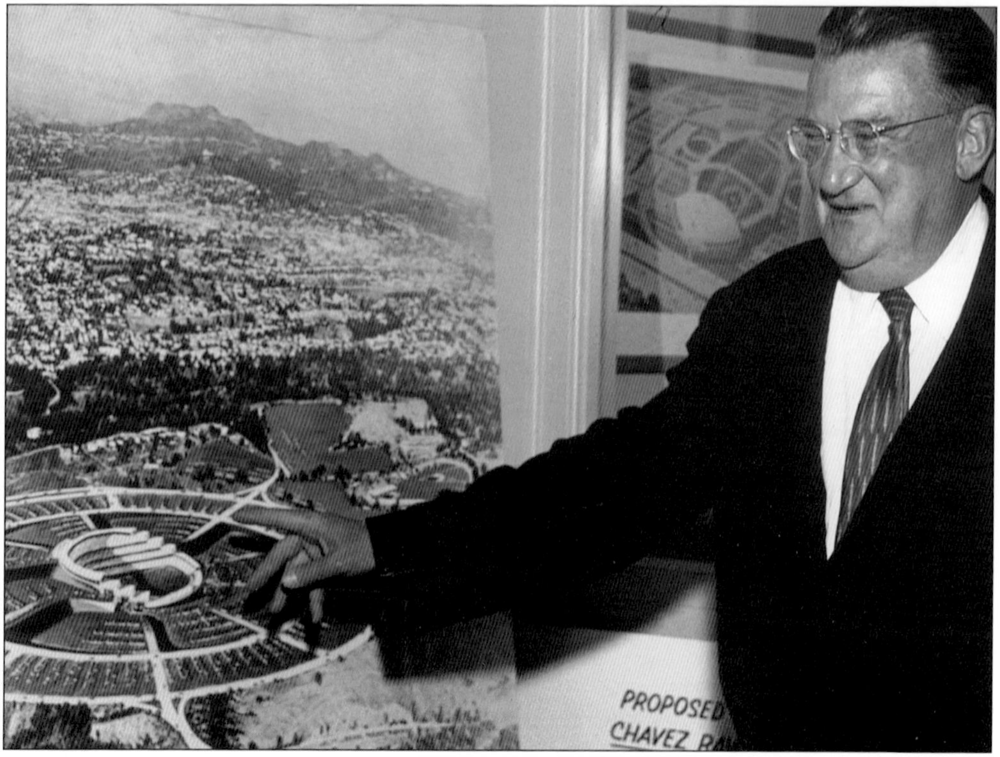

WALTER O'MALLEY. The president of the Los Angeles Dodgers points to a model of a proposed ballpark in the hills of Los Angeles known as "Chavez Ravine" in 1958. The 56,000-seat stadium opened on April 10, 1962, and more than 115 million fans have since attended Dodger baseball games.

Contents

ACKNOWLEDGMENTS

For this book, special thanks to my colleagues in the Dodger front office, including Communications Vice President Derrick Hall, External Affairs Vice President Tommy Hawkins, and the members of the publicity and broadcasting departments: Paul Gomez, Chris Gutierrez, Dave Tuttle, John Olguin, Josh Rawitch, Rachelle Smith, and Donna Carter. Thanks to the staff at the O'Malley-Seidler LLP, including Brent Shyer, Robert Schweppe, Tasha Noriega, Max Lane, and Dianne Mesa.

As a former *Pasadena Star-News* beat reporter, my admiration to the many talented media members I have worked alongside, including Bob Keisser, Kevin Modesti, Ross Newhan, Terry Johnson, Gordie Verrell, Ben Platt, Joe Hendrickson, Ken Gurnick, Bill Plaschke, Kevin Bronson, Larry Goren, Ron Lewis, Randy Hill, and Joe Resnick. Matt McHale, the champion mentor of the Pasadena newsroom, took a high school intern to his first stadium event using a media pass—a glorious rained-out affair on August 18, 1983 in which I met everyone in the press box over the course of four hours while waiting for a Mets-Dodgers game never played.

And gold stars for faculty members along the way who offered encouragement in school, including Jack Smith, Andrew Boyd, Greg Ring, John Ukropina, Paul Smith, Cynthia Rawitch, Mary Ida Phair, Gretchen Foulger, Jack Dalton, Sandi Iverson, Mikki Bolliger, and Reiko Ikkanda, who was skeptical of a life in sports but pushed good typing skills.

From 1956 to 1987, three men worked as Dodger publicity directors, serving as a liaison between the organization and the fans, generating storylines, photo themes, and any miscellaneous item requiring class and creativity. The contributions of Arthur E. "Red" Patterson, Fred Claire, and Steve Brener remain cornerstones to any history project involving the Dodger organization.

INTRODUCTION

Any sports stadium in the United States is a melting pot of personalities, opinions, vocations, and generations. And most adults still carry their childhood memories to the ballpark as their favorite player or heart-thumping game can suddenly materialize with the blink of an eye.

This book is about Dodger Stadium, the revolutionary 56,000-seat structure that opened in 1962 and evolved into a cultural landmark in Southern California with a breathtaking view of Los Angeles to the south, green tree-lined Elysian hills to the north and east, and the San Gabriel Mountains beyond.

"It's still the most beautiful ballpark in the major leagues," said Dodger Hall of Fame broadcaster Vin Scully. "Over the years, the backdrop beyond the outfield has increased in beauty and the landscape is so inspiring, especially at twilight on those cool summer evenings. There isn't anything to distract a baseball fan when coming to a game at Dodger Stadium. The ballpark is surrounded by beauty and everyone can focus on the game. Even fortysomething years after it was built, the stadium is a tribute to Walter O'Malley's vision."

There is also a special place within Dodger Stadium, tucked away from the obvious landmarks and carefully preserved and packaged like a grandparents' cedar chest in a dusty attic. Assembled in a special storage area are rows of four-drawer metal cabinets, filled to the brim with manila-colored files and photos of Dodger players, executives, and press conferences. This is the heart of the organization with its roots in New York, a storied and colorful Brooklyn franchise that joined the National League in 1890. These photographs chronicle the West Coast memories generated from more than four decades of Dodger baseball games in Los Angeles, along with concerts and other unique events at Walter O'Malley's dream stadium.

Within the piles of photographs are images frozen in time, capturing the range of emotions felt by players and coaches on a daily basis while trying to perform against their world-class colleagues. The sport's premise is a split-second confrontation highlighting the ultimate power and physical exertion. Only a camera's lens can reveal the maximum exertion during a pitcher's release point and the batter's wooden bat slicing through the air on a frantic pendulum, hoping to make square contact on a round baseball.

When the mix of mathematical geometry, aerodynamic physics, and pure luck are in alignment, the resulting photos can become works of art: Ron Cey's eyes looking toward the horizon as a probable home-run ball takes flight; the spindly 6-foot-4 frame of Ramon Martinez in his prime, unfolding like a flower as his right arm slowly readies for the bull-whip delivery.

Along with the Rembrandts, there are the outtakes, the "blooper" photos that confirm major leaguers are indeed human—batting swing sequences that won't be found in any textbook, first basemen digging the ball out of the dirt with their eyes closed, teammates bumping one another in the shallow outfield as the ball rolls away.

The gladiators, though, do not battle in a private arena. During their confrontations, kids in the grandstands yearn for popcorn, cotton candy, or a Dodger Dog before returning to the souvenir booth. Their parents might talk about the day's events while a young couple in the next row might not even know the visiting team's identity or the current score.

For seven decades, the Dodgers have utilized the talents of team photographers who focused their attention on the entire ballpark experience. They enjoy special access to the world of Major League Baseball, which includes the airplane flights, bus rides, closed clubhouse meetings, workout rooms, the kitchen area, card games, and players rehabilitating injuries. Current Dodger photographers Jon SooHoo, Juan Ocampo, and Jill Weisleder have added digital cameras to their arsenal, which can translate into thousands of images per month.

This edition also contains the work of past Dodger photographers Frank Worth, L. Andrew Castle, Andrew Bernstein, Art Foxall, Mark Malone, Don Ploke, Darryl Norenberg, Mike Cronin, Richard Kee, Craig Molenhouse, and Alvin Chung, Their portraits share a common thread, as the basic layout of the script on the front of the uniform hasn't changed in appearance since the early 1930s. The artful "Dodgers" worn by Babe Ruth in the Brooklyn first-base coaching box in 1938 is in the same style as the jersey presented to Edwin Jackson on his 20th birthday when he made his major league debut in September 2003.

In Brooklyn, the most famous photo taken by Barney Stein wasn't an action shot. Instead, it was the portrait of utter dejection following a 1951 playoff loss to the New York Giants at the Polo Grounds on Bobby Thomson's ninth-inning home run. Just outside the Brooklyn clubhouse, disconsolate pitcher Ralph Branca lies face down on a set of concrete steps, exposing only his unlucky No. 13 uniform back as he stretched out and burying his head within his crossed arms. Coach Cookie Lavagetto sits alongside staring aimlessly into the distance, still clutching near his left shoe the stubble remainder of a postgame cigarette.

And the frames snapped before and after the famous picture, or the same moment captured from a different angle, provide a unique sidebar to the storylines that blend into folklore. Berstein's 1988 World Series photo on page 89 of Kirk Gibson, raising his right fist in triumph while hobbling up the first-base line, punctuates the most memorable moment in Southern California sports history. But a sequence of batting shots taken from the third-base photo well location reveal Gibson muscled a home-run swung while standing on his front foot, which even with photographic proof doesn't seem possible against a star relief pitcher, Oakland's Dennis Eckersley, in the bottom of the ninth inning. So sit back and enjoy a decade-by-decade look at Dodger Stadium—the construction, Opening Day pageantry, Hollywood Stars, community events, musical performances, behind-the-scene personalities, and playoff drama. Those metal file cabinets from the ballpark's archives are slowly opening and a photographic journey is about to begin!

ONE

Construction

The dream of a grand baseball stadium materialized amidst the frustration, inspiration, and determination of Walter O'Malley, whose creation of Dodger Stadium would become a jewel in a four-decade career in the major leagues. While representing the Brooklyn Trust Company, O'Malley also owned Dodger season tickets to Ebbets Field in New York during the early 1940s. When he left his successful law practice to become a vice president and general counsel for the Dodgers in 1946, O'Malley wrote to New York–based architect Emil Praeger and asked for ideas about "enlarging or replacing our present stadium."

Thus began a 10-year campaign by O'Malley to find a new ballpark for the Dodgers. Although successful on the field with either first- or second-place finishes in all but one season from 1946 to 1956, the Dodgers' cozy Ebbets Field was an aging facility in the middle of a Flatbush neighborhood and had a 32,000-seat capacity and parking for 700 cars. O'Malley succeeded Branch Rickey as team president in November 1950.

In a May 26, 1955 letter to architect Buckminster Fuller, O'Malley outlined ideas for a potential domed ballpark, having earlier spoken to representatives from the Owens-Corning Fiberglass Corp. about working with their rigid corrugated product. O'Malley envisioned a year-round facility immune to inclement weather because of a dome constructed of translucent material, which would open a new horizon for baseball. In his closing line to Fuller, O'Malley wrote, "I am not interested in building just another park." And O'Malley hoped to stay in Brooklyn. He explored numerous plans for a site at the intersection of Atlantic and Flatbush Avenues and felt the confluence of transportation (all major subways, Long Island Railroad) to the ballpark would boost attendance and improve the surrounding areas.

Despite the desire of the city to have a major league team, Los Angeles voters on June 1, 1955 rejected a proposition using $4.5 million in bonds to fund the building of a municipal baseball stadium. O'Malley saved a newspaper clipping from this topic because if the Dodgers were to relocate to the West Coast, O'Malley would have to build his own ballpark.

Meanwhile, O'Malley announced his intentions for the Dodgers to play seven "home" games in New Jersey's Roosevelt Stadium in 1956. O'Malley served notice to New York officials he was serious about leaving Ebbets Field following the 1957 season.

In February 1957, O'Malley purchased the Chicago Cubs' minor league franchise, the Los Angeles Angels, along with their home ballpark, Wrigley Field. O'Malley secured the territorial rights to the Los Angeles market and had a home if the team was unsuccessful building a new stadium in Brooklyn.

During his negotiations with New York officials, O'Malley also met with Los Angeles representatives after the 1956 World Series. On a May 2, 1957 helicopter tour, O'Malley was shown the land where he immediately envisioned freeway access from all directions.

In September, Los Angeles agreed to exchange 300 acres of land in Chavez Ravine to the Dodgers in return for the Dodgers' commitment to build a 50,000-seat stadium. The Dodgers also exchanged the deed to Wrigley Field to the city and agreed to pay a property tax estimated at $345,000. The contract also included a commitment from the city to spend $2 million on grading for the area and $2.74 million from the county for the construction of access roads.

The Chavez Ravine at one time was designated as a Federal Public Housing project in the early 1950s. When the project failed, residents were later offered independently assessed valuations for the properties and were evicted. The 169 acres had been sold by the federal government back to the City of Los Angeles in 1953 for $1,279,204 with the proviso that it be used for a "public purpose."

On October 7, 1957, the Los Angeles City Council, by a vote of 10-4, adopted an ordinance that entered the city into a contract with the Dodgers. The next day, the Dodgers announced their intentions to move to Los Angeles in a historic West Coast expansion of baseball as the Giants also moved from New York to San Francisco. The Dodgers would play their first four seasons in Los Angeles at the Los Angeles Memorial Coliseum while a series of legal challenges and court battles delayed the construction project.

Chavez Ravine was a difficult site because of a network of washes, gullies, and gulches that were interlaced with hills and twisting roads. More than 8 million cubic yards of earth were moved to reshape the area. The northern face of the rock and sandstone hill was cut down and shaped into a rough amphitheater and benches were cut into the sloping floor to support the stadium foundations and pedestals. To control erosion, a two-inch-thick concrete was sprayed over the area. The 124-foot-high grandstand has three major cantilever tiers built on 78 precast bents.

The actual construction of Dodger Stadium didn't begin until after Labor Day 1960, which left only 19 months to move the remaining 5.5 million yards of dirt en route to building the stadium.

On September 3, 1959, a $646,890 contract for grading the site of Dodger Stadium was awarded by the Board of Public Works to Vinnell Constructors of Alhambra, which submitted the lowest bid among the 11 submitted and was 9.8 percent under the city's estimate.

Jack Yount, the Vinnell contractor in charge who specialized in concrete projects and had experience with freeway interchanges in Southern California, never imagined his company would be asked to build the ballpark using Praeger's design and O'Malley's input. The specialty of the company was installing the sewers and drainage areas associated with any municipal project involving large amounts of concrete. But O'Malley feared a deal with another company might lead to delays with subcontractors. He wanted Yount to personally supervise the building of the ballpark and wanted the structure made of concrete instead of steel. On August 25, 1960, O'Malley signed a contract with Vinnell for the entire construction of the 56,000-seat stadium.

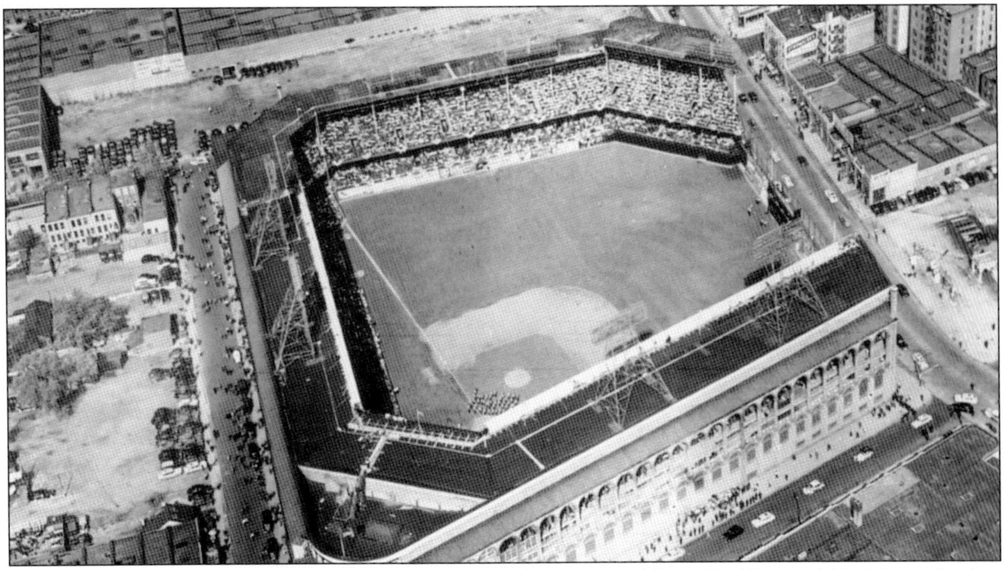

Ebbets Field. The Brooklyn Dodgers began playing at Ebbets Field in 1913. Named after team president Charles H. Ebbets, who owned the team from 1898 until his death in 1925, the ballpark was located in the Flatbush section of Brooklyn on the block bounded by Sullivan Place, Bedford Avenue, Montgomery Street, and McKeever Place. The original seating capacity was 25,000 and was later expanded to 32,000. The first televised game in baseball was broadcast from Ebbets Field in 1939. One of the most significant moments in sports and American history occurred in Brooklyn on April 15, 1947 when Hall of Famer Jackie Robinson broke the sport's color barrier with his major league debut at Ebbets Field.

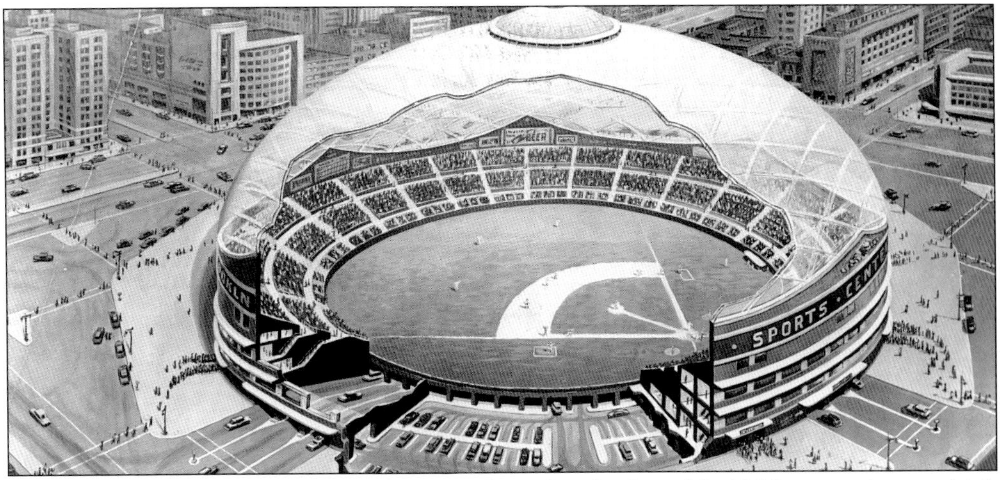

A Dome Grows in Brooklyn. That was the title of a June 20, 1956 press release, which began "Future home games of the Brooklyn Dodgers may be played under a giant plastic dome, according to current plans to replace the team's hallowed but decaying Ebbets Field. Preliminary designs of a dome have been made by famed architect Buckminster Fuller. Artist Frank Tinsley envisions the completed stadium in a picture (above) published in the July issue of Mechanix Illustrated Magazine." The proposed location was a 500-acre site beside the Long Island Rail Road's Brooklyn terminal. After a 10-year campaign to find a new ballpark site failed, the Dodgers moved to the West Coast following the 1957 season along with the Giants, who relocated from New York to San Francisco.

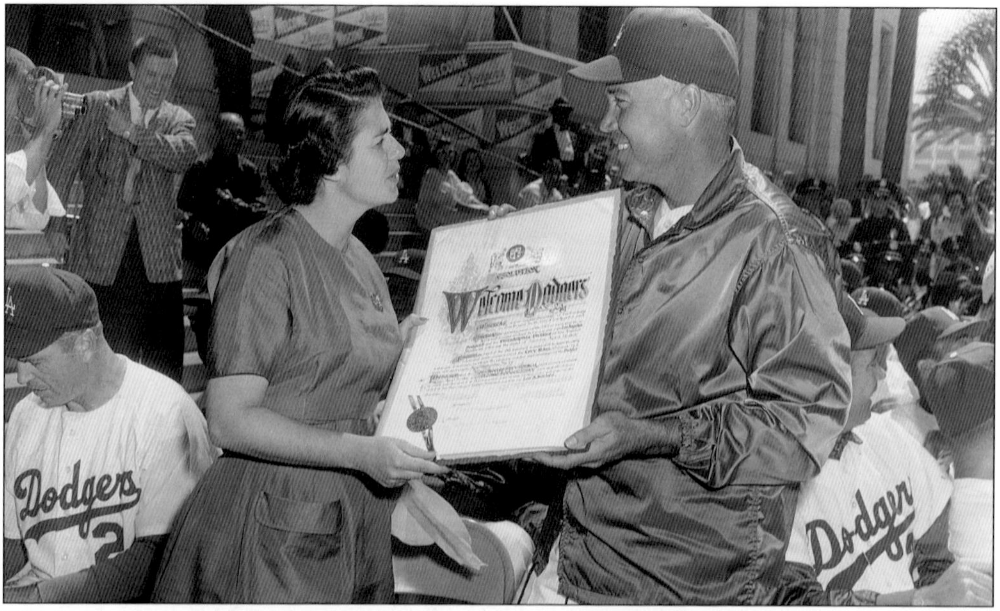

WELCOME TO LOS ANGELES. Rosalind Wyman, a member of the Los Angeles City Council and one of the early supporters of the city's efforts to invite a major league franchise to the West Coast, greets Dodger outfielder Duke Snider during Opening Day 1958 ceremonies at City Hall. At the podium, Dodger President Walter O'Malley presented a signed home plate from Ebbets Field to Los Angeles Mayor Norris Poulson, who threw out the ceremonial first pitch that April 18 afternoon at the Coliseum as Los Angeles defeated San Francisco, 6-5.

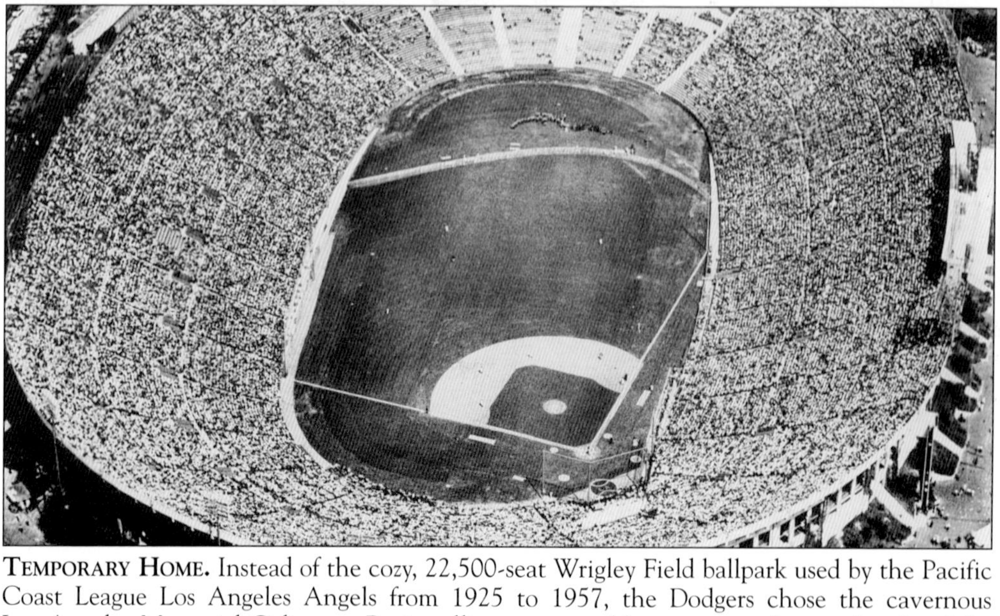

TEMPORARY HOME. Instead of the cozy, 22,500-seat Wrigley Field ballpark used by the Pacific Coast League Los Angeles Angels from 1925 to 1957, the Dodgers chose the cavernous Los Angeles Memorial Coliseum. By installing a removable screen on the north side of the Coliseum, it was possible to configure the football layout into a makeshift baseball field. A 42-foot-high screen had to be installed because of the short 251-foot left field fence. Los Angeles drew 78,762 fans for its Opening Day in 1958, and all three home games during the 1959 World Series drew more than 92,000.

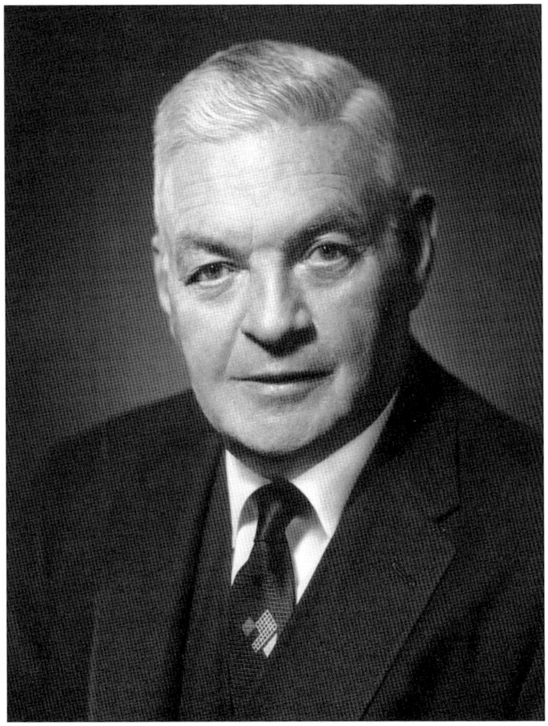

Emil Praeger. The former Navy Captain served in both World Wars and developed the original design of a concrete floating breakwater as a member of the Committee for Planning Normandy Invasion Facilities. A consulting engineer for the renovation of the White House and United National General Assembly, Praeger began his association with Walter O'Malley in 1946 when O'Malley began his quest for a new ballpark. Dodger Stadium in Los Angeles was the 11th site on which they mulled over plans and blueprints.

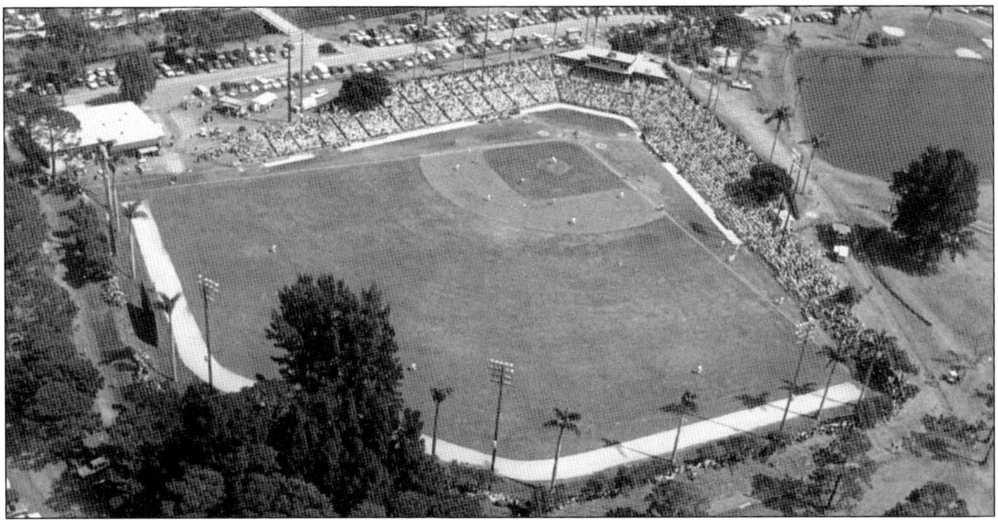

Their First Project. Captain Emil Praeger designed Holman Stadium at Dodgertown in Vero Beach, Florida. The Dodgers moved their spring training headquarters to the former Naval Air Station in 1948. Holman Stadium, which opened in March 1953, was built by excavating 20,000 cubic yards of sand, marl, and muck. The fill formed in mounds that were compacted and rolled, over which four-inch reinforced concrete was poured to make the stands. Walter O'Malley desired a stadium that had perfect sightlines—no poles to obstruct the customer's view of the field. He also wanted an intimate ballpark, especially capturing the feeling of bringing the players and fans close together during spring training. The idea of digging a hole and reshaping large amounts of earth instead of building a ballpark on existing flat ground would become one of the key points to the Dodger Stadium project.

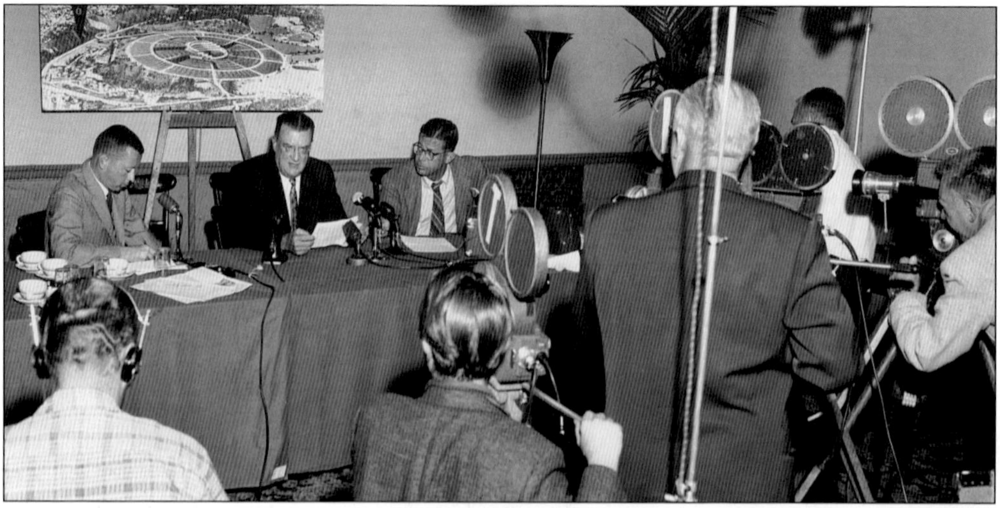

PROPOSITION B. When the Dodgers moved to Los Angeles, a coalition opposed the city's ordinance to approve the contract for Walter O'Malley's stadium construction project on the 300-acre Chavez Ravine site, and they collected enough signatures to force a vote of the electors on the referendum known as Proposition B. "I was not aware of a thing called a referendum," O'Malley said. "We don't have them in New York." On June 3, 1958, the referendum produced the largest non-Presidential election turnout in Los Angeles history as 62.3 percent of the city's registered voters cast ballots. The referendum favored the Dodgers by 25,785 votes with more than 670,000 total votes cast.

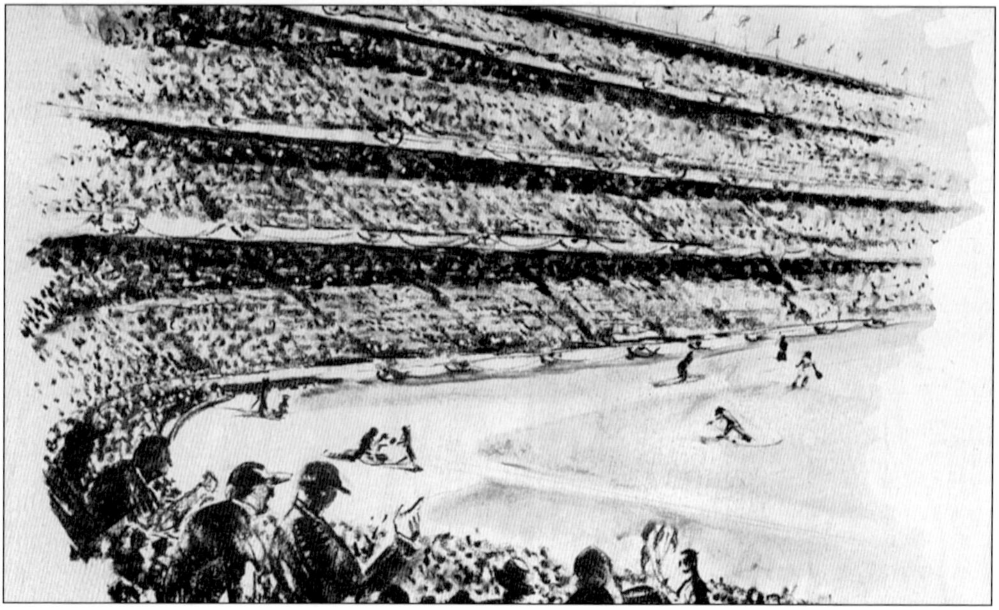

AN EARLY SKETCH. In the official game program, fans at the Los Angeles Memorial Coliseum in 1959 received a sneak preview of the Dodgers' new ballpark. O'Malley's original map submitted in 1959 to the City Council included what the *Los Angeles Mirror* described as "a myriad of commercial enterprises; auto service center, novelty and souvenir shops, restaurants and car wash centers." The plans also proposed a Dodger Hall of Fame, botanic garden, a mall, drive-in ticket offices, and quarters for both staff and visiting teams.

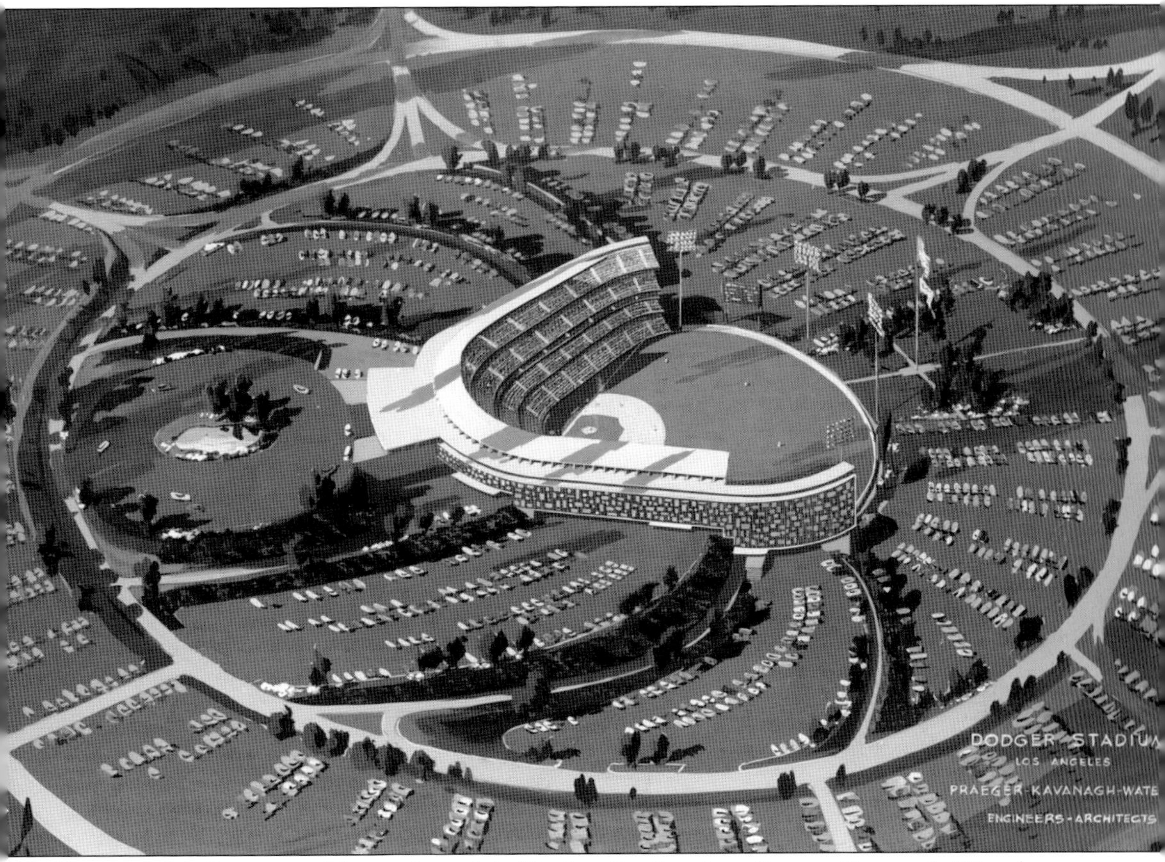

THE MODEL BALLPARK. This early model of Dodger Stadium from Praeger-Kavanagh-Waterbury Engineers in 1959 showcases some of the early stadium designs. The outfield pavilions were later added to the blueprints and the general admission level was reduced in seating capacity. The dugout seats were inspired by a similar layout of the dugout seats at Korakuen Stadium in Tokyo, where the Dodgers played during their 1956 Japan goodwill tour.

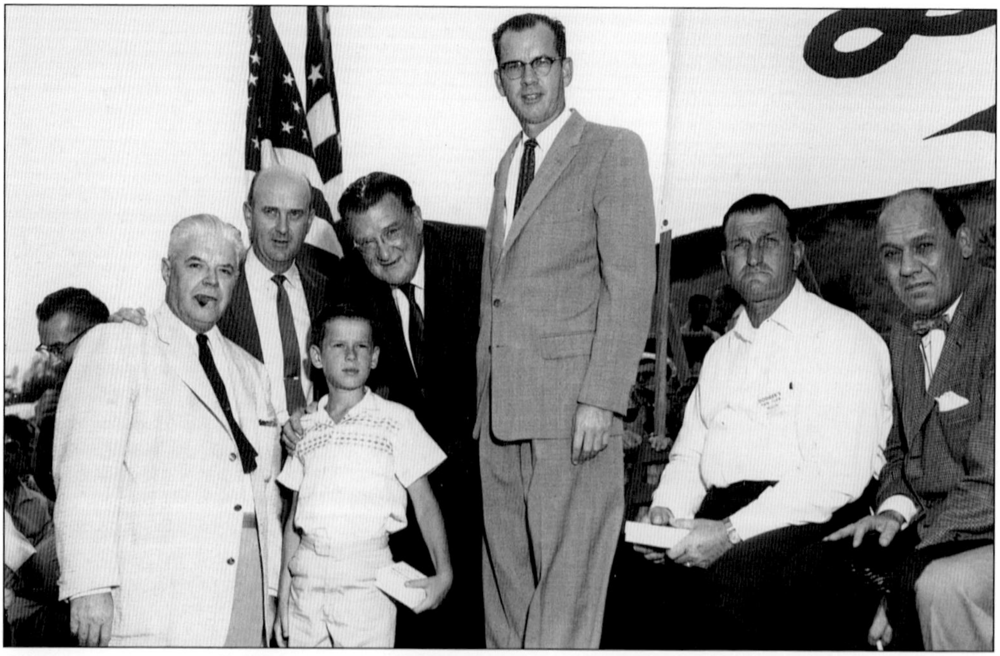

GROUNDBREAKING CEREMONY. Nearly 15 months after Proposition B was approved by Los Angeles voters, groundbreaking ceremonies at Chavez Ravine were held on September 17, 1959. From left to right are Robbie Robinson, publisher of the *Southside Journal*; Councilman Gordon Hahn; Jimmy Hahn, the first honorary batboy for the Dodgers and future mayor of Los Angeles; Walter O'Malley; Supervisor Kenneth Hahn; Dodger fan club president Warren K. Countryman; and Dodger Vice President E.J. "Buzzie" Bavasi.

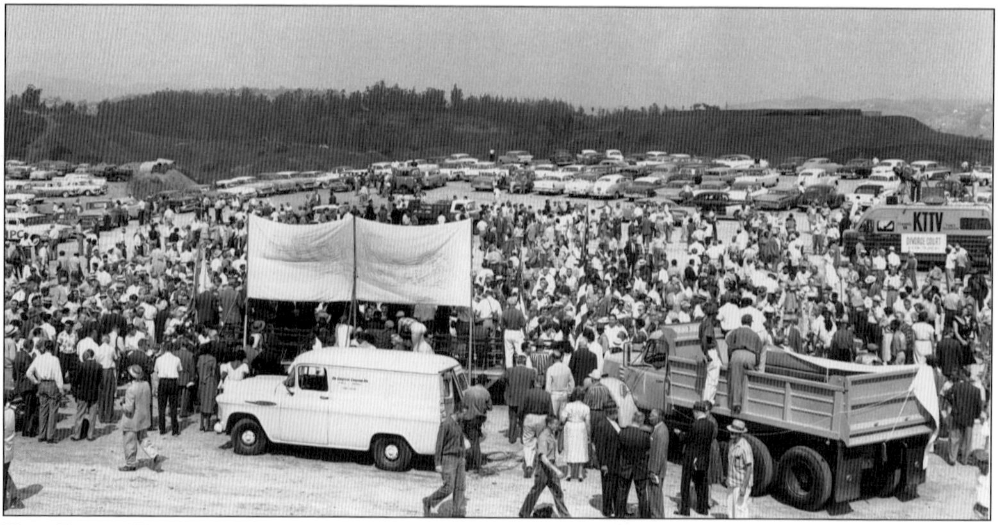

THE FIRST "DODGER STADIUM" CROWD. More than 500 fans gathered for the groundbreaking ceremonies. In the early 1950s, *Herald-Examiner* sportswriter Vincent X. Flaherty began to lobby in print for a major league franchise in Los Angeles. City officials met with Washington Senators owner Calvin Griffith in 1956 and with the Dodgers following the World Series, although the team still hoped for a new ballpark in New York. On October 7, 1957, the Los Angeles City Council voted 10-4 in favor of a motion officially asking the Dodgers to relocate to Los Angeles.

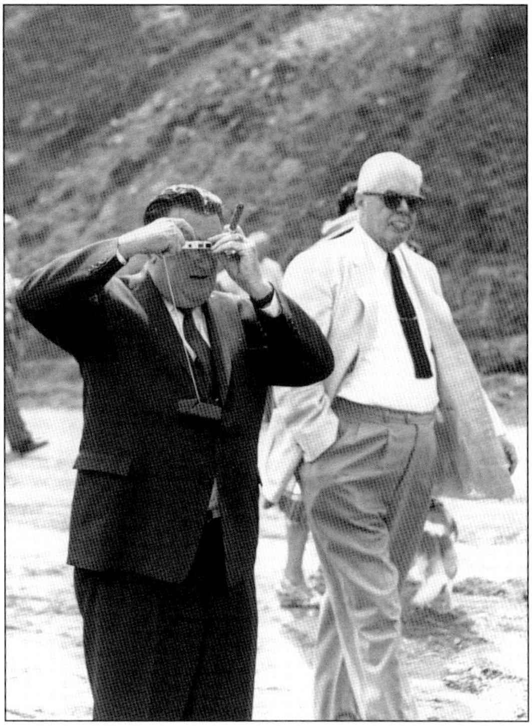

CANDID CAMERA. Walter O'Malley surveys the Chavez Ravine construction site on September 17, 1959. Dodger Stadium would become the first sports structure to be built on numerous levels, each connecting to an adjacent parking lot and eliminating vertical climbing—designed for the maximum comforts of the public. It was also the first privately financed stadium since Yankee Stadium, which was built by a brewery in 1923.

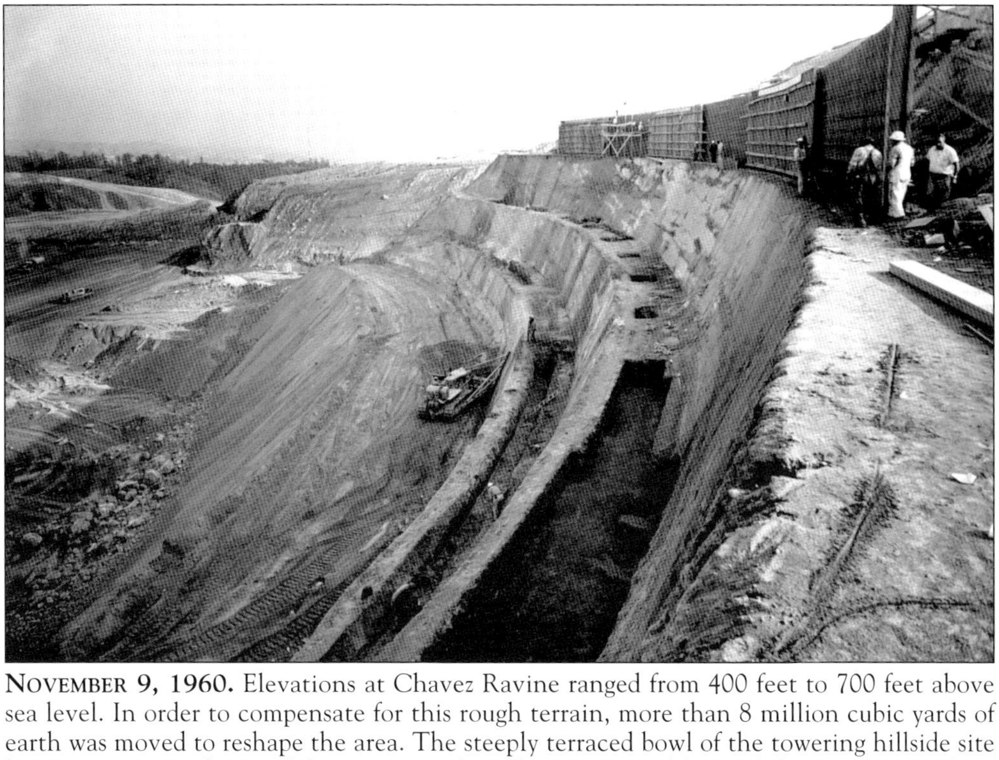

NOVEMBER 9, 1960. Elevations at Chavez Ravine ranged from 400 feet to 700 feet above sea level. In order to compensate for this rough terrain, more than 8 million cubic yards of earth was moved to reshape the area. The steeply terraced bowl of the towering hillside site became an integral part of the main grandstand structure and located the stands on a slope in the shelter of a U-shaped hill.

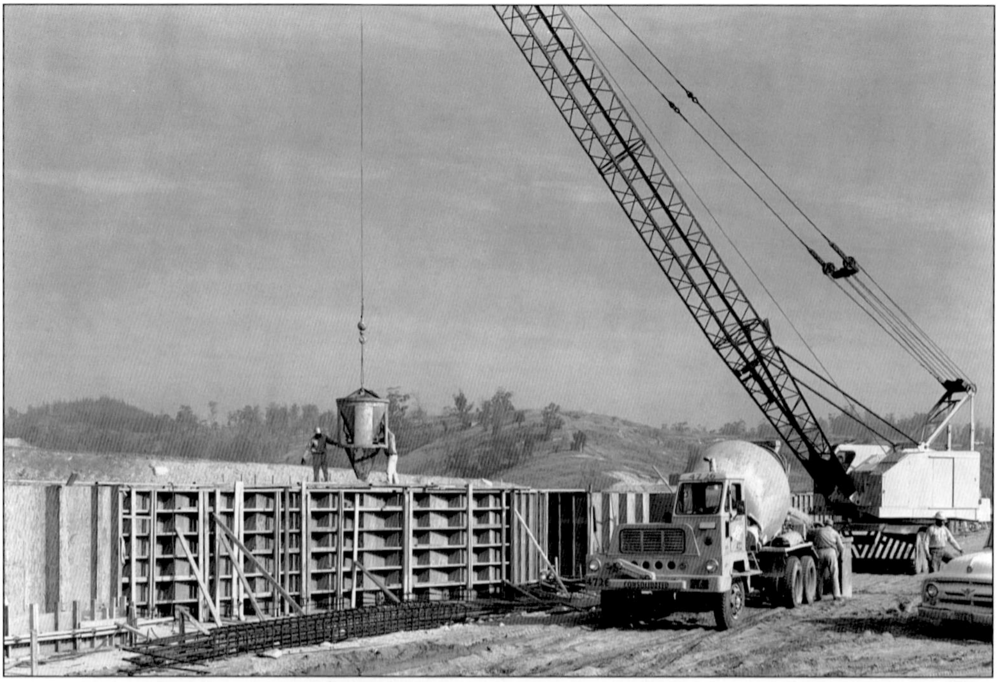

DECEMBER 5, 1960. Vinnell Constructors of Alhambra built a six-acre casting yard. The concrete casting beds were 3 inches thick, 50 feet wide, and between 200 and 400 feet long. Vinnell cast the 22-foot-long seat units in steel side forms and cured them with steam. All other concrete members were cast in wood forms and covered with curling compound. The consulting engineers planned a casting yard on the job because there was available space and some of the members, especially the 32-ton frames, were too large to truck into the site.

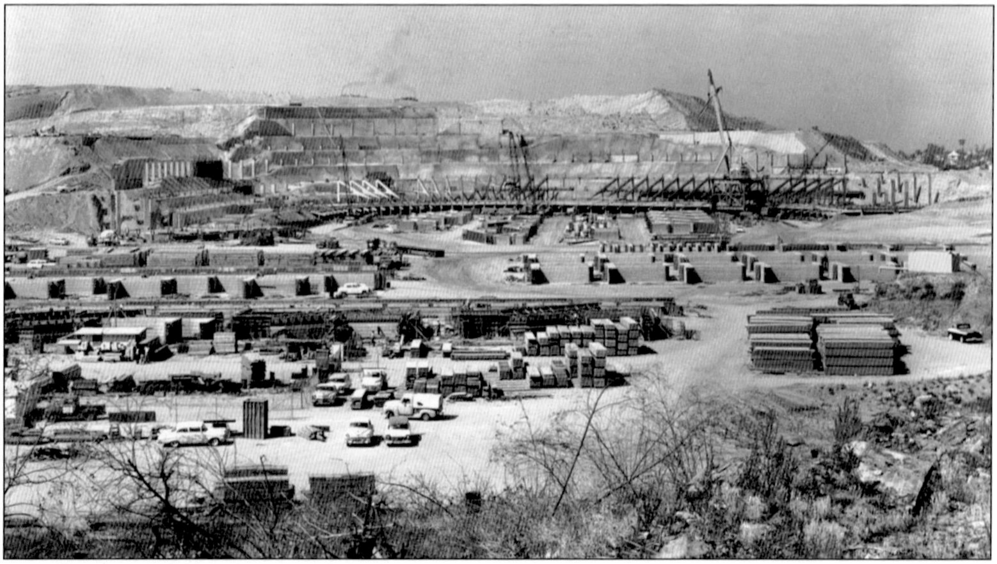

MAY 8, 1961. There were more than 25,000 separate pieces used to build Dodger Stadium. Each piece of concrete was marked and catalogued so the erection crew could find it. Vinnell Constructors also used fiberglass molds instead of steel. The pieces were cast on the property and a special $150,000 one-time-use crane was assembled at the stadium to put the pieces into place.

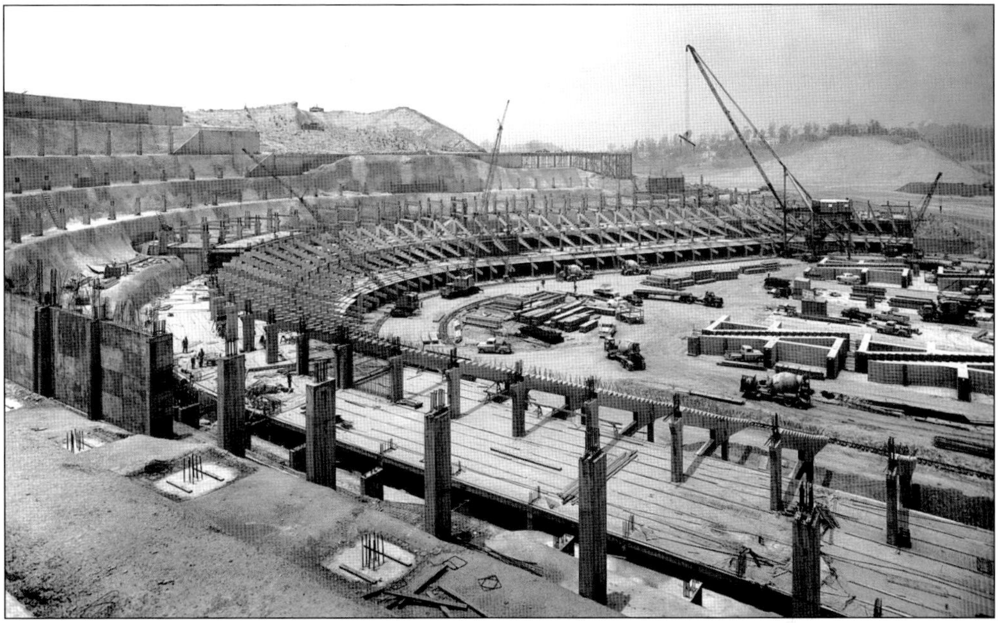

JUNE 7, 1961. As the stadium began to take shape, Walter O'Malley announced that it would have 52,000 seats and could be expanded in stages to boost capacity to 67,000 and eventually 80,000. O'Malley made it clear expansion might not be necessary. He later settled on a 56,000-seat capacity.

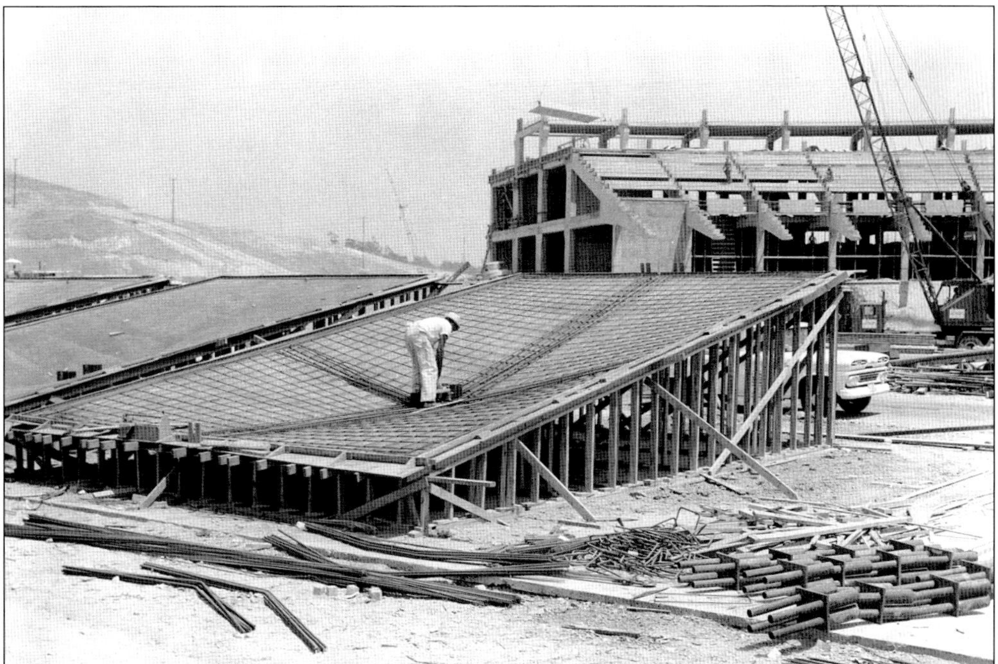

JULY 10, 1961. A view, looking east, shows completed and partially completed roof units. During construction, the Los Angeles Angels joined the American League in 1961, played their inaugural season at Wrigley Field, and would move into the new ballpark in 1962.

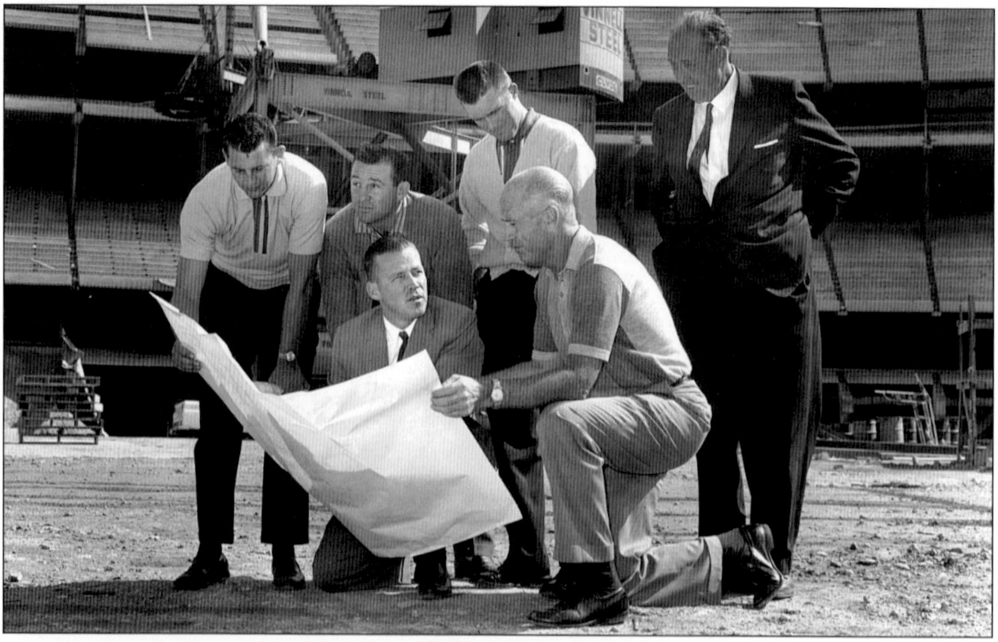

PLAYERS INSPECTING THEIR FUTURE HOME. From left to right, Larry Sherry, Norm Sherry, Dodger Vice President Dick Walsh, Ron Fairly, Manager Walter Alston, and general contractor Jack Yount examine the ballpark blueprints during a 1961 winter tour of the stadium construction site. The group met at "home plate."

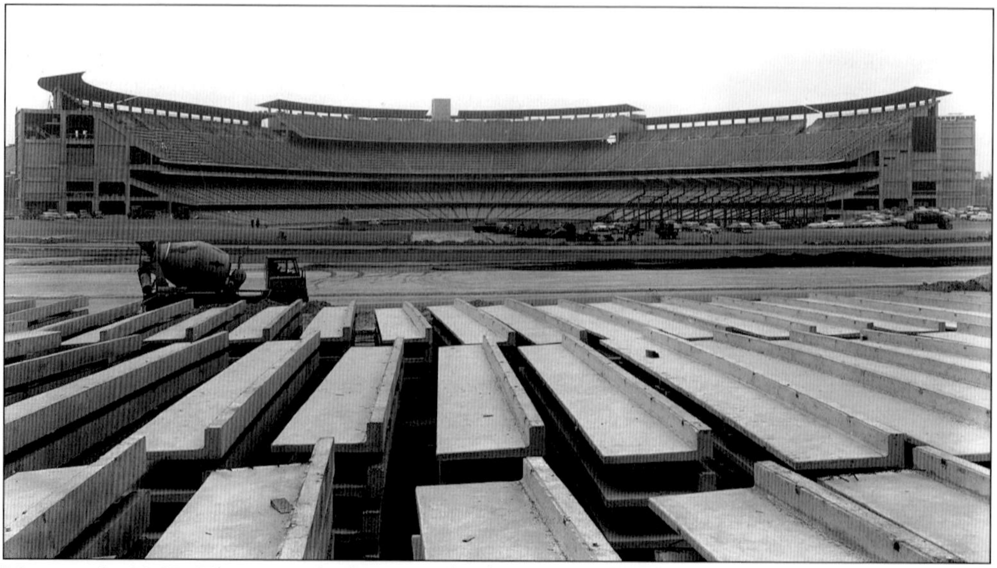

MARCH 5, 1962. This view, looking north, shows completed seat units for bleachers in the foreground. Note only the framework for the Left Field Pavilion is in place. Torrential rains hit Southern California in February 1962 and threatened the project's target date for Opening Day on April 10. The field was graded and ready for sod when the first rains came in February. It took 10 days to dry out and reconditioning for the field to be graded again. After 150 square feet of sod was installed, another five-day series of storms washed away the topsoil, causing an estimated $500,000 in damages.

TWO

1960s

It was a personal challenge for Walter O'Malley to make his ballpark a special destination among an already large list of Southern California attractions, landmarks, and amusement parks. There were behind-the-scene brainstorming and planning sessions with professional architects, co-workers in the Dodger front office, and general baseball fans. And there were plenty of ideas swirling in O'Malley's mind. He jotted notes in 1958 with questions, observations, and plans about everything from locker room blueprints to the menus at the various concession stands.

"Don't ever doubt that Walter is a showman," Dodger vice president Dick Walsh told the *Los Angeles Times* in October 1960. "Walter knows that baseball today demands more than three outfield walls and a covered stand. Chavez Ravine will have every innovation known to baseball—and a few known only to Walter."

The daybreak above Dodger Stadium on the morning of April 10, 1962 marked the dawn of a new era in Major League Baseball and Southern California sports history. After an exhaustive construction process and a longer period of anticipation that stretched back to the Dodgers' original arrival in Los Angeles in 1958, the team was finally going to play a home game in its own ballpark.

In an editorial titled "A Date With the Dodgers," the *Los Angeles Herald-Examiner* previewed the opening of the new ballpark as Los Angeles hosted the defending National League champion Cincinnati Reds in a 1 p.m. matinee.

It seems only a few yesterdays in the past that the glamorous, fantastic, romantic, and at times almost unbelievable Dodgers streamed across the country and thereby transformed themselves from the Brooklyn Dodgers of baseball history into the Los Angeles Dodgers.

In doing so, they wrote another chapter of baseball history—they brought big league baseball to this city, an event which a few years earlier had seemed almost impossible.

In addition to the seating for 56,000 fans, there was parking for 16,000 automobiles on 21 terraced lots adjacent and at about the same elevations as the five different seating levels on the 300-acre site. By employing the cantilever theory, every seat in the column-free stadium afforded a spectator a completely unobstructed view of the symmetrical playing field.

Herald-Examiner artist Karl Hubenthal penned a cartoon in O'Malley's honor. The "It's His Oyster" sketch portrayed a smiling O'Malley opening a giant-sized baseball, containing the sparkling "pearl" of a new stadium.

The headline in the *Los Angeles Times* sports section on April 10 was "Palmer Rallies to Win Masters Golf," but right below was the headline "At Last It's Play Ball in Chavez Ravine Today!" along with a picture of starting pitchers Don Drysdale, Sandy Koufax, and Johnny Podres from the previous day's workout. The players, coaches, and estimated 5,000 fans in the grandstands enjoyed the sneak preview of the new Dodger Stadium.

"It's the most gorgeous thing I've seen in my life," said Dodger shortstop Maury Wills. "The infield is perfect. It's nice and firm and true. It's bound to get better, too. They've done a wonderful job on it." Mrs. Gene Autry, whose husband's Los Angeles Angels American League franchise would also share Dodger Stadium from 1962 to 1965, said, "I want to thank Mr. O'Malley for paying so much attention to the beauty of the ballpark."

During the public dedication ceremonies, broadcaster Vin Scully raved about the acoustics as the stadium's public address system was in stereo. The system was installed by a West German company using plans from the same engineer who designed the acoustical system in the La Scala Opera House in Milan.

"Even when I saw the plans and watched the park grow, I still can't believe it," Commissioner Frick said. "It's like a dream come true." Giles said the ballpark exceeded his already high expectations. "It is a material expression of the future of the Dodgers and Major League Baseball in Los Angeles," Giles said. "I think it took a lot of courage on Mr. O'Malley's part." And O'Malley himself told *Los Angeles Times* columnist Sid Ziff, "I'm pretty relaxed and very pleased for the first time in weeks. I haven't slept for a month."

Although the Dodgers dropped the opener, 6-3, on a three-run home run by Cincinnati's Wally Post, the energy and excitement with the new ballpark was just beginning. Aerial photographers in helicopters chronicled a better view of the 52,564 patrons and a circular maze of automobiles with the downtown Los Angeles skyline in the background.

"All the minor problems were expected and conquered," wrote John Hall in the *Los Angeles Times*. "The main thing is the gates are open. Los Angeles has itself a major league ballpark, a truly remarkable stadium that is obviously destined to be recognized as the finest in the world. And those who were there will never forget how it all started on opening day."

One of the biggest stories of the first week was lack of drinking fountains, but the planners also forgot to install electrical outlets in the clubhouses. The Dodgers were a hit on the field and at the box office, but O'Malley and his staff continued to analyze the new venue to better accommodate the comfort and overall experience of the fans.

In November 1962, O'Malley embarked on a $1.5 million beautification program, originally slated as a five-year project, to be packed in one off-season. The bare hills in the back of the stadium were covered with California golden poppy, along with a solid sea of blue and purple flowers. Palms and eucalyptus worth more than $104,000 were planted in the front area of the ballpark. The hills in the background were laced with pipe for the sprinkler system. Poppy seed, containing its own fertilizer and hormones, was shot in with a gun.

"Everything will be in bloom by June," O'Malley predicted. "The setting will not just be beautiful, but dramatically beautiful so that people will come out raving."

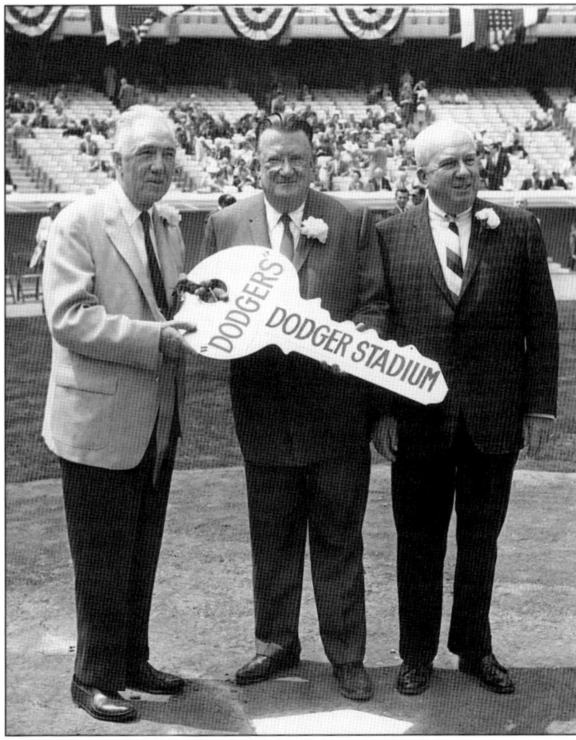

KEY TO THE BALLPARK. Baseball Commissioner Ford C. Frick and National League President Warren Giles flank Walter O'Malley during stadium dedication ceremonies on April 9, 1962. An estimated crowd of 2,000 attended the civic event and listened to Teddy Buckner's Dixieland band while a small army of painters, construction workers, and electricians completed last-minute details. Batting practice was canceled because the protective screen could not be located, so Manager Walter Alston's squad improvised with infield drills. On his way to the ballpark that afternoon, the tailpipe on Duke Snider's car fell off. The Dodger outfielder instinctively picked up the hot pipe and he nearly missed the following day's game due to burns on his fingers.

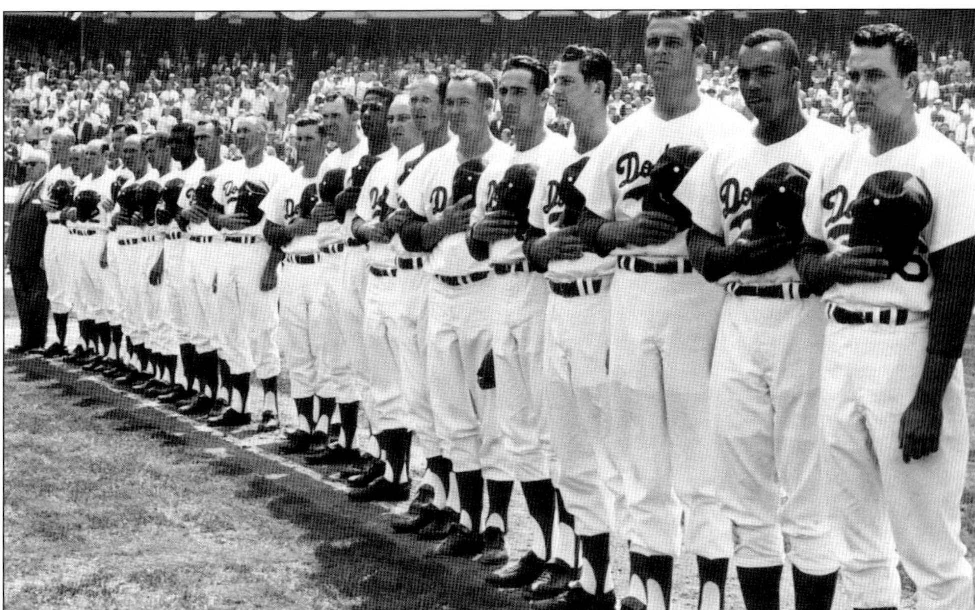

NATIONAL ANTHEM. The Dodgers stand along the third-base line on Opening Day in 1962 as the national anthem is performed by Alma Pedroza, accompanied by Johnny Boudreau's band. Kay O'Malley, wife of the Dodger president, threw out the ceremonial first pitch to catcher John Roseboro. Also honored was Mrs. James (Dearie) Mulvey, Dodger stockholder who traveled from her New York home to visit Los Angeles. Mrs. Mulvey witnessed the Dodgers' first game at Ebbets Field in 1913.

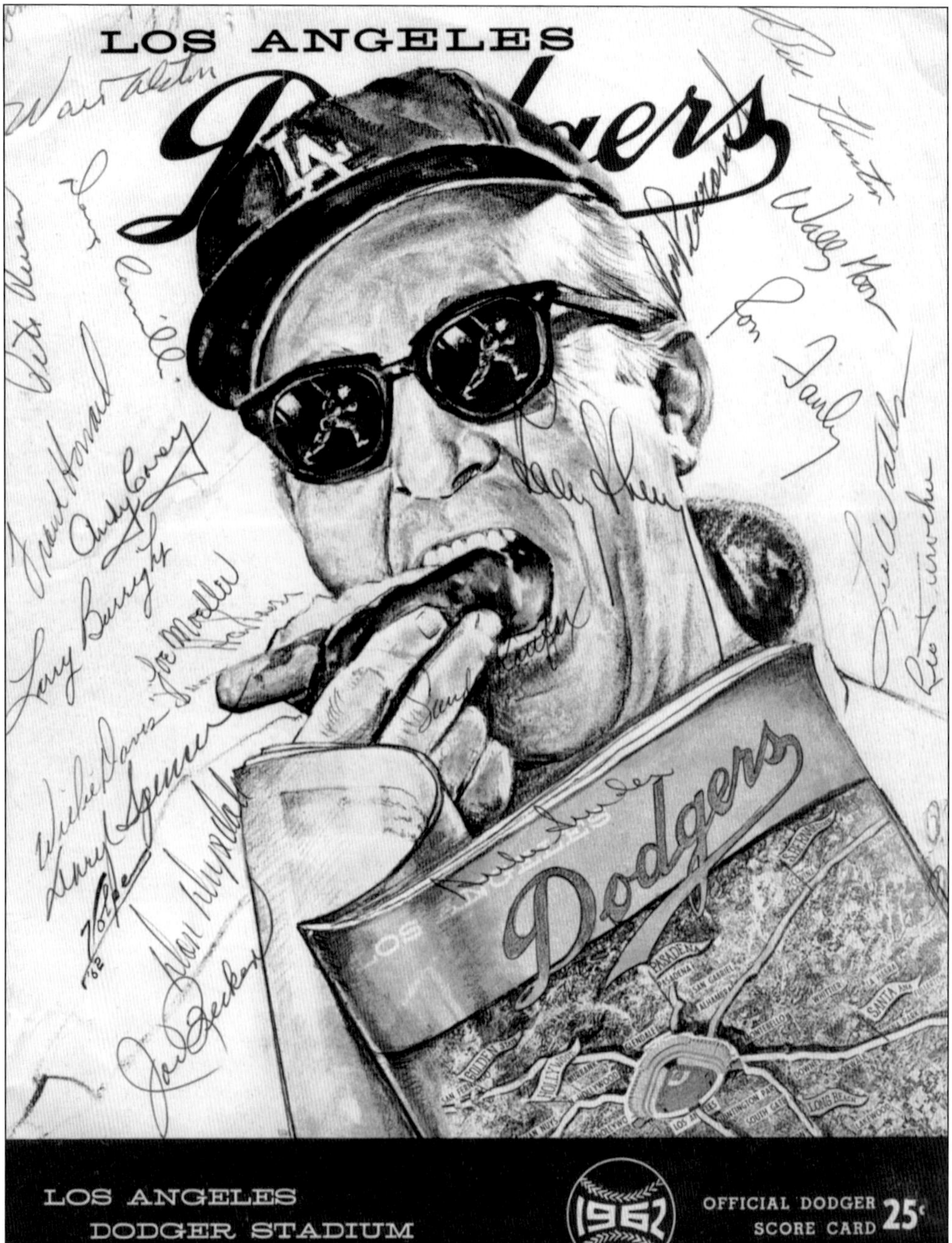

OPENING DAY, 1962. The first game program at Dodger Stadium features a self-portrait by artist Nicholas Volpe. Scott Morgan, a 12-year-old Dodger fan and a family friend of Dodger scout Kenny Myers, collected signatures of players and coaches in the clubhouse prior to the game. The Dodgers starting lineup was Maury Wills, SS; Jim Gilliam, 2B; Wally Moon, LF; Duke Snider, RF; John Roseboro, C; Ron Fairly, 1B; Daryl Spencer, 3B; Willie Davis, CF; and Johnny Podres, P.

SOUVENIR TICKET. There was a special die-cut ticket with a picture of Dodger Stadium on April 10, 1962. A similar design was utilized for the Los Angeles Angels' American League season-opener against the Kansas City Athletics on April 17. Coin-shaped tokens initially were used for general admission in the pavilions, but that practice was discontinued after the 1962 season. "Coin horders" purchased extra admissions in anticipation of sold-out games with the San Francisco Giants in September, causing overflow crowds.

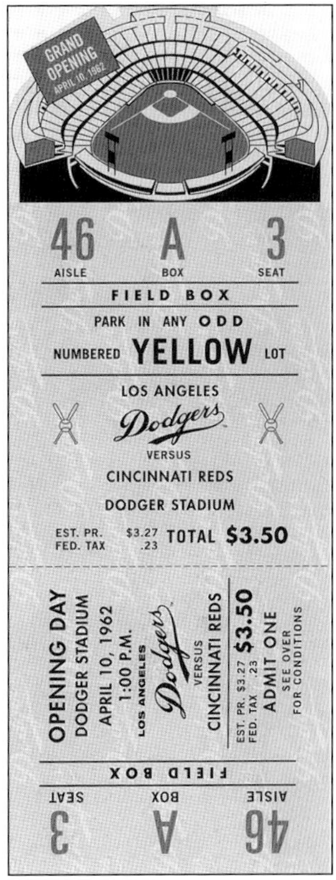

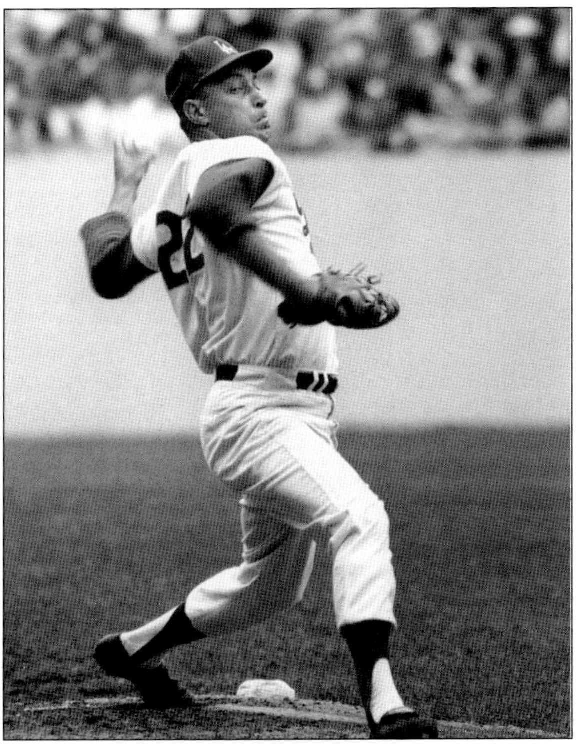

JOHNNY PODRES. The Dodgers' Opening Day starter in 1962 took the advice of Los Angeles Police Chief William Parker, who urged fans to carpool and arrive early after studying maps of the new stadium access roads. Podres left his headquarters at the Mayfair Hotel at 8:55 a.m. The cab ride lasted just 10 minutes, leaving Podres plenty of time before the first pitch. Podres, the hero of the Brooklyn Dodgers' 1955 World Series Game 7 victory over the New York Yankees, suffered a 6-3 loss against the defending National League champion Cincinnati Reds on a three-run home run by veteran Wally Post.

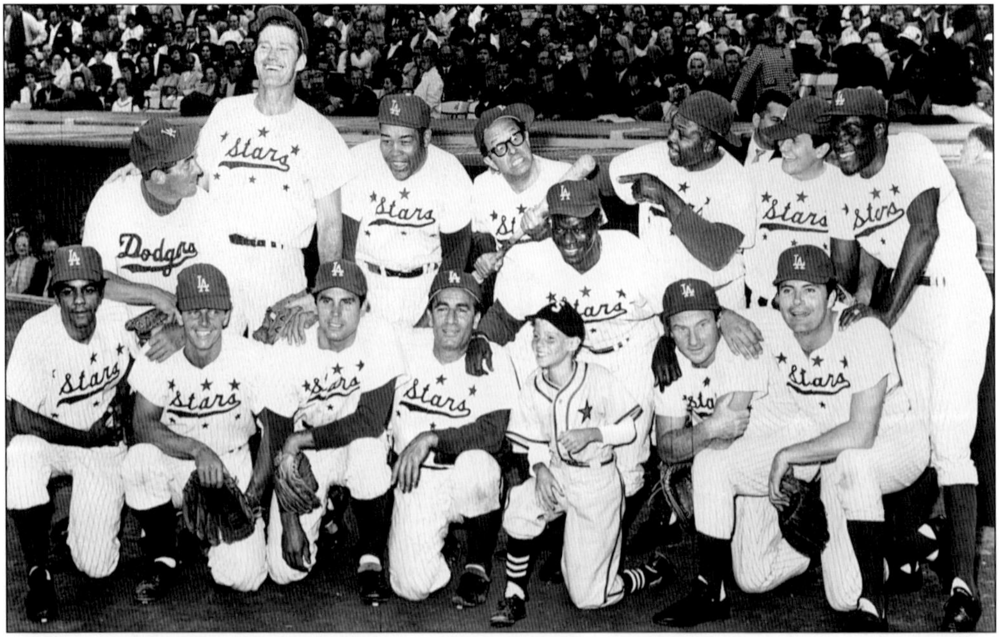

HOLLYWOOD STARS. The exhibition games started in the 1940s as World War II benefit games in Pacific Coast League ballparks and continued at the Coliseum. The first Dodger Stadium "Stars" game, held in 1962, included, from left to right, (top row) Dean Martin, Chuck Connors, Joe Louis, Phil Silvers, Nat King Cole, Archie Moore, Pat Boone, and Rafer Johnson, (bottom row) Johnny Mathis, Peter Brown, Mike Dante, John Beradino, Jay North, Jack Warden, and Max Baer Jr.

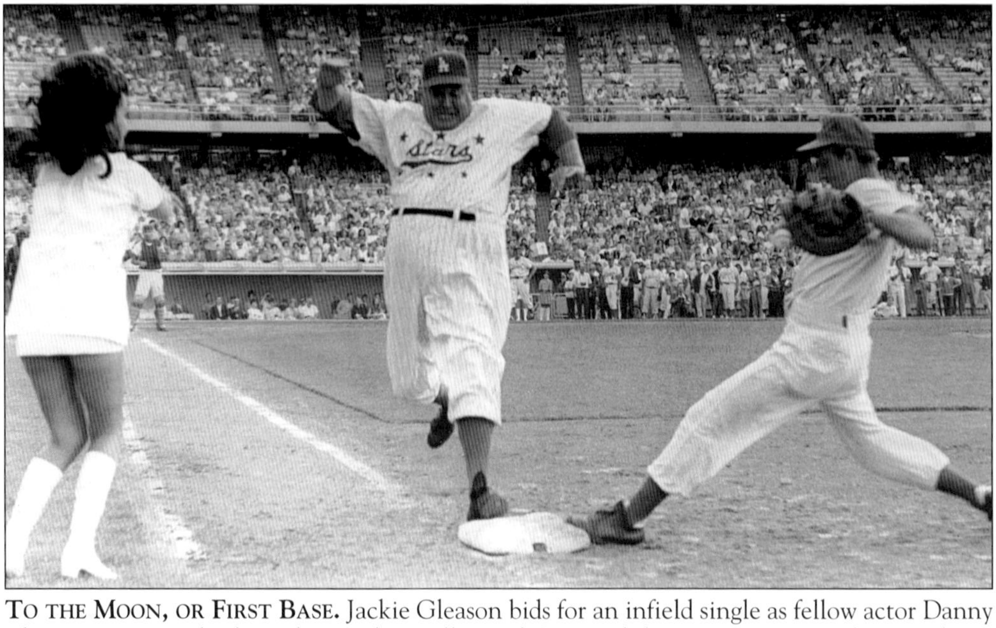

TO THE MOON, OR FIRST BASE. Jackie Gleason bids for an infield single as fellow actor Danny Thomas races to the base during the Hollywood Stars exhibition game at Dodger Stadium. Coaching first base is actress Annette Funicello.

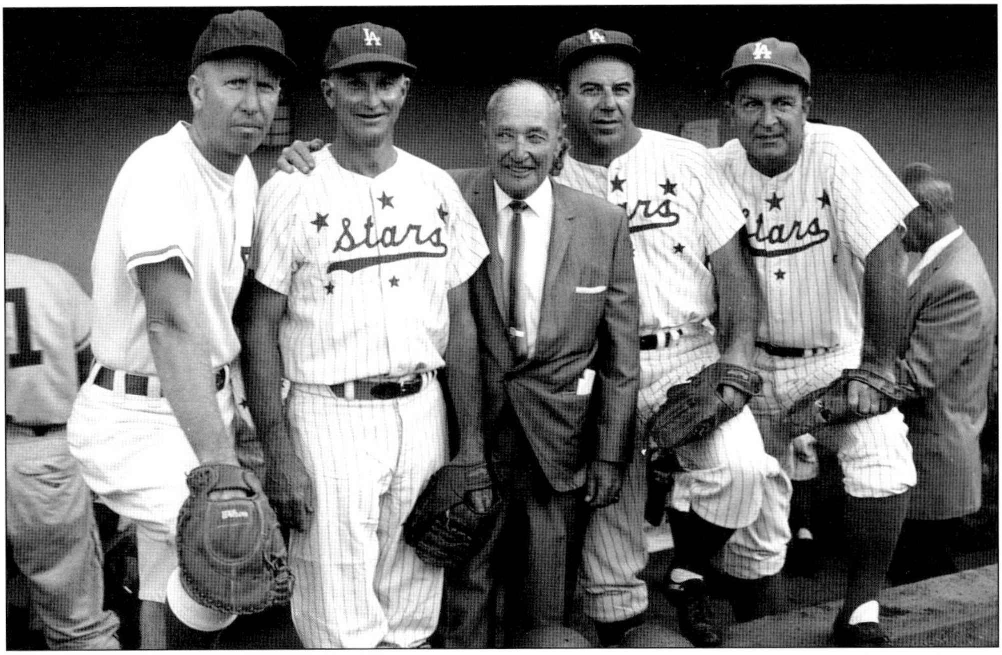

PACIFIC COAST LEAGUE REUNION. On September 11, 1962, the Dodgers saluted former standout players from the Pacific Coast League's Hollywood Stars and Los Angeles Angels. In the "Stars" third base dugout are, from left to right, Chuck Stevens, Gene Hadley, Fred Haney, Murray Franklin, and Frank Kellert. Haney was a Hollywood Stars broadcaster in the 1940s, won a World Series as Milwaukee Braves manager in 1957, and later served as the first general manager for the major league Angels franchise.

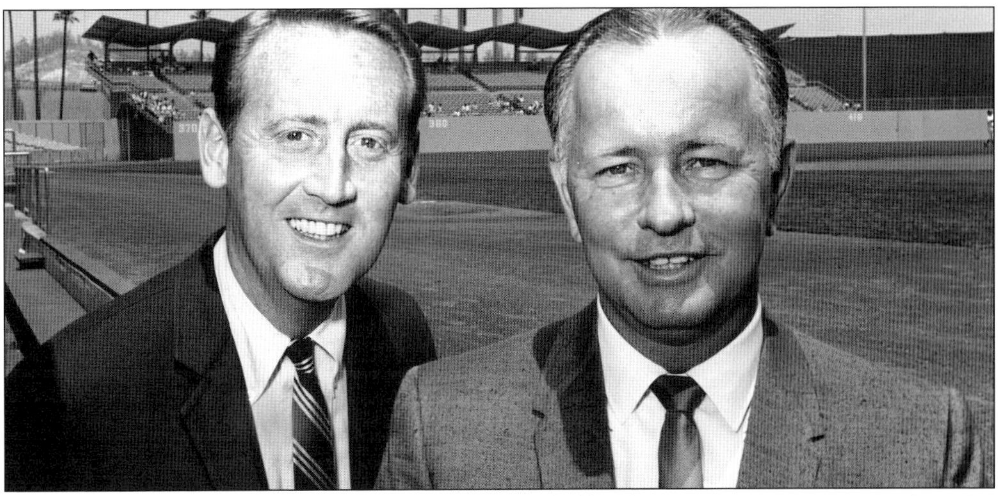

VIN AND JERRY. Bringing a transistor to the radio ballpark was necessary at times when the Dodgers played at the huge Los Angeles Memorial Stadium because the playing field was so far away from some vantage points. At Dodger Stadium, the popular radio team of Vin Scully and Jerry Doggett became the new soundtrack. The partnership lasted a record 32 seasons, which was Doggett's tenure from 1956 to 1987. Scully, the Hall of Famer who once was voted the "Most Memorable Personality" in Dodger Stadium history in fan balloting in 1976, joined the franchise in 1950.

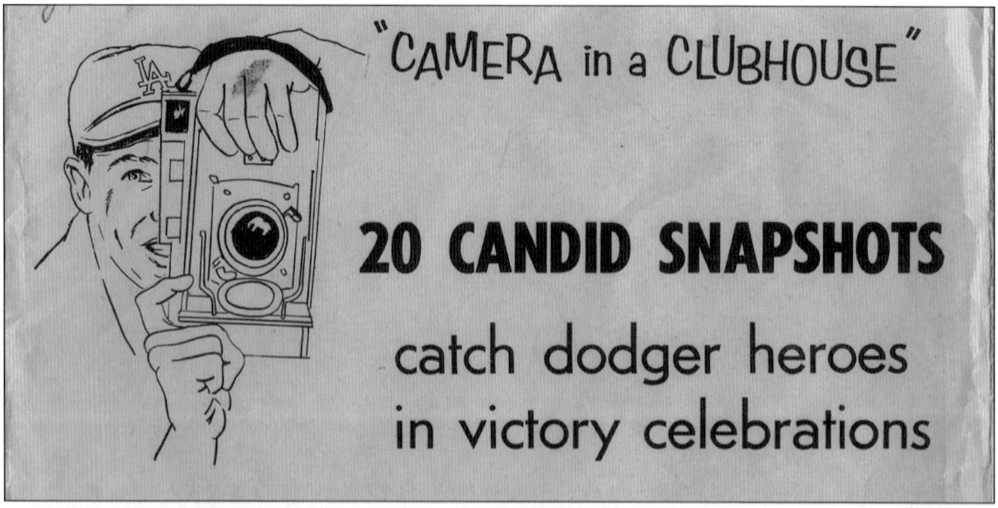

THE CLUBHOUSE CAMERA. One of the most unique novelties sold at Dodger Stadium was "Camera in the Clubhouse," a packet of black-and-white photos taken by infielder Andy Carey in 1962. The shots revealed a rare look at the Dodger players' celebrations, including the use of shaving cream to spell out milestones on bare-chested heroes Maury Wills (104 stolen bases), Tommy Davis (153 RBI), Frank Howard (31 home runs), and others donning funny hats and costumes while mugging for Carey's camera. In his message to fans, Carey explained, "It started out as a gag, but we thought you would like to see how the Dodgers relax after winning games during a red-hot pennant race. All of these pictures have been taken on a Polaroid Land Camera. Hope you enjoy our behind-the-scene hi-jinx as much as we enjoyed the victories which went with them."

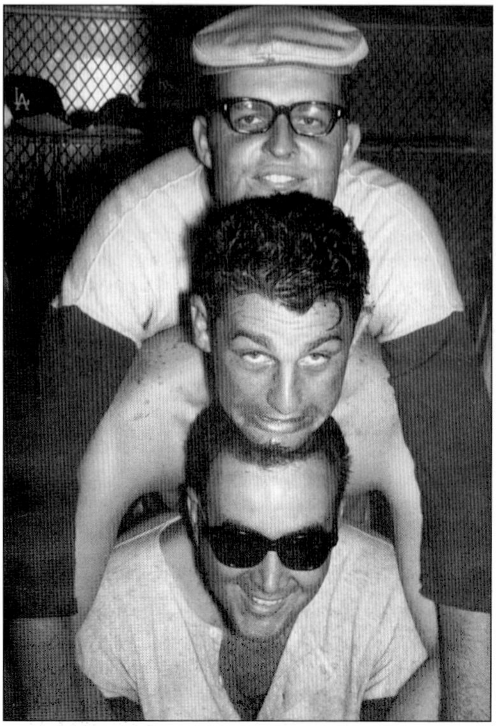

TRIPLE PLAY. Can you recognize these Dodger pitchers? From top to bottom, Don Drysdale, Larry Sherry, and Ron Perranoski form a totem pole following a Dodger victory. Drysdale won a career-high 25 games in 1962, along with the National League's Cy Young Award. Drysdale may have been fearsome to opposing hitters during his 14-year Hall of Fame career, but "Big D" turned into a big ham for Andy Carey's clubhouse camera. He also broke into a warm smile when teammates presented a special baseball field–themed cake to salute his 20th victory on August 3.

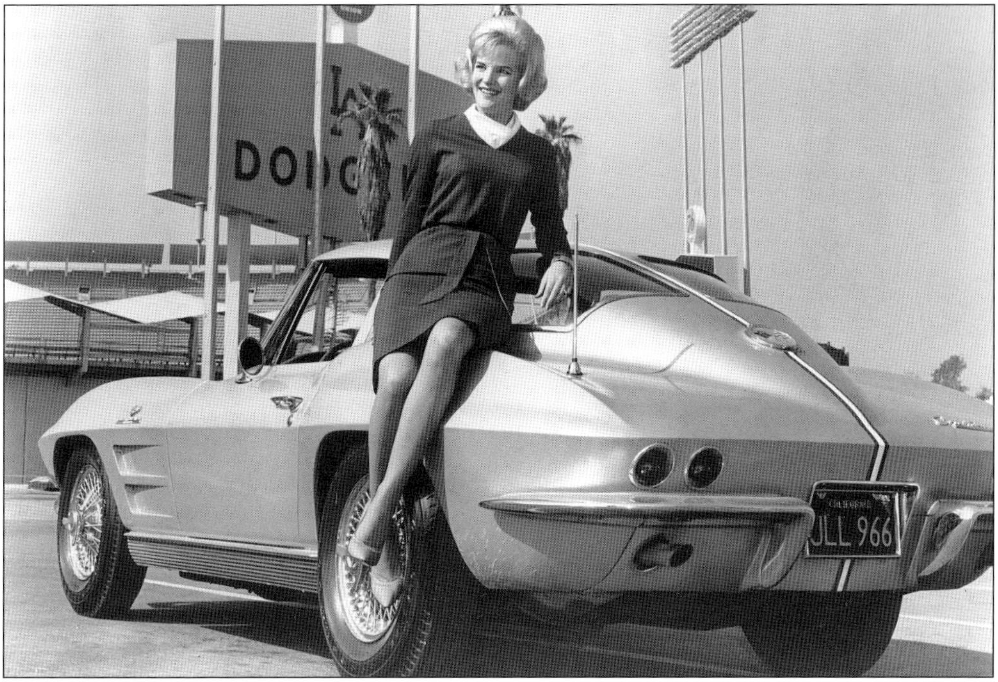

A Day at the Races. After drawing more than 5 million fans for the Dodgers and Angels home games in 1962, Dodger Stadium hosted a series of road races in March 1963. The 1.3-mile course snaked along the perimeter of the parking lot with 12 turns as cars reached top speeds of 120 miles per hour and an average speed of 70. Three sets of bleachers were placed around the ballpark to watch the 120 drivers who were invited by the sponsoring California Sports Car Club. Lee Moeller, the official "Road Race Queen," models the Corvette pace car.

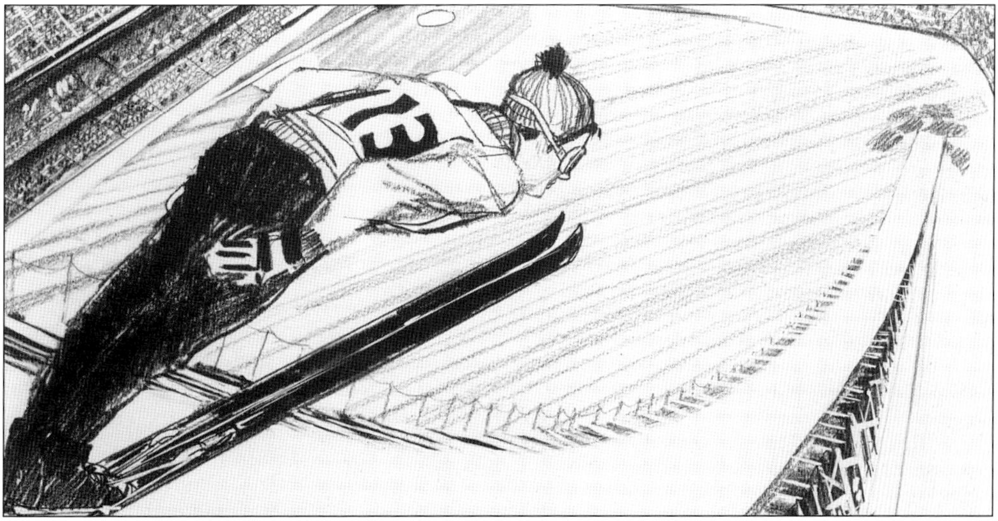

Stadium Ski Jump. In addition to boxing matches and road races, some of the early non-baseball events at Dodger Stadium included an international ski show in 1963. The daily shows consisted of two jumping events, a slalom race, and fashion show. The roster of participating athletes included Minnesota native Gene Kotlarek, the reigning U.S. distance record holder (322 feet) who was expected to contend for a gold medal at the 1964 Olympics in Innsbruck, Austria.

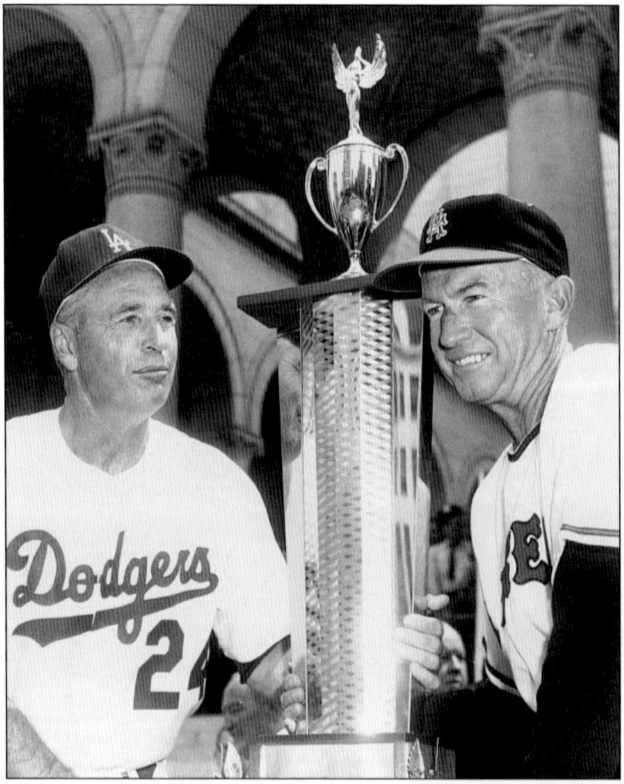

THE FREEWAY SERIES. Los Angeles managers Walter Alston (Dodgers) and Bill Rigney (Angels) admire a trophy during a 1963 Opening Day rally at City Hall. For the better part of four decades, the Dodgers and Angels have staged this popular exhibition series prior to the start of the regular season. From 1962 to 1965, the Angels used the Dodger Stadium facility but preferred the name "Chavez Ravine" on their promotional materials.

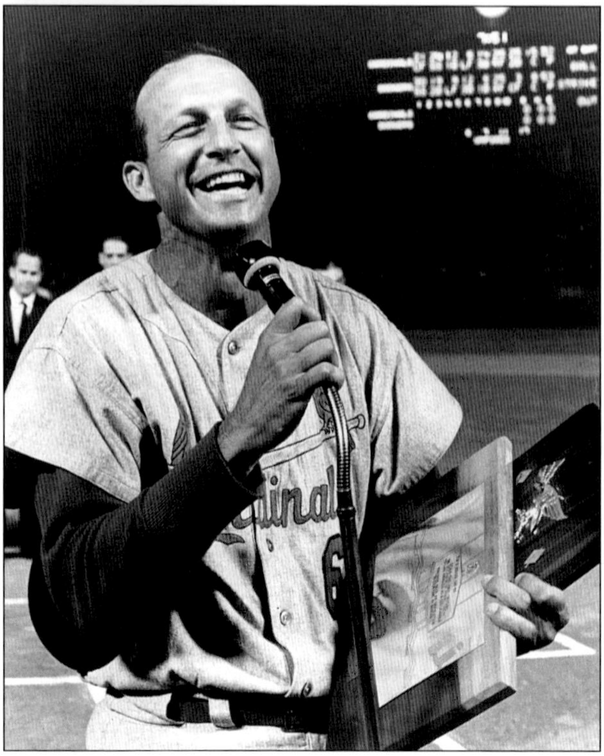

STAN MUSIAL NIGHT. One of the first opposing players honored at Dodger Stadium was Hall of Fame outfielder Stan "The Man" Musial, who played for the St. Louis Cardinals from 1941 to 1963. Musial, who retired with a National League record 3,630 career hits, acquired his nickname during a hitting spree in a 1946 doubleheader against the Dodgers at Ebbets Field. When Musial approached the plate in the second game, fans chanted, "Here comes the man. Here comes the man." St. Louis columnist Bob Broeg wrote about the incident and a nickname was born.

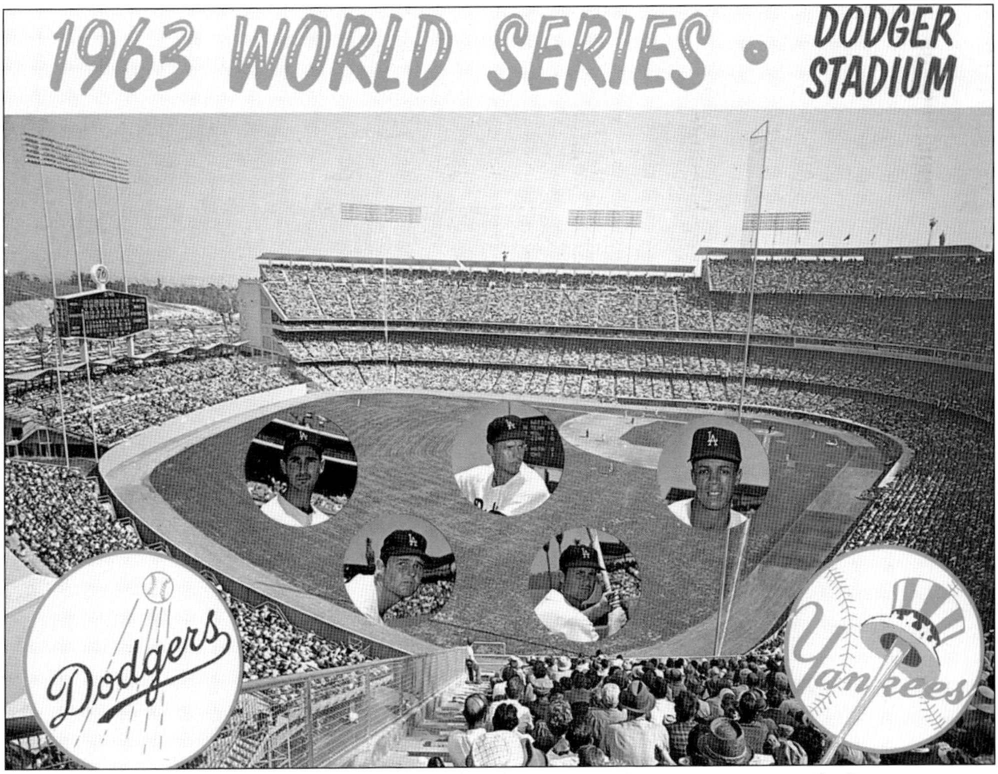

The Fall Classic. In 1963, Los Angeles won the pennant by six games over St. Louis to earn a World Series berth against their October rivals. This souvenir placard pictures Dodger stars Sandy Koufax, Frank Howard, Maury Wills, Don Drysdale and Ron Fairly.

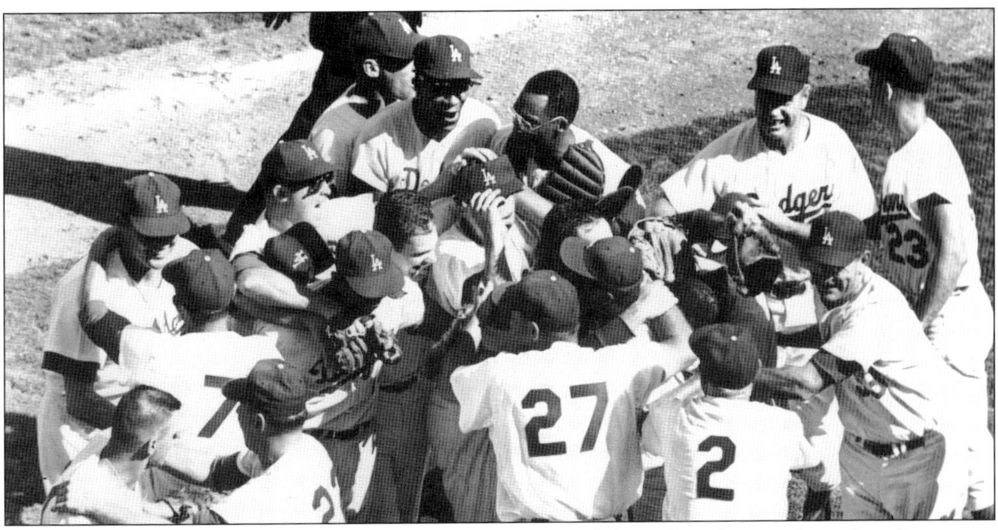

Dodgers Sweep Yankees. When Los Angeles stunned their October rivals with a four-game World Series sweep in 1963, it marked the only time the Dodgers clinched a championship in their home ballpark. Sandy Koufax pitched a complete game in Game 4 and scattered six hits during a 2-1 victory. With his fifth-inning home run against Yankees' starter Whitey Ford, Frank Howard became the first player to hit a fair ball on the Loge Level.

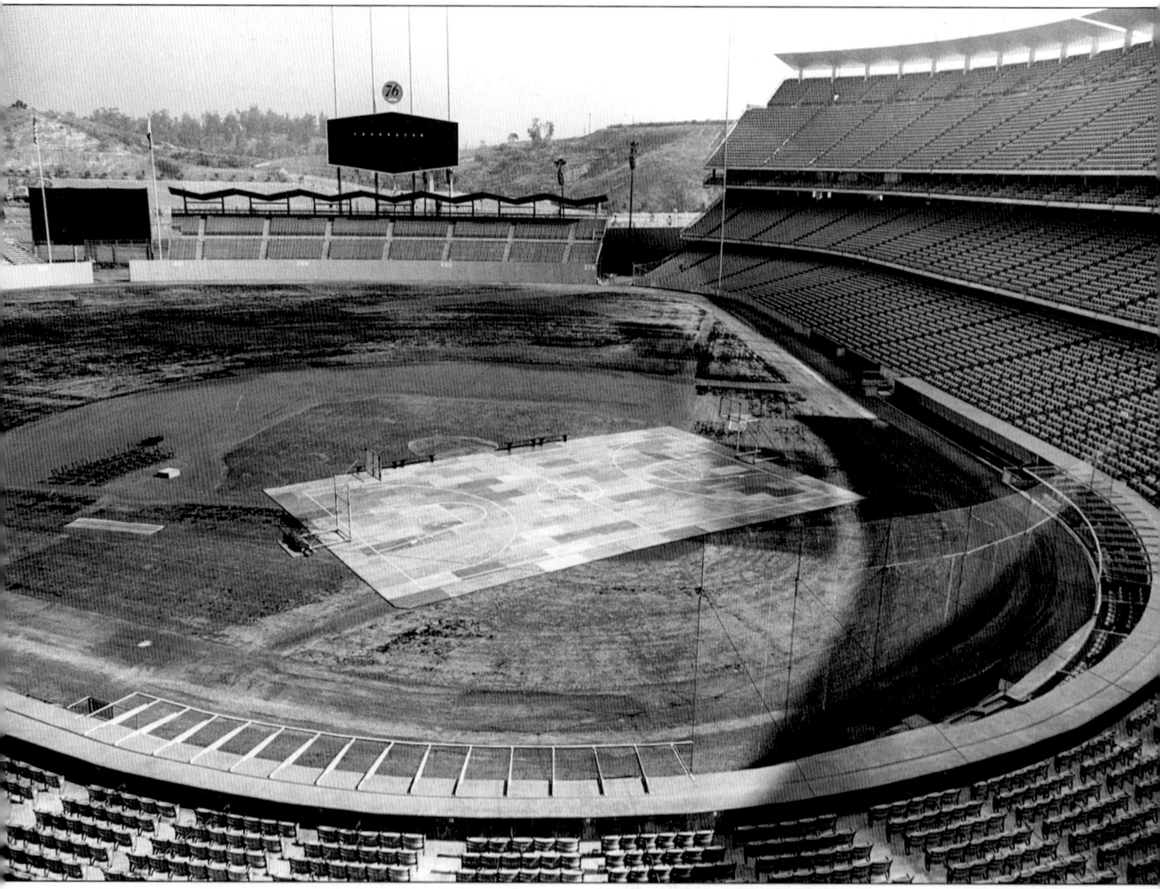

HARLEM GLOBETROTTERS. The world-famous basketball ambassadors, including Meadowlark Lemon, Tex Harrison, Connie Hawkins, and dribbling specialist Tim Mitchell, played an exhibition game in front of 12,405 on February 2, 1964. A full-sized court was installed on the infield grass, just as a boxing ring was built for a series of championship fights in 1963. The floor, imported from the defunct Los Angeles Jets, also featured an exhibition game between the World Champion Dodgers and the National Football League's Chicago Bears, including linebacker Dick Butkus and tight end Mike Ditka. Participating Dodgers included Tommy Davis, John Werhas, John Roseboro, Roy Gleason, and Ken McMullen. The Angels' Dean Chance and Bo Belinsky each scored two point for the Globetrotters' "Atlantic City Sea Gulls" opponent.

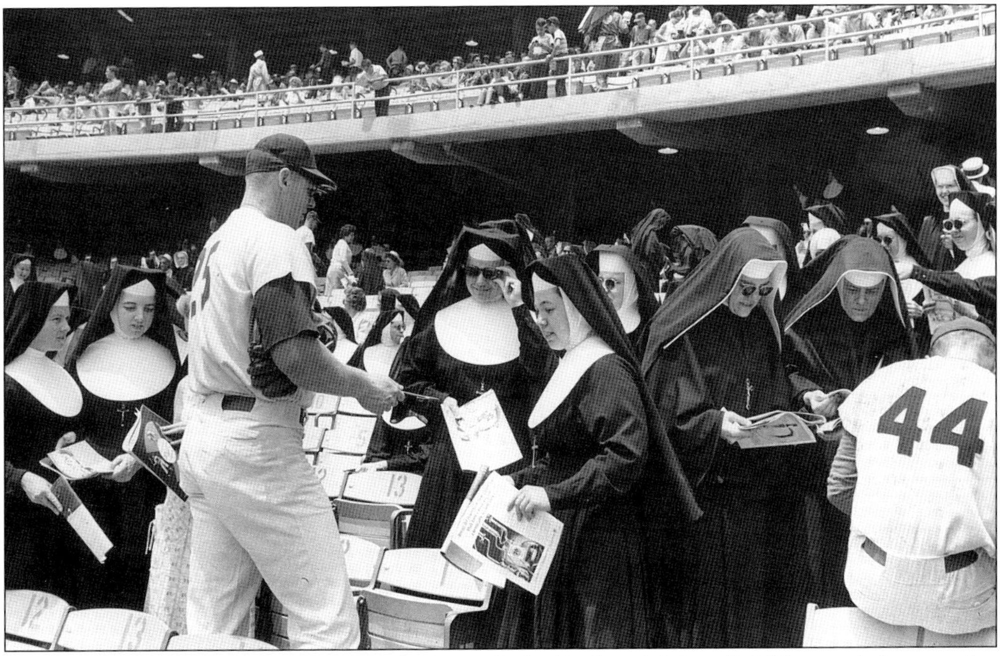

BIG MAN IN DODGER DUGOUT. Frank Howard, the Dodgers' 6-foot-7, 258-pound slugger, who was an All-America in both baseball and basketball at Ohio State, signs autographs during Nun's Day at the ballpark. Howard hit 123 home runs for Los Angeles from 1958 to 1964. "Hondo" was traded to the Washington Senators in exchange for pitcher Claude Osteen and later won two American League home run titles.

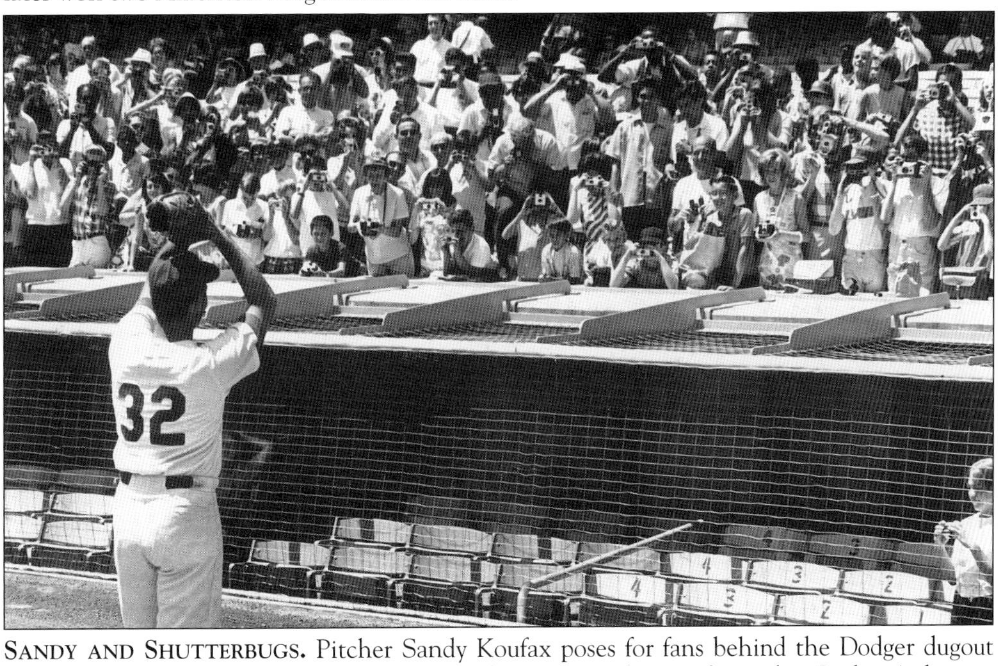

SANDY AND SHUTTERBUGS. Pitcher Sandy Koufax poses for fans behind the Dodger dugout during a Camera Day promotion. This tradition carried over from the Dodgers' days at Brooklyn's Ebbets Field and at the Los Angeles Memorial Coliseum. Because of overwhelming crowds at Dodger Stadium, club officials later moved the fans onto the field.

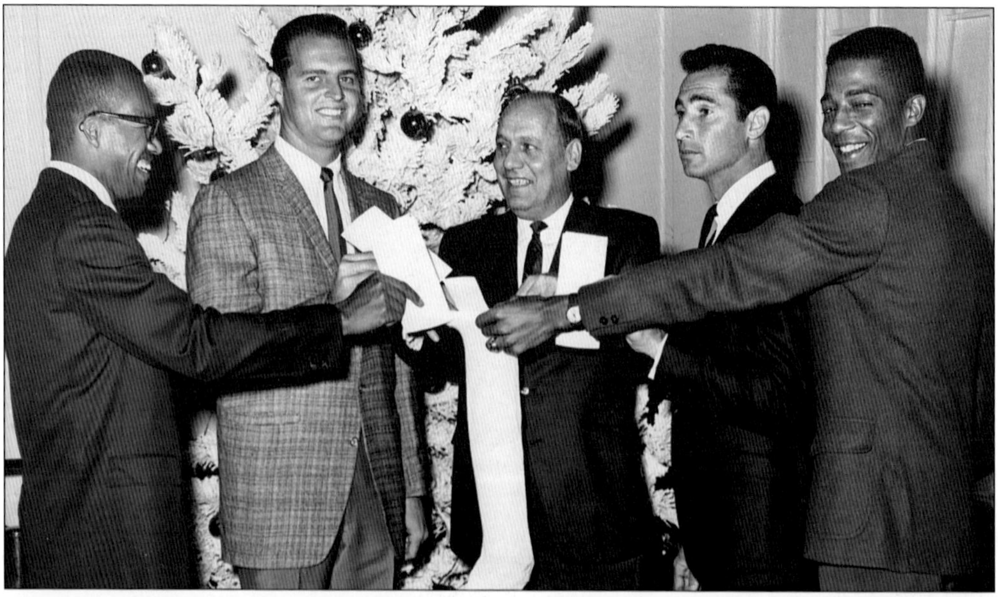

Holiday Cheer with Buzzie. During a winter break at Dodger Stadium, Tommy Davis, Don Drysdale, Sandy Koufax, and Willie Davis place their contracts for the upcoming 1965 season in the Christmas stocking of Executive Vice President and General Manager Emil "Buzzie" Bavasi. The Dodgers would win a championship, but the next round of negotiations wasn't as easy. Koufax and Drysdale staged a well-publicized holdout prior to reporting to spring training in 1966.

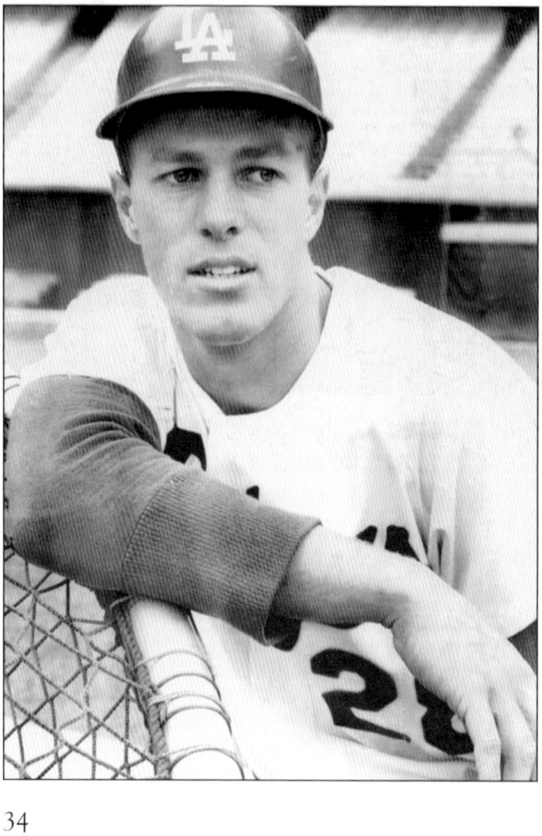

Wes Parker. One of the biggest surprises for the Dodgers in the 1960s was the sudden development of first baseman Wes Parker, who received no signing bonus in 1963 after attending Claremont College in Southern California. Parker's self-confidence and hard work paid off. He spent only one season in the minor leagues and appeared in 124 games as a rookie in 1964. Parker won six Gold Gloves during his nine-year career with Los Angeles. Parker's finest season at the plate was in 1970—a .319 batting average with 10 home runs and 111 RBI in 161 games. Parker also became a favorite of Dodger Stadium fans, often hitting fly balls to youngsters in the parking lot after ballgames.

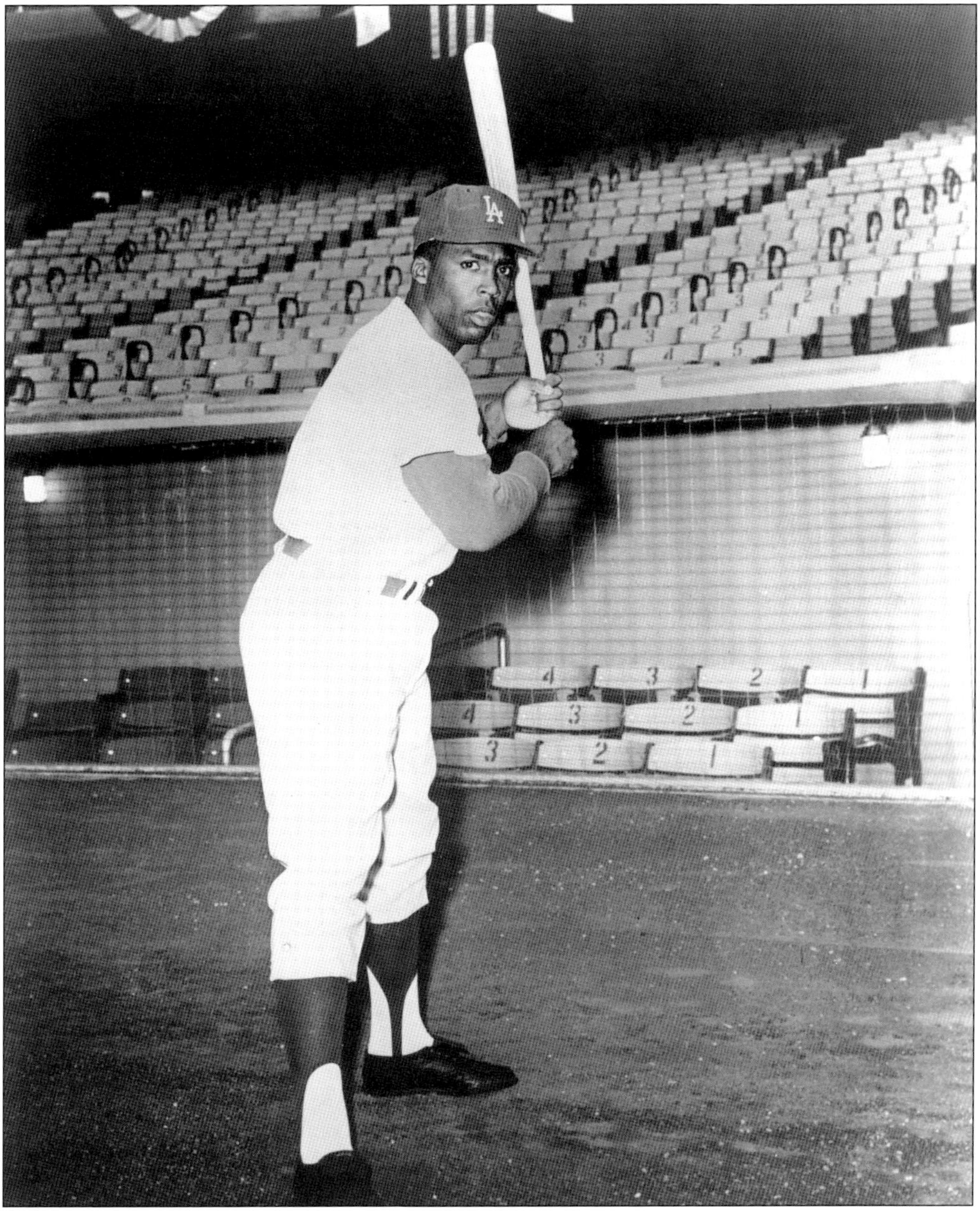

CLASSY CATCHER. Following Roy Campanella's automobile accident in January 1958, John Roseboro became a fixture behind home plate for the Dodgers through 1967. The Ohio native appeared in four World Series and compiled a lifetime .249 batting average in 14 major league seasons. The roof above the dugout seats, shown in the background of this photo, was later padded when Roseboro's catching counterpart, Minnesota Twins' backstop Earl Battey, struck his throat while chasing a foul ball during the 1965 World Series.

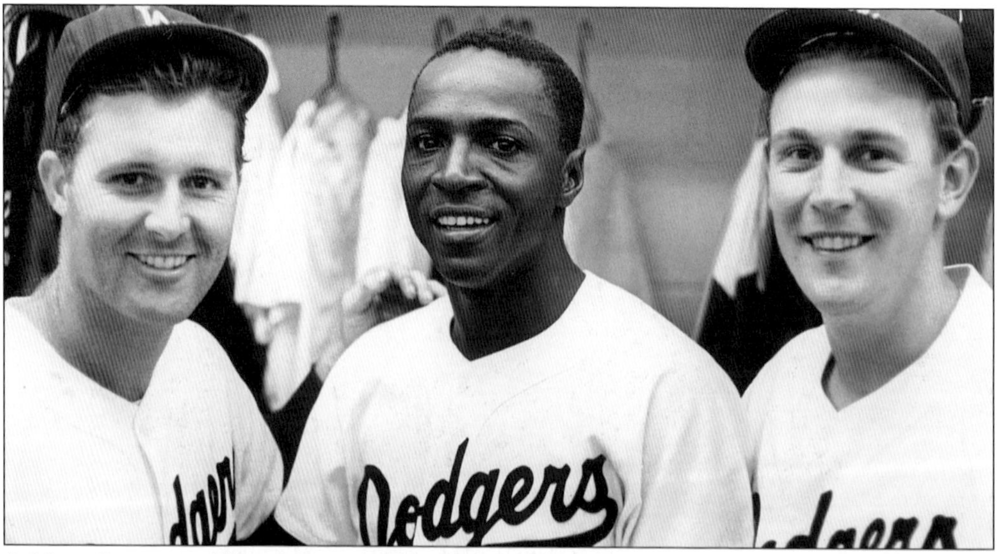

A NEW CATALYST. Tommy Davis' ankle injury early in 1965 opened the door for 30-year-old outfielder Lou Johnson, recalled from Triple-A Spokane. Johnson wasted no time contributing during a 3-2 victory in 10 innings over the Astros on May 10. Flanking Johnson are Ron Fairly, whose hit scored Johnson with the winning run, and Bob Miller, who relieved Johnny Podres for the win. Johnson, who spent a decade in the minors, would emerge as a hero of the Dodgers' 1965 World Series victory over Minnesota, blasting a home run in the deciding Game 7.

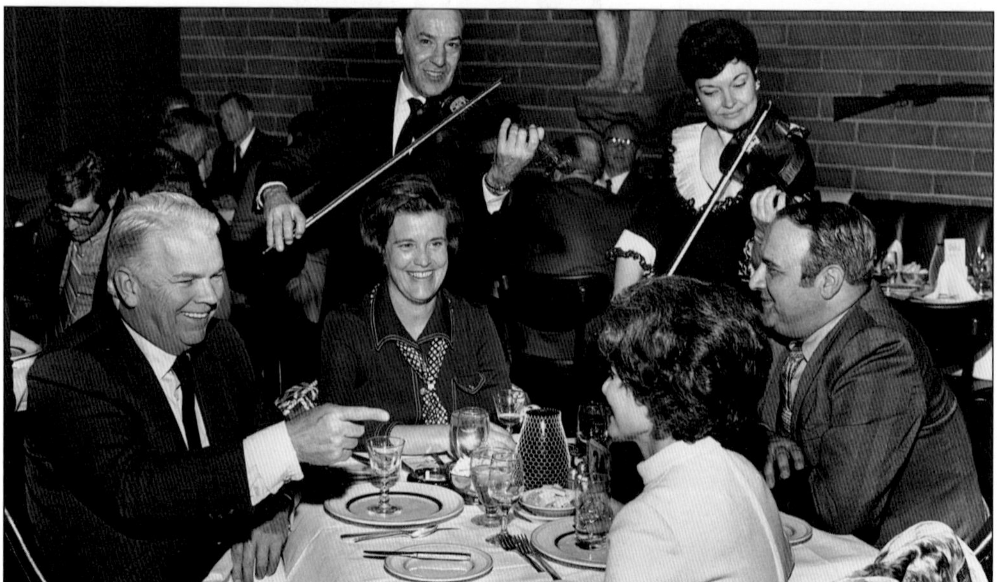

THE STADIUM CLUB. The Stadium Club restaurant for season-ticket holders on the Club and Dugout Levels overlooks the right-field corner of the ballpark. Picture windows offer fans a breathtaking view of the ballpark as they enjoy their food before or during a Dodger game. One of the first charter members in 1962 was Robert E. Cobb, the former owner of the Pacific Coast League's Hollywood Stars whose famous "Cobb Salad" was on the menu at his Hollywood landmark, the Brown Derby. In addition to fine cuisine, the Stadium Club featured unique decorations and other artifacts from Walter O'Malley's safari expeditions.

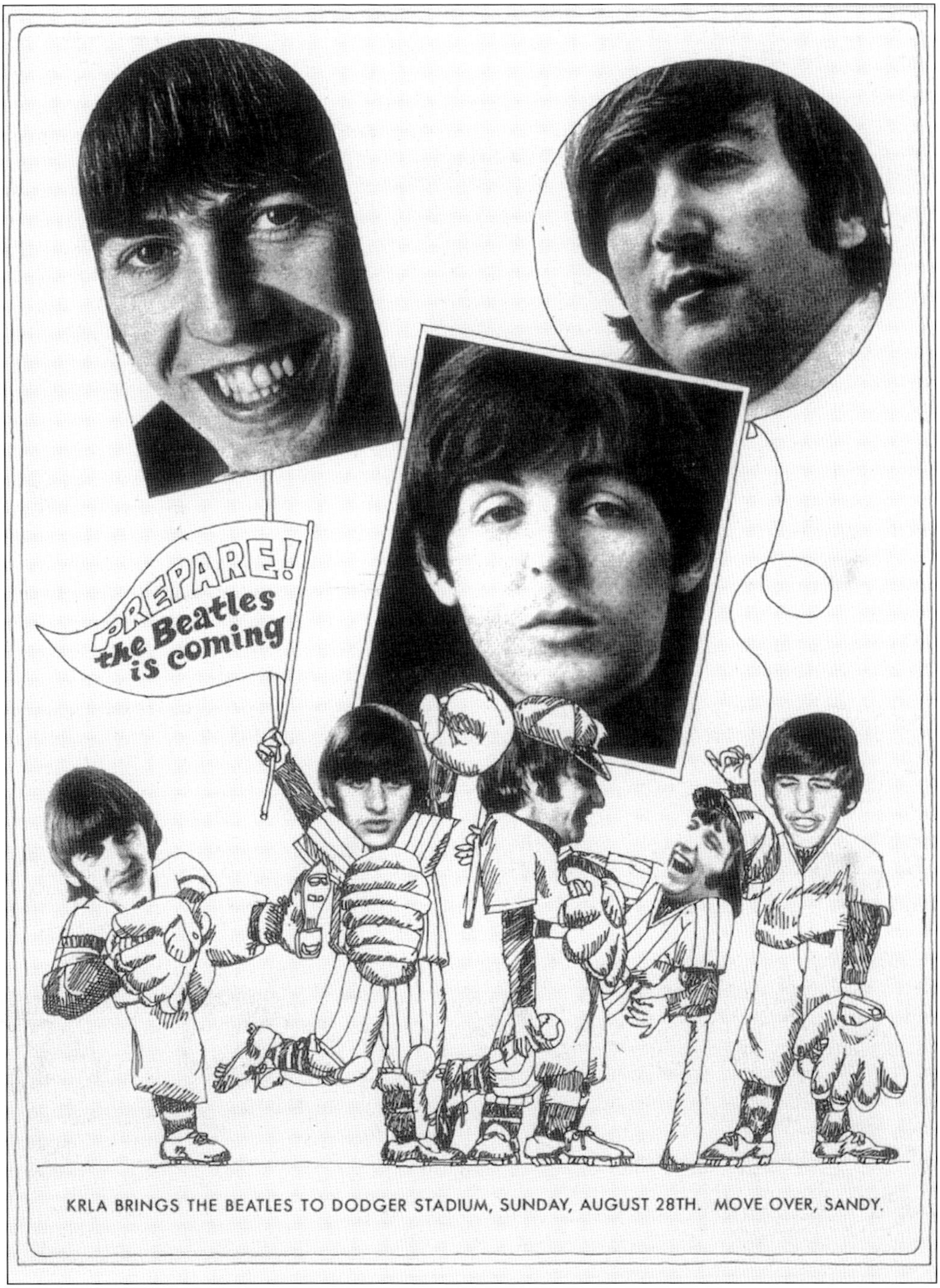

THE BEATLES. The famous band arrived in an armored car for their concert at Dodger Stadium on August 28, 1966. The Sunday evening event was sponsored by radio station KRLA and field box seats cost $6. Two days later, John Lennon, Ringo Starr, Paul McCartney, and George Harrison performed their final concert together at San Francisco's Candlestick Park.

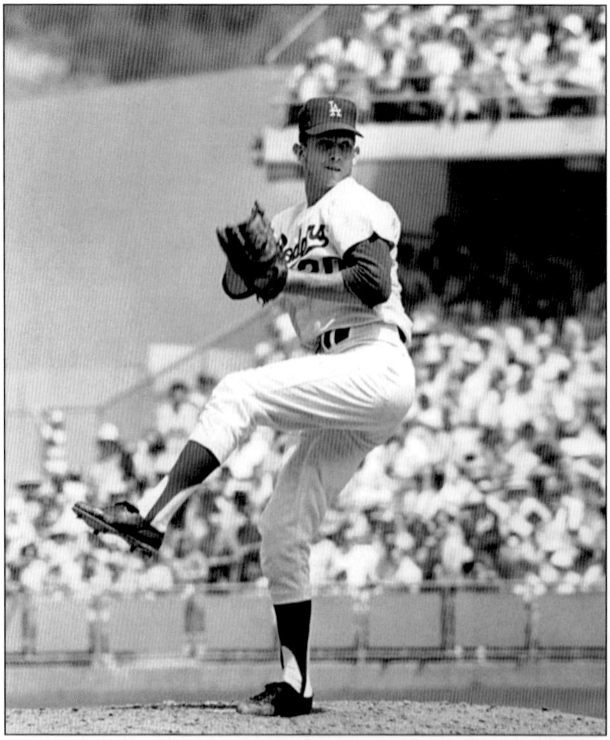

DON SUTTON'S ROOKIE SEASON. At age 21, right-hander Don Sutton joined a Dodger starting rotation that featured Sandy Koufax, Don Drysdale, Claude Osteen, and Johnny Podres. Sutton posted a 12-12 record in 1966, but didn't appear in the World Series because of a strained muscle in his forearm. When the Dodgers retired Sutton's uniform No. 20 upon his election to the Hall of Fame in 1998, Sandy Koufax attended the ceremony at Dodger Stadium. According to Sutton, Koufax told him, "You're the only 300-game winner I ever played with."

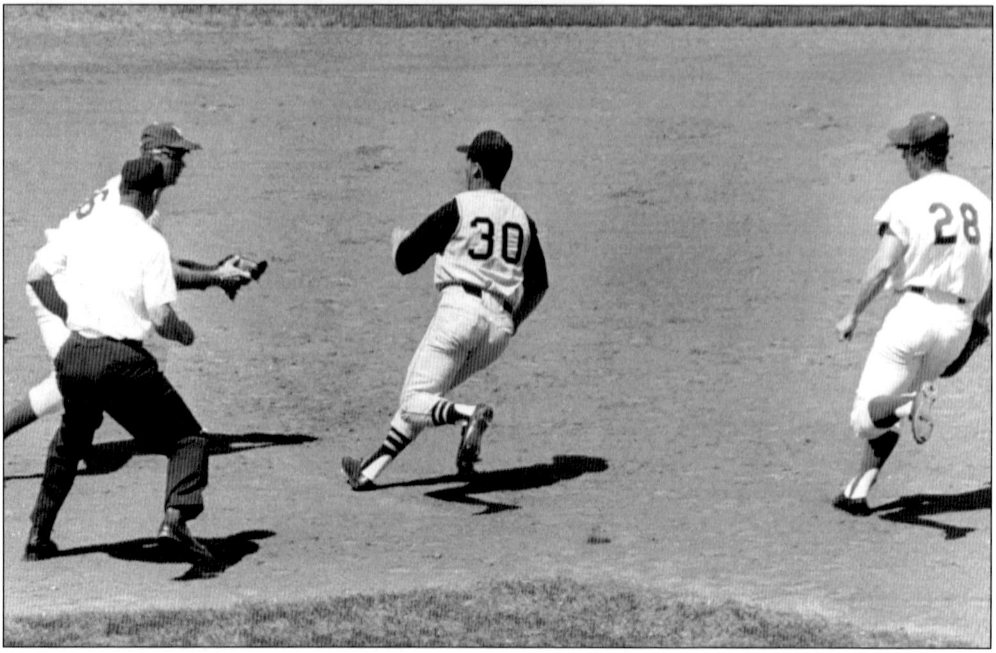

FAMILIAR FACE, DIFFERENT UNIFORM. After he left the team in the middle of their 1966 Japan tour, the Dodgers traded speedster Maury Wills to the Pittsburgh Pirates. On June 4, 1967, Wills was caught in a rundown between infielders Gene Michael and Wes Parker. Wills, who signed his first professional contract with the Dodgers in 1951, returned to Los Angeles for his final four seasons from 1969 to 1972.

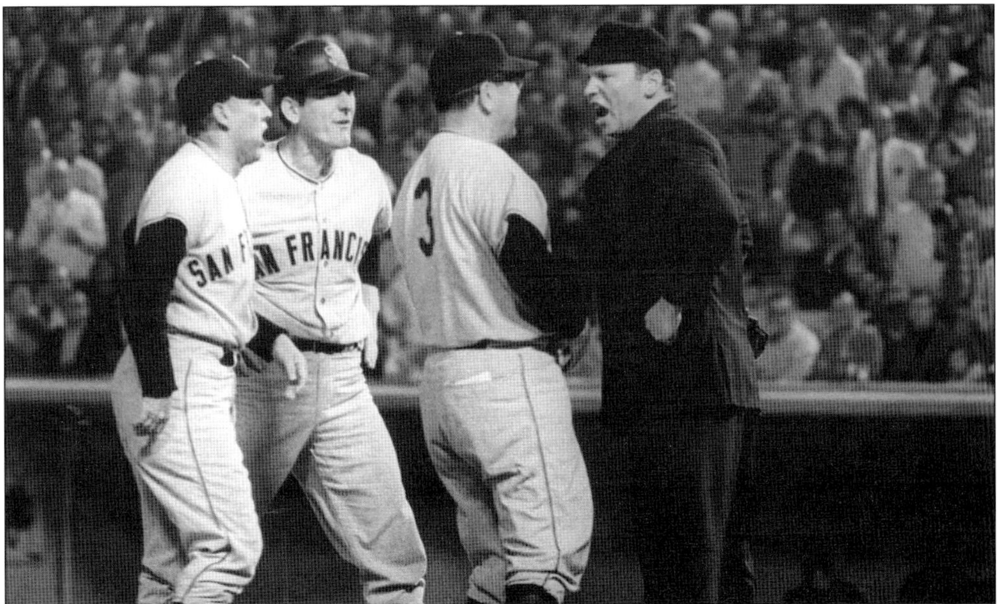

A Giant Argument. The flashpoint of Don Drysdale's record $58^2/_3$ consecutive innings in 1968 occurred at Dodger Stadium on May 31 when home plate umpire Harry Wendlestedt ruled San Francisco batter Dick Dietz failed to attempt to get out of the way of a bases-loaded pitch. Instead of awarding first base and ending Drysdale's streak, the umpire ruled the pitch a strike, triggering an argument with Dietz, Coach Peanuts Lowery, and Manager Herman Franks. Dietz eventually flied out and Drysdale retired the next two batters to escape the jam.

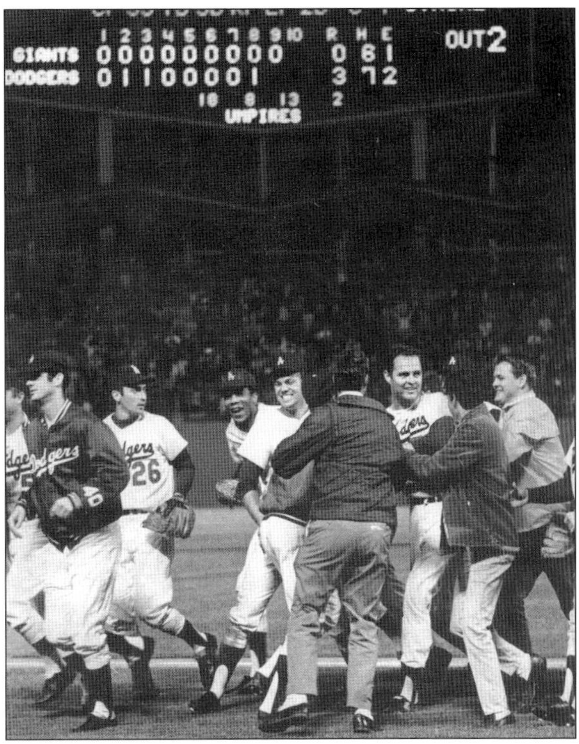

The Streak Continues. Having survived the Dick Dietz controversy, Don Drysdale is mobbed by teammates after his sixth consecutive shutout, a major league record. The 3-0 triumph over San Francisco was also the 200th career victory for Drysdale, who began his career with the Brooklyn Dodgers at age 19 in 1956. Drysdale's 54 consecutive scoreless innings at that point was just two shy of Walter Johnson's string of 56 scoreless innings with the 1913 Washington Senators.

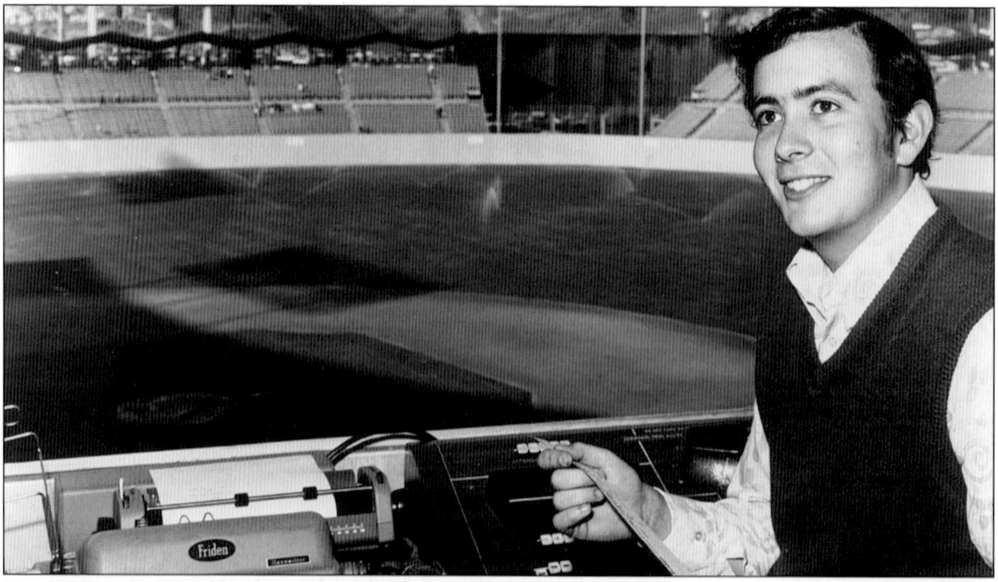

The Famous Scoreboards. The scoreboards at Dodger Stadium were designed for baseball information and public announcements instead of the "bells and whistles" style of the famous "exploding scoreboard" at Bill Veeck's Comiskey Park in Chicago. The Dodger scoreboards were 75 feet by 34, featured 17,000 lights, using enough electricity to light up 200 houses or 100,000 Christmas trees. Barry Stockhamer (pictured) began his Dodger career as a scoreboard operator and eventually became a vice president in charge of marketing.

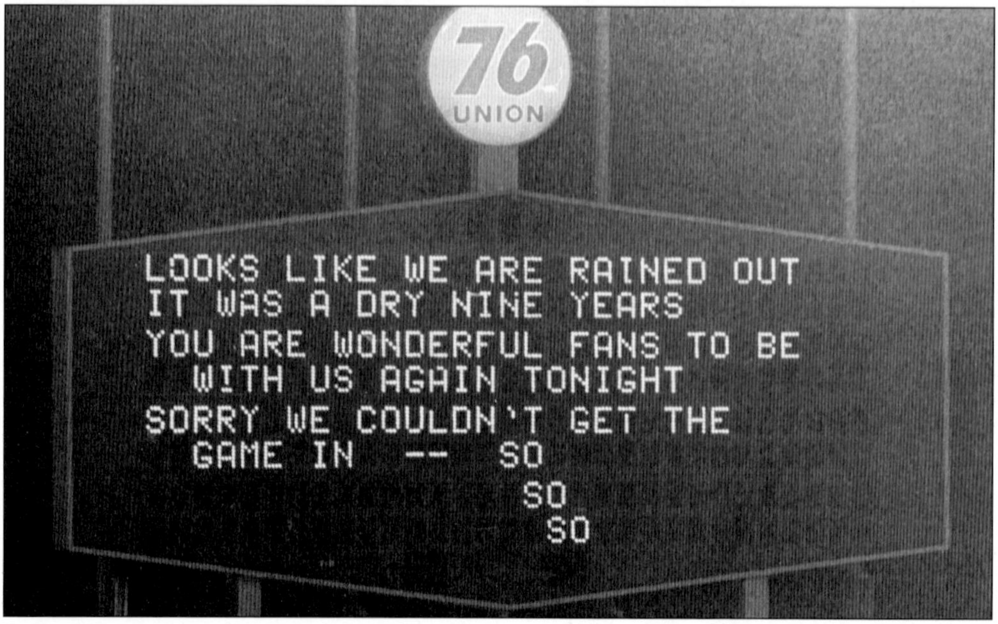

Rare Waterworks. During the Dodgers' first 18 seasons on the West Coast, only one game was postponed due to weather when rains wiped out the scheduled matchup with the St. Louis Cardinals at Dodger Stadium on April 21, 1967. Los Angeles would play 724 consecutive home games until the second stadium rainout on April 12, 1976. The club also staged 856 consecutive games without a rainout from 1988 to 1999.

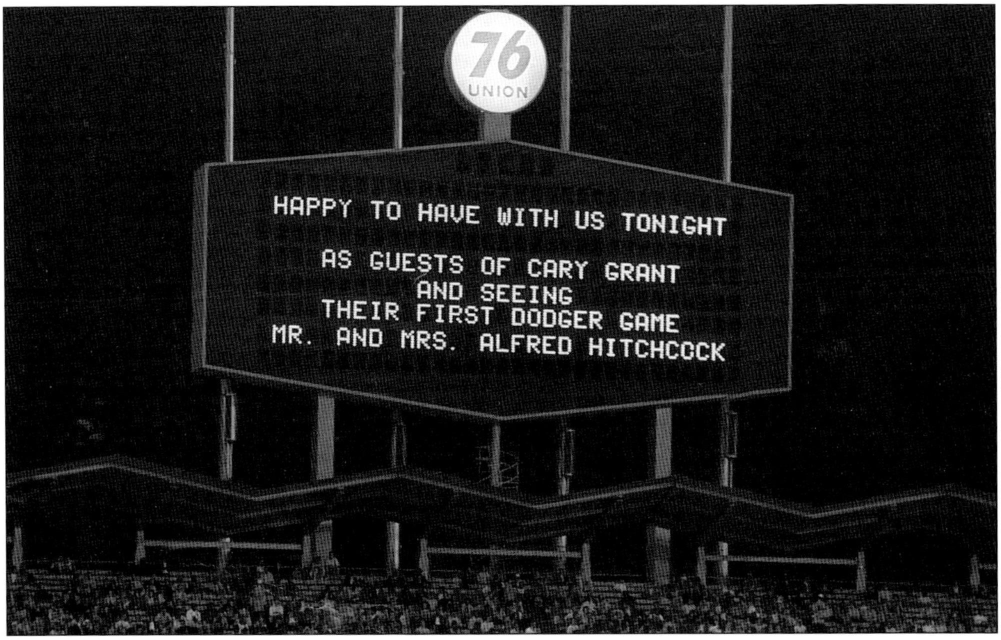

STAR SIGHTINGS. One never knew which Hollywood star might drop by the ballpark in the 1960s. Of course, everyone found out if the famous guests were greeted on the scoreboard.

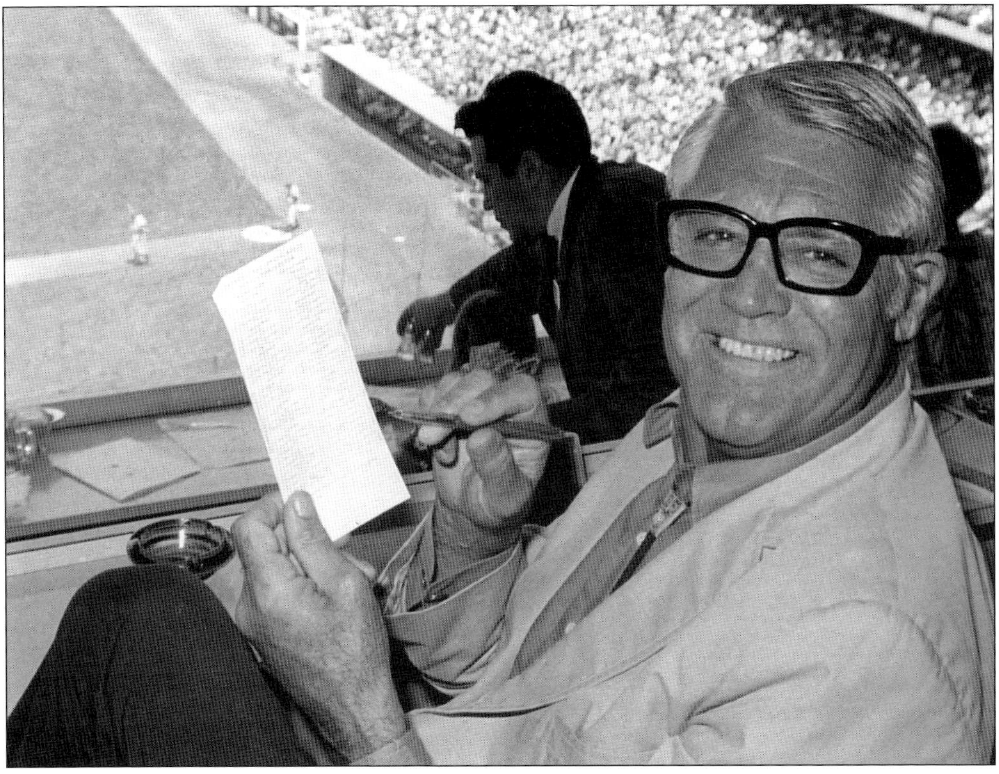

CAST YOUR BALLOT. Actor Cary Grant scans a list filled with hopeful stars—the candidates for the All-Star Game during the annual fan balloting program.

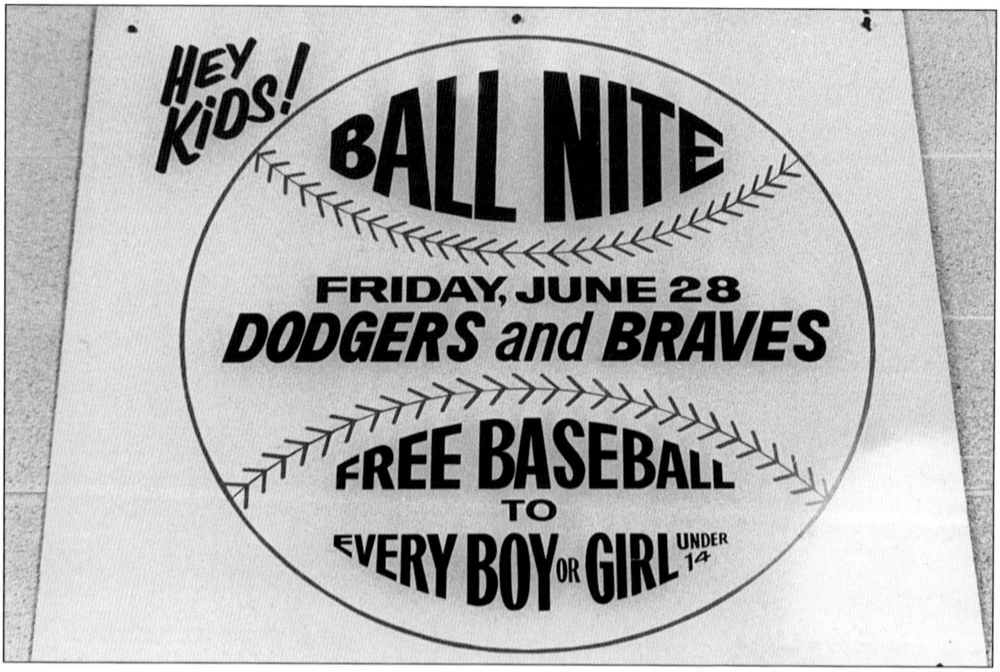

BALL DAY SIGN. Dating back to their roots in Brooklyn, the Dodgers traditionally have staged special promotional giveaway days for their fans. This sign from 1968 advertises Ball Night.

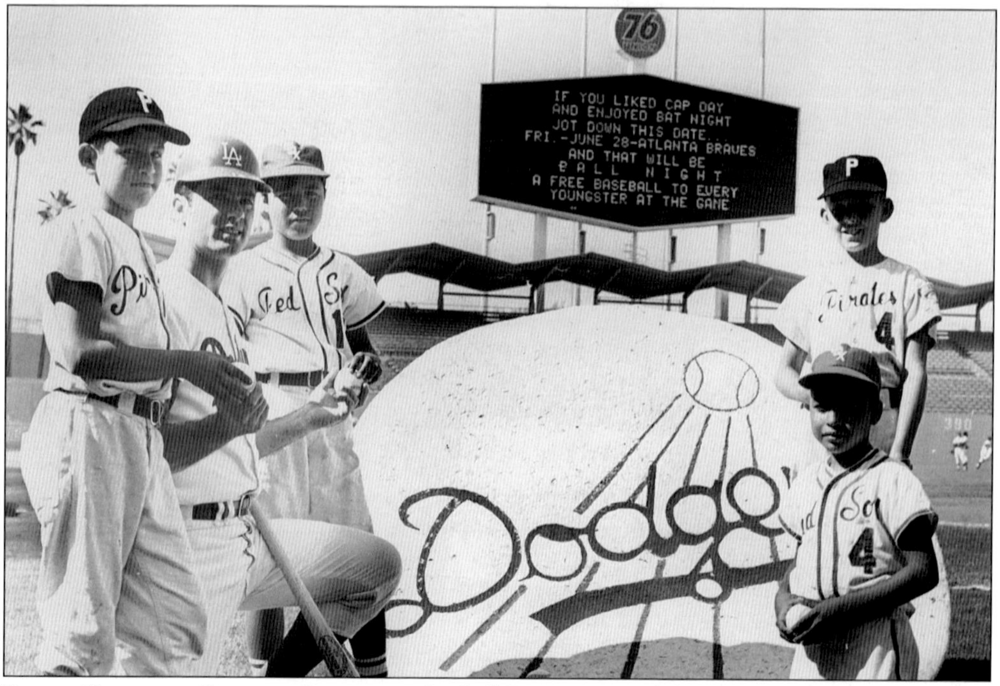

ROCKY DAYS AS A DODGER. Promoting the Ball Day event with local Little Leaguers at Dodger Stadium is veteran outfielder Rocky Colavito, who batted .204 in 40 games with Los Angeles. Colavito split the 1968 campaign with the Dodgers and New York Yankees and the six-time All-Star retired after the season at age 35.

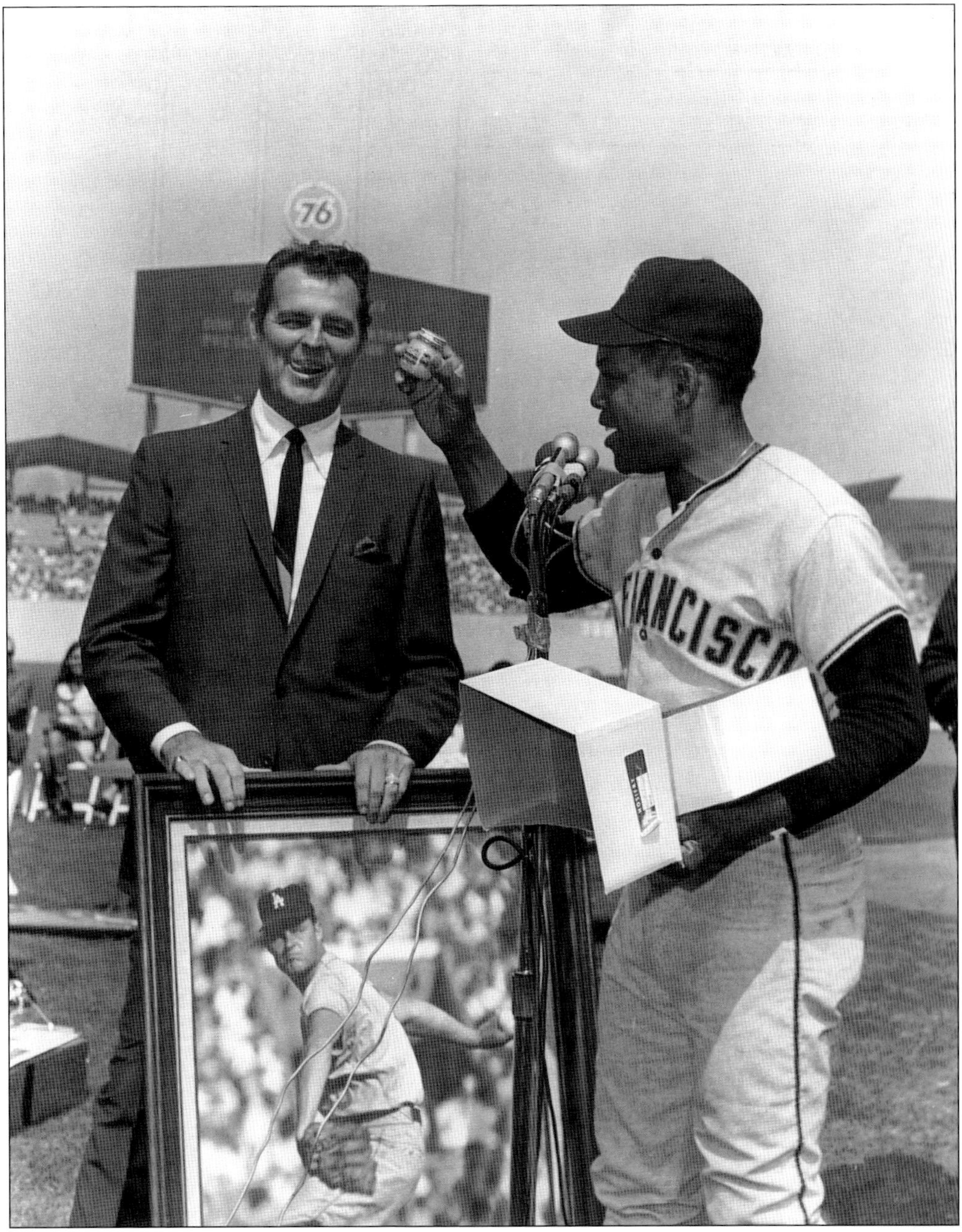

THE SAY HEY SPITTER. During Don Drysdale Day ceremonies at Dodger Stadium in 1969, Giants slugger Willie Mays presents the pitcher with a jar of Vaseline. "Big D" flashes a mischievous grin, but Mays couldn't get a confession at the podium. Drysdale retired at age 32 as the Los Angeles all-time leader in victories (209), games started (465), strikeouts (2,486), innings (3,432.1), shutouts (49), and games (518). When Drysdale went to Walter O'Malley's office to confirm his retirement on August 10, he watched a few innings of the Dodger game in the stands and heard an unfamiliar sound. "In all the years I pitched, it was as if I'd become immune to the sound of bat hitting ball and ball hitting mitt," he said. "It had always been a magnetic click for me and I saw my whole childhood again. I knew then that all my dreams had come true."

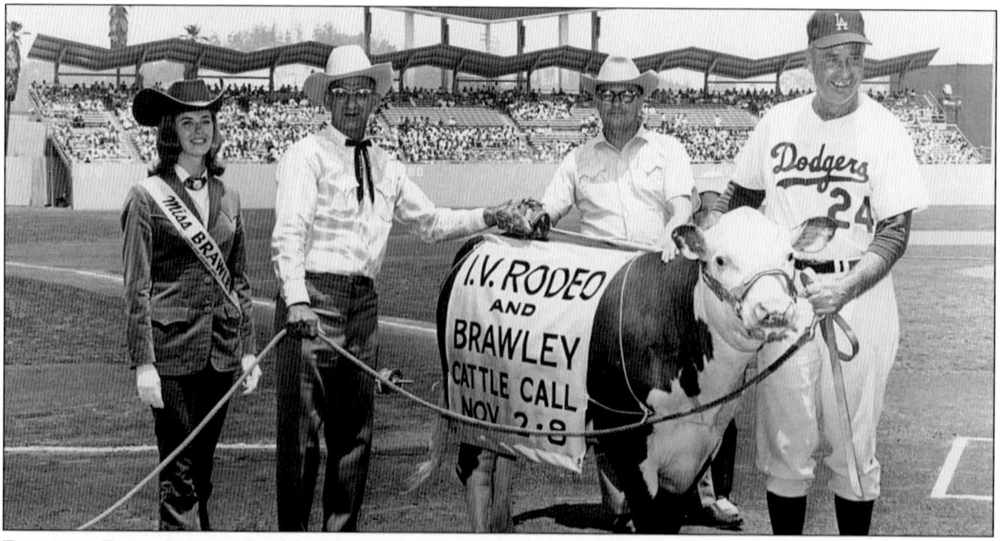

DODGER BUM STEER. Dodger Stadium hosts many community-related events in conjunction with every ballgame. Pregame guests are introduced to the crowd and have a chance to take their picture with a player or coach in uniform. In this event, Manager Walter Alston meets participants promoting an upcoming a Brawley rodeo.

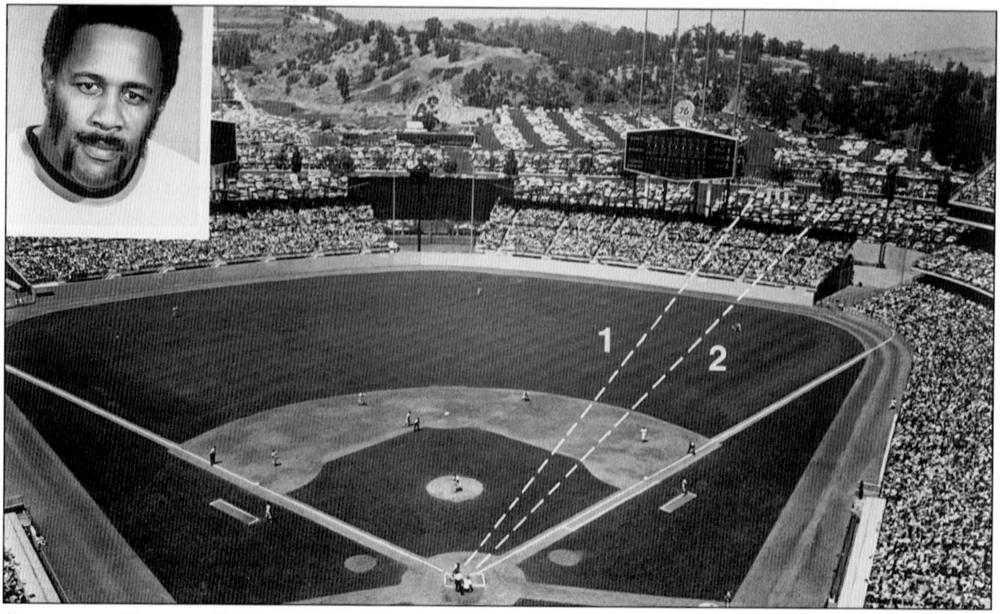

STARGELL CLEARS ROOF. On August 6, 1969, Pittsburgh Pirates outfielder Willie Stargell became the first player to hit a home run out of Dodger Stadium. Stargell's blast off Los Angeles pitcher Alan Foster traveled past the 370-foot sign and landed about 506 feet, 6 inches away. Stargell turned the trick again on May 8, 1973 when his blast off Andy Messersmith hit the right field pavilion roof and landed 470 feet from home plate. The only other opponent to hit a home run completely out of Dodger Stadium was St. Louis Cardinals' first baseman Mark McGwire, who hit a 483-foot home run to left-center off Jamie Arnold on May 22, 1999. Mike Piazza is the lone Dodger to perform the feat, connecting against Colorado Rockies reliever Frank Castillo for a 478-foot home run on September 21, 1997.

THREE

1970s

There was a changing of the guard in March 1970 when Walter O'Malley became chairman of the board and turned over control of the Dodgers to his son Peter, who became the 10th team president in team history. Peter O'Malley began working for the Dodgers full-time in January 1962 when he was named director of Dodgertown, the team's spring training facility in Vero Beach, Florida. He was president of the team's Triple-A Spokane affiliate from 1965 to 1966 and returned to Los Angeles in 1967 as vice president in charge of stadium operations.

When Dodger Stadium celebrated its 10th season in 1971, O'Malley staged the first Oldtimers Day as heroes of the 1960s were invited, along with some familiar faces from Ebbets Field in New York and the Los Angeles Memorial Coliseum. The Oldtimers Day participants took part in a luncheon at the Stadium Club and played an exhibition game on the field. In 1972, the Dodgers retired the uniform numbers of Hall of Famers Sandy Koufax (32), Roy Campanella (39), and Jackie Robinson (42).

In the front office, Fred Claire took over public relation duties from Arthur E. "Red" Patterson as another former baseball reporter who excelled as a team publicist. Patterson worked for the *New York Herald Tribune*; Claire wrote for newspapers in Long Beach, Pomona and Whittier. While attending San Jose State College, Claire once wrote a story in 1955 for *Baseball Magazine* titled, "Make Way for the Coast League," discussing the merits of a league hurt by rumors about major league franchises moving to California.

"Not only have the stories taken up space which could have been used for promotion of the coast circuit, they have led thousands of fans to believe that the Pacific Coast League is nothing but a grave yard for worn out major league ballplayers, discouraging countless ticket buyers," Claire wrote. "Without a doubt the west coast is the fastest growing section in the United States and if left alone, and given a fair shake, could support a third major league, as impractical as it may sound."

Claire encouraged Dodger team photographers to utilize the beauty of the ballpark in the stadium portraits. And the team's 1972 yearbook cover displayed five different angles of the ballpark, along with its flowers and palm trees.

The concept of a privately financed stadium was a benefit to the Dodgers in terms of stability. When the Braves moved to Milwaukee in 1953, they enjoyed success on the field and record attendance figures in their new ballpark. But attendance dwindled with a decade and by the middle of the 1965 season, the Braves tried to buy out their lease. The National League made the Braves stay in Milwaukee for the season, but they could move to Atlanta in 1966. The lame-duck Braves drew only 555,584 fans in a ballpark that once drew 2.2 million in 1957.

At their box office, the Dodgers suffered a drop in attendance from 2.6 million during Sandy Koufax's final year as a player in 1966 to 1.5 million in 1967, when the ballclub finished in eighth place. But Walter O'Malley knew the "novelty" of a new ballpark would wear off and that a competitive product would ensure the fans would attend Dodger games. Attendance at Dodger Stadium climbed over the 2 million mark by 1971 and jumped to 2.6 million in 1974 when the Dodgers won their first pennant in nine years in 1974 with a spectacular 100-62 season, highlighted by newcomers Jimmy Wynn in the outfield and Mike Marshall in the bullpen, along with their young infield of Steve Garvey, Davey Lopes, Bill Russell, and Ron Cey. The impact of the fan support was evident in 1974 when Garvey wasn't listed on the All-Star Game ballot and he became only the second "write-in candidate" elected to a starting position, joining Rico Carty of the 1970 Braves.

"As a kid growing up in Los Angeles, you saw the Dodgers on television and heard them on the radio," said Bobby Castillo, who broke into the majors with the Dodgers in 1977. "My dad used to drop us off as kids to come up to the ballpark and this is where your Sunday afternoon was. When we played in the streets, everyone wanted to play for the Dodgers."

The familiar faces at the ballpark also became part of people's everyday lives. The broadcasting team of Vin Scully and Jerry Doggett was in the middle of a 32-year tenure together and the core of young players would continue performing into the next decade.

In the dugout, low-profile Walter Alston retired in 1976 after 23 seasons and handed the reins to the bombastic, energetic Tommy Lasorda, who had spent 27 years in the Dodger organization as a player, scout, minor league manager, and major league coach. Fans reading the 1977 yearbook at Dodger Stadium received an entire page of famous "Lasorda-isms," including his proclamation "I bleed Dodger Blue." The capitalization of the color became a key jingle around Dodger Stadium and a 1978 season ticket brochure featured the headline "The Dodger Blue And You. . . ."

And visiting his father's office was a special treat for Mark Brewer, a current Dodger minor league pitching instructor whose father, Jim, was a Los Angeles relief pitcher from 1964 to 1975. "Every time I go to Dodger Stadium, I get emotional, thinking about the things that happened when I was growing up, and I wouldn't change any of it for the world," said Mark Brewer, an Oklahoma native who played hide-and-seek with other children of Dodger players when the ballpark was empty. "I knew everyone at the stadium: the security guards, the ushers, the usherettes. We were on a first-name basis with everybody. I can still smell the same smells when I was a youngster and it brings back memories of smelling the stale beer after the game, the peanuts on the floor. But previous to the game, walking in and hearing the echoes and knowing every inch of that place was going to be clean and healthy."

MARTIN LUTHER KING JR. MEMORIAL. Following the death of Rev. Martin Luther King Jr. in 1968, Major League Baseball sponsored an East-West All-Star Game at Dodger Stadium. The exhibition was staged near the conclusion of spring training and every team sent representatives to Los Angeles to participate. Dr. King's widow, Coretta Scott King, attended the 1970 game in the box seats behind the dugout. During batting practice, comedians Bill Cosby and Danny Kaye met the All-Star players. In the background covering the event was KNBC sports reporter Tommy Hawkins, a former Los Angeles Lakers basketball player who later joined the Dodgers in 1987 as a vice president of communications.

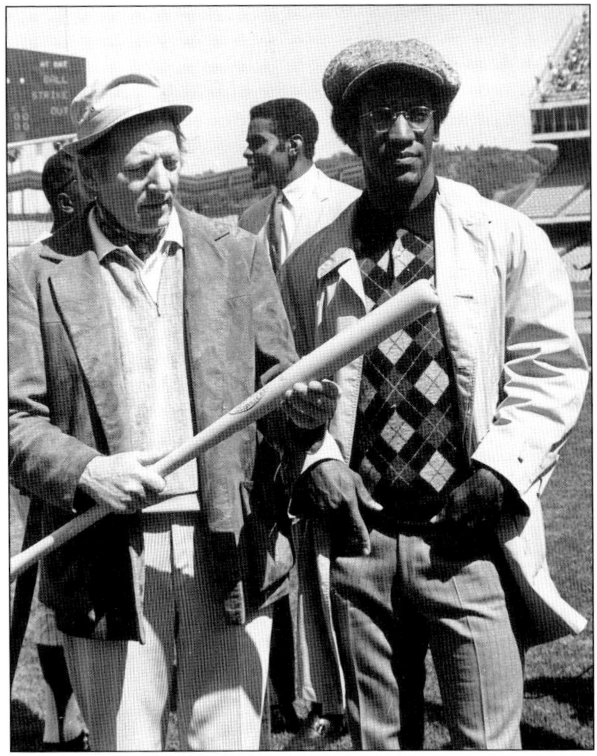

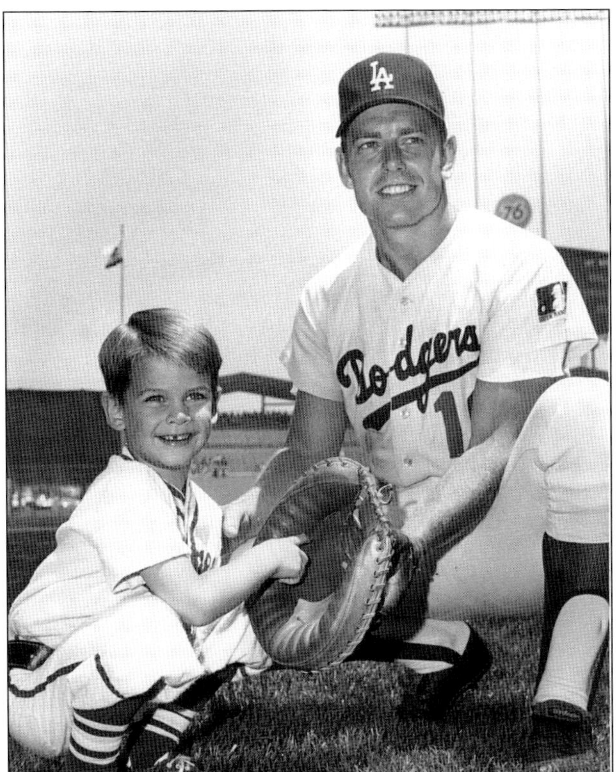

FATHER AND SON. Catcher Jeff Torborg and his son Doug get ready for the annual Dodger Family Game. Torborg played in Los Angeles from 1964 to 1970. The former All-America selection at Rutgers caught Sandy Koufax's perfect game in 1965 and Bill Singer's no-hitter in 1970. Traded to the California Angels, Torborg caught pitcher Nolan Ryan's first career no-hitter in 1973.

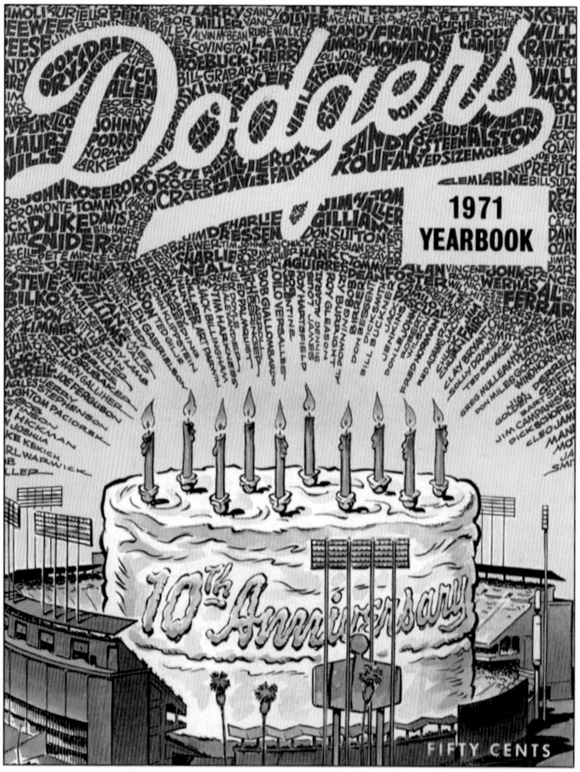

THE FIRST DECADE. Karl Hubenthal, the *Los Angeles Herald-Examiner* political cartoonist whose sports illustrations are among the most famous in Southern California history, salutes Dodger Stadium's 10th season on the cover of the team's 1971 yearbook. One of Hubenthal's early mentors was *Herald* cartoonist Willard Mullin, who later created the "Dodger Bum" character when he moved to New York.

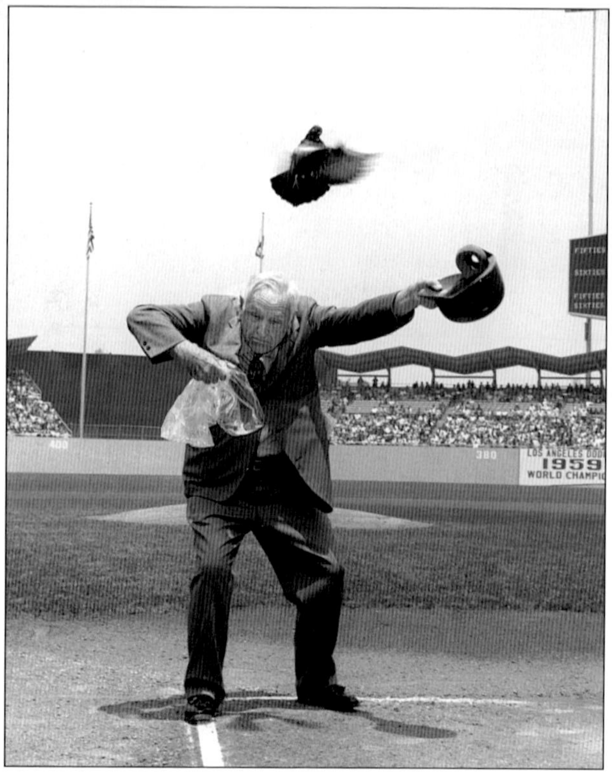

CASEY STENGEL. In addition to his Hall of Fame managerial skills—winning 10 pennants and 7 World Series titles in 12 years with the New York Yankees—Casey Stengel was a colorful player who broke into the majors with a four-hit game for the Brooklyn Dodgers in 1912. Dealt to the Pittsburgh Pirates in 1918, Stengel was booed by Dodger fans upon his first game at Ebbets Field. But Stengel found a sparrow before his second at-bat and when he doffed his cap to the crowd, boos turned into waves of laughter. For Oldtimers Day at Dodger Stadium in 1971, Stengel performed his hidden-bird trick to the delight of the Los Angeles crowd.

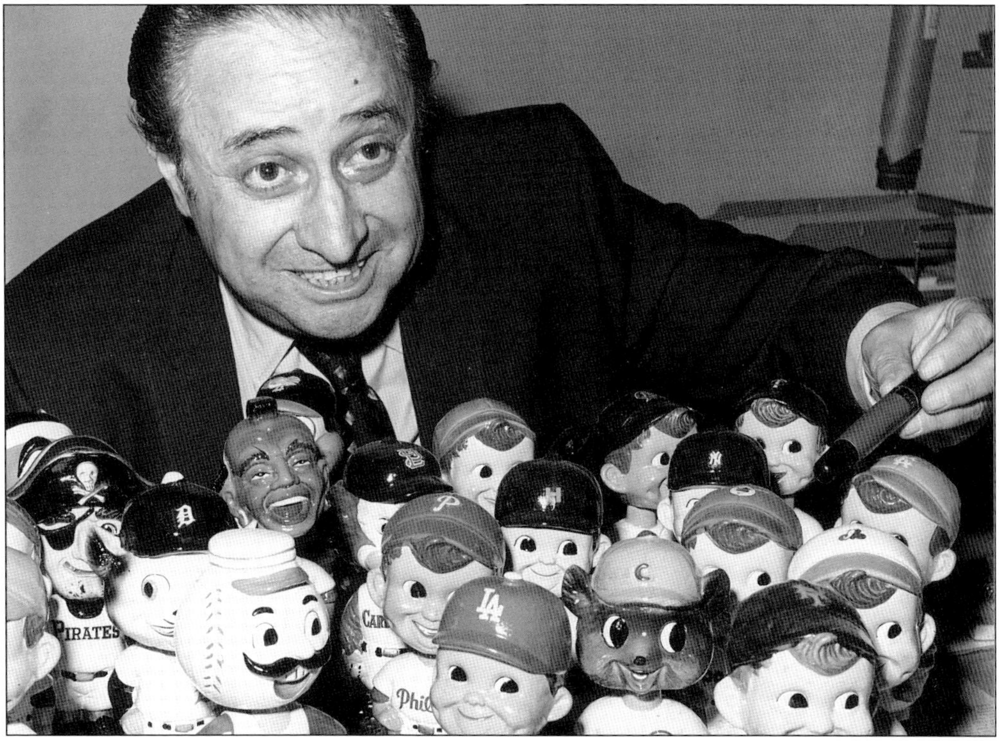

(*above*) **THE KING OF NOVELTY ITEMS.** When the Dodgers moved to the West Coast in 1958, the only major addition to the front office was Danny Goodman, who had 30 years of experience in the concessions business. He managed concessions for the minor league Newark Bears from 1933 to 1937 and moved to California in 1938 to handle concessions for the Pacific Coast League's Hollywood Stars. During his tenure with Los Angeles, the Dodgers offered "Danny Goodman Specials," which featured surplus merchandise with a specific theme.

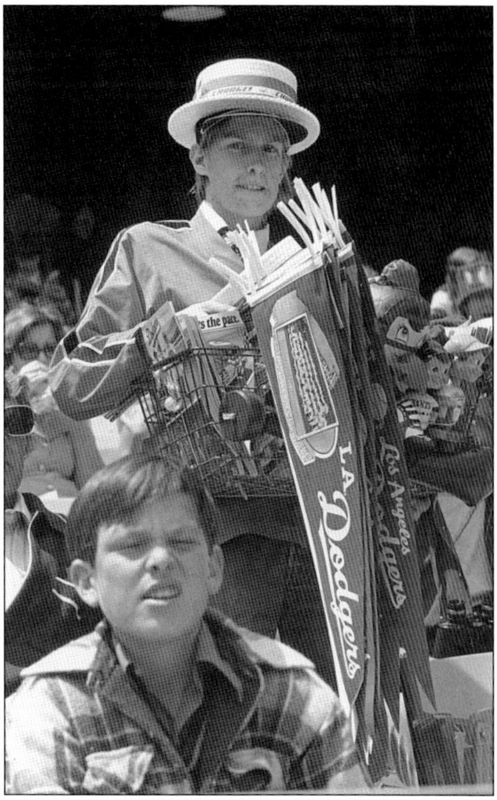

(*right*) **GET YOUR SOUVENIRS.** A stadium vendor is ready for any sale with an abundant supply of bobble heads, pennants, and other Dodger items. In the early 1970s, Danny Goodman's department stocked a variety of items with the Dodger logo, including ash trays, beach balls, money clips, comb and file sets, pearl bracelets, trinket boxes, voodoo dolls, "Wee Willie Dagger," terry cloth bibs, baseball radios, models of the team's Electra II airplane, bookmarks, "Happy People Dolls," aprons, hair pins, and ladies clutch bags.

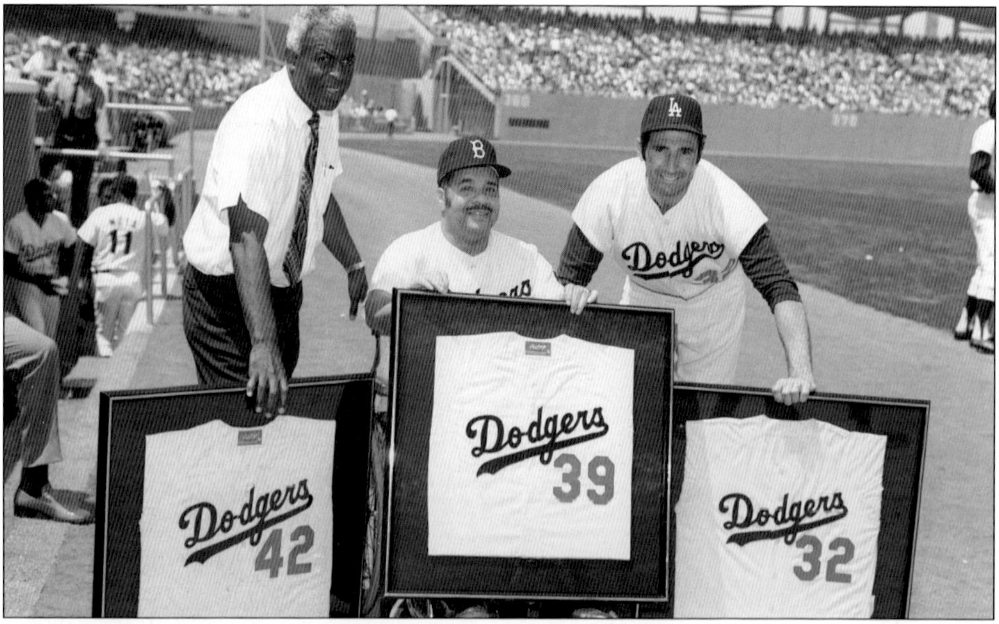

HALL OF FAME TRIO. On June 4, 1972, the Dodgers retired the first three uniform numbers in team history, saluting pitcher Sandy Koufax (32), Roy Campanella (39), and Jackie Robinson (42), who were the only players who spent their entire playing careers with the Dodgers and ended up in the Hall of Fame. The Dodgers traded Robinson to the New York Giants following the 1956 season, but he opted to retire after a historic 10-year career in which he compiled a lifetime .311 batting average and made six World Series appearances. The Oldtimers Day ceremony would be the final Dodger Stadium appearance for Robinson, who passed away four months later at age 53.

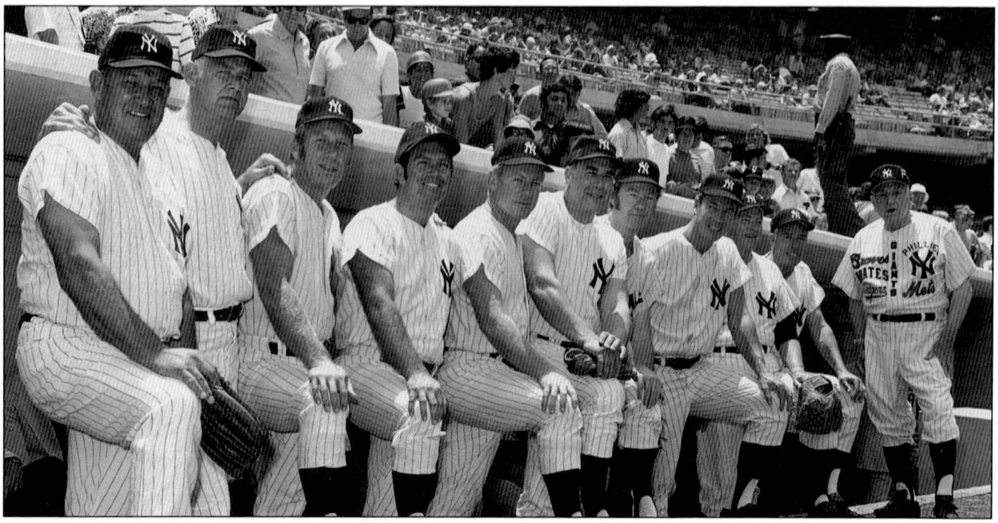

THE MIGHTY YANKEES. Several members of the New York Yankee pennant-winning ballclubs assembled for the Dodgers' Oldtimers Day ceremonies in 1972. From left to right are Allie Reynolds, Don Larsen, Mickey Mantle, Bobby Richardson, Whitey Ford, Vic Raschi, Gil McDougald, Andy Carey, Bill Dickey, Joe DiMaggio, and Manager Casey Stengel. Stengel wore a uniform with logos from all his major league affiliations.

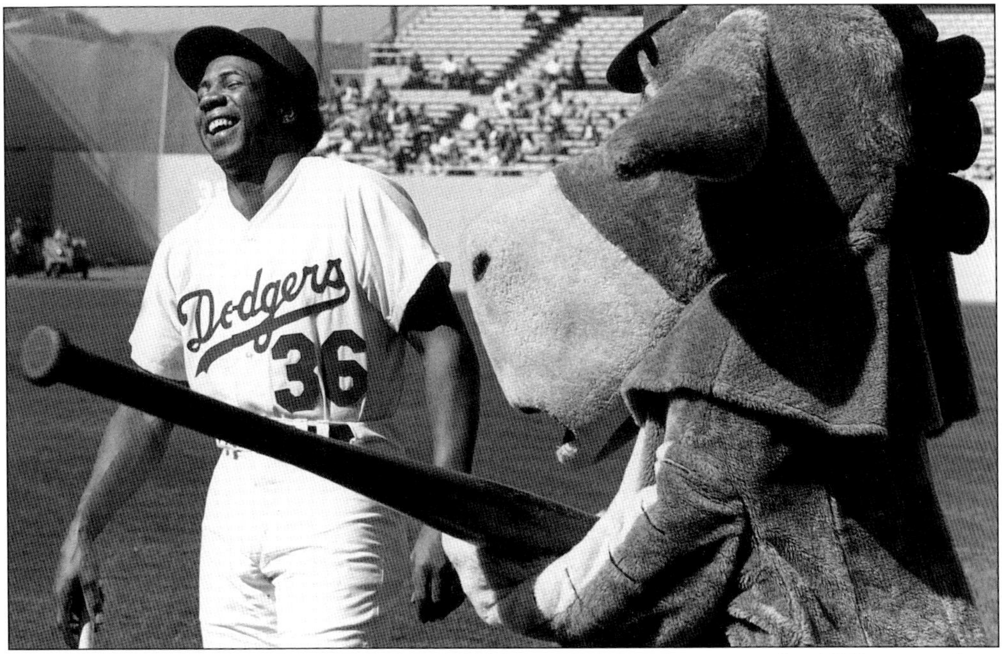

FRANK ROBINSON. The Hall of Fame outfielder was acquired prior to the 1972 season from the World Champion Baltimore Orioles. In his first game with the Dodgers, Robinson smiled when a cartoon character offered an oversized bat for the annual workout exhibition with the University of Southern California. The 1972 campaign would be Robinson's only appearance in a Dodger uniform and the last National League stop of his career. Robinson batted .251 with 19 home runs and 59 RBI in 103 games. The Hall of Famer hit career home runs No. 504 through 522 in a Dodger uniform, the highest in Los Angeles history.

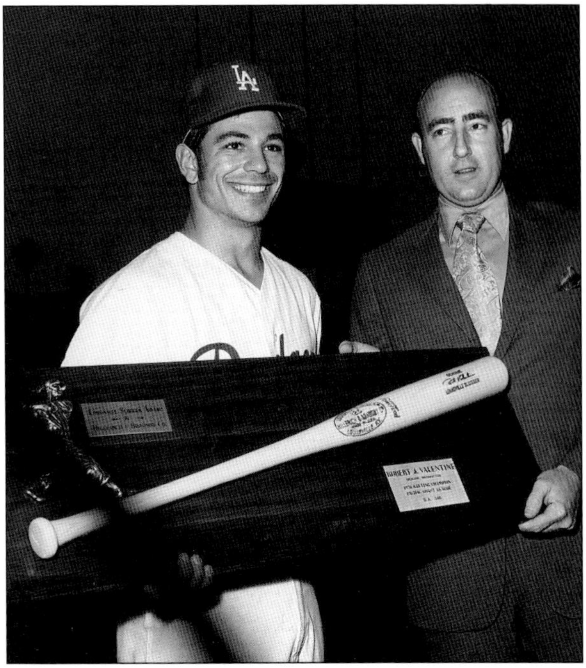

TOP PROSPECT. Infielder Bobby Valentine led Pacific Coast League hitters with a .340 average at Triple-A Spokane in 1971. Valentine, receiving his silver bat award from *Long Beach Press-Telegram* beat reporter Gordon Verrell, appeared in a career-high 119 games with Los Angeles in 1972, batting .274 with three home runs and 32 RBI. He also played four positions: second base, third base, shortstop, and outfield. The Dodgers dealt Valentine to the Angels prior to the 1973 season as part of a seven-player trade.

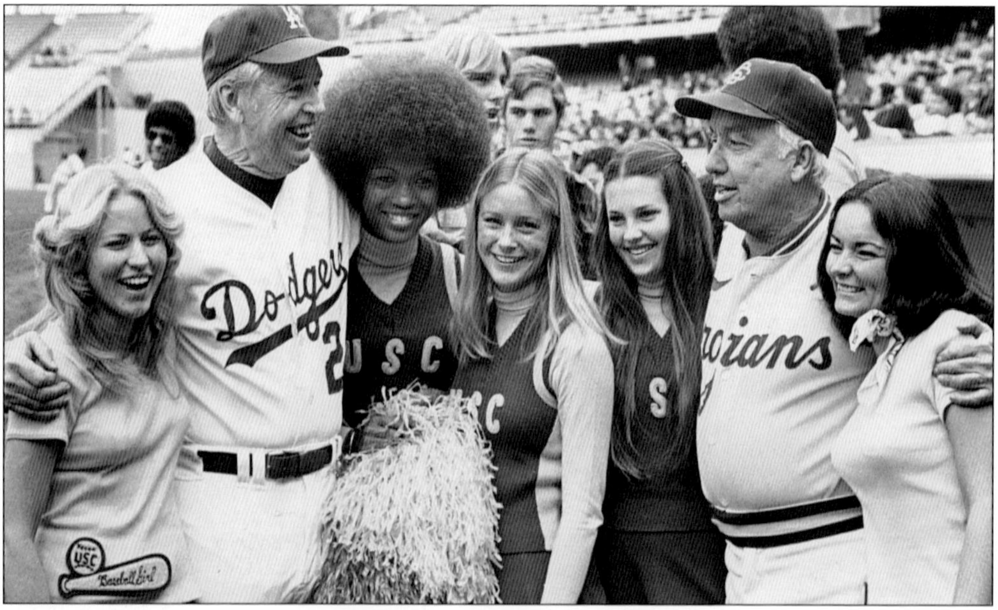

WINTER WORKOUT. For three decades, the Dodgers played an annual exhibition game against the University of Southern California. The 1965 Dodger-USC workout featured the only Heisman Trophy winner to play at Dodger Stadium—running back Mike Garrett, an outfielder who later was selected by Los Angeles in the amateur draft. The Trojans were led by Head Coach Rod Dedeaux, who was a member of the 1935 Brooklyn Dodgers and captured a record 11 national championships at USC. For this 1972 exhibition game, Dedeaux and USC cheerleaders gather around Los Angeles Manager Walter Alston.

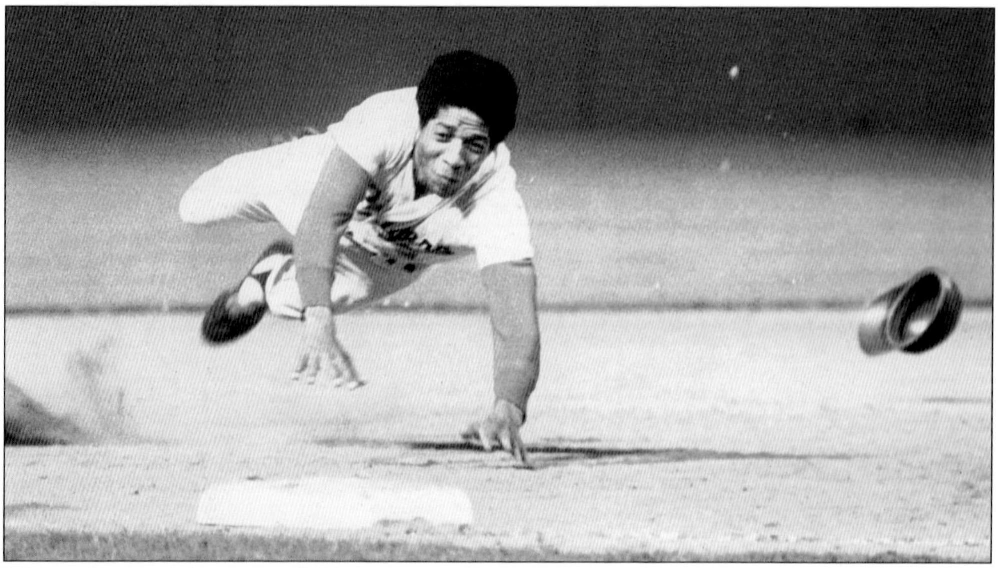

WILLIE DAVIS. The center fielder spent 14 seasons in a Dodger uniform and established Los Angeles career records for hits (2,091), extra-base hits (585), at-bats (7,495), runs (1,004), triples (110), and total bases (3,094). Davis hit in a club-record 31 consecutive games in 1969. Davis also became the first Los Angeles player with six hits in one game during a 19-inning marathon against the Mets at Dodger Stadium.

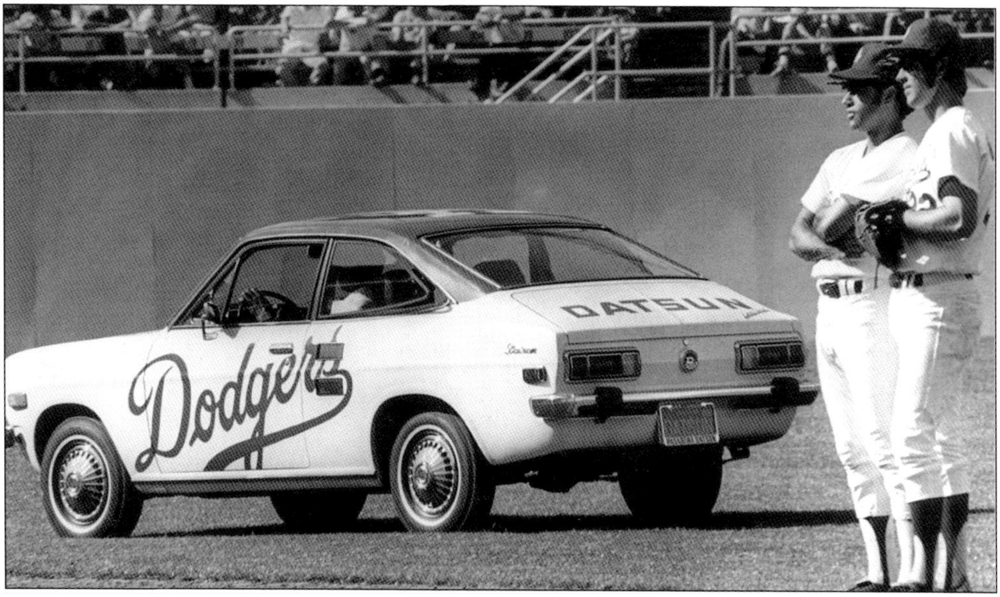

BULLPEN SHUTTLE. In the early 1970s, golf carts with baseball-shaped shell and oversized hat became the standard mode of transportation for most relief pitchers arriving for work. By 1973, the Dodgers used an automobile to make such necessary pitching changes. The car was parked in the bullpen and usually made the circular drive around the warning track. Infielders Bill Buckner and Davey Lopes watch as the car makes another delivery.

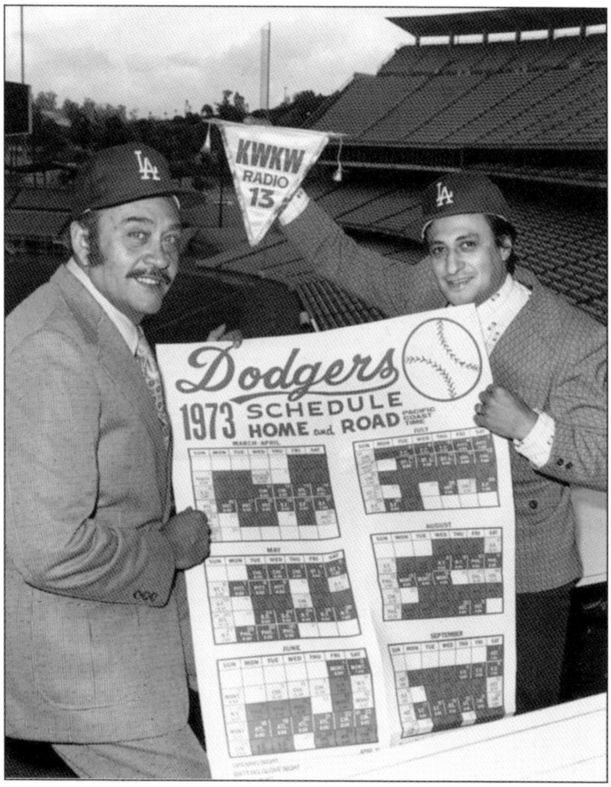

THE SPANISH VOICE OF THE DODGERS. Preparing for the 1973 season, broadcasters Rudy Hoyos and Jaime Jarrin hoist their banner for KWKW 1330, the Spanish flagship radio station of the Dodgers. Dodger games have been broadcast in Spanish since their arrival to Los Angeles in 1958. Hoyos spent nine seasons with Los Angeles from 1973 to 1981. Jarrin, who joined Los Angeles in 1959, was named to the broadcaster's wing of the Baseball Hall of Fame in 1997.

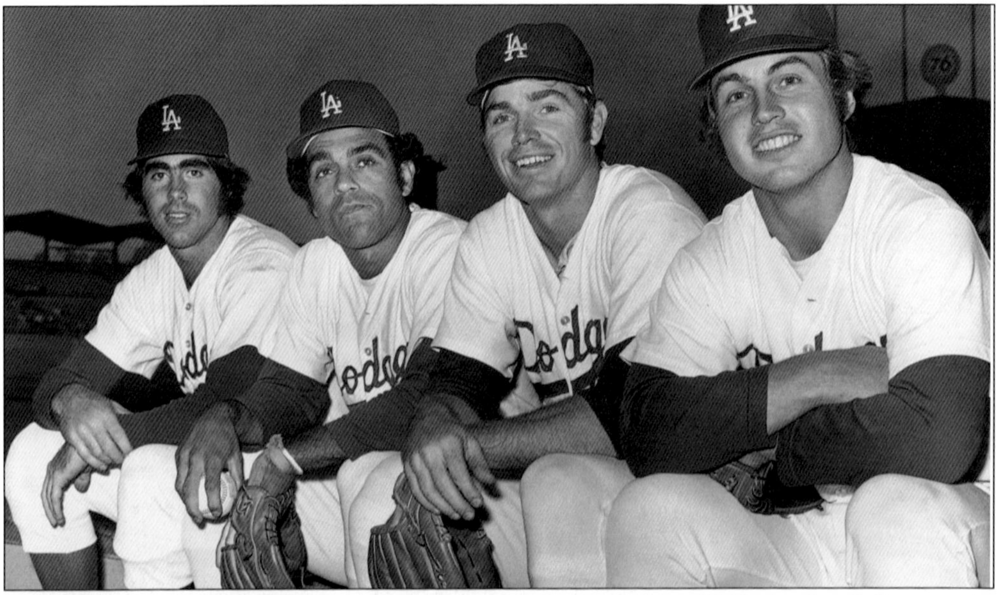

THE NEW INFIELD. The retirement of veterans Maury Wills and Wes Parker following the 1972 season opened the door for some of the top minor league prospects, including, from left to right, Bill Buckner, Davey Lopes, Bill Russell, and Ron Cey. Russell and Lopes originally were outfielders when they signed with the Dodger organization, but switched to the infield under the tutelage of coach Monty Basgall. Because scatter-armed Steve Garvey was a liability at third base, Manager Walter Alston switched him to first base in the middle of the 1973 season and dispatched Buckner to left field.

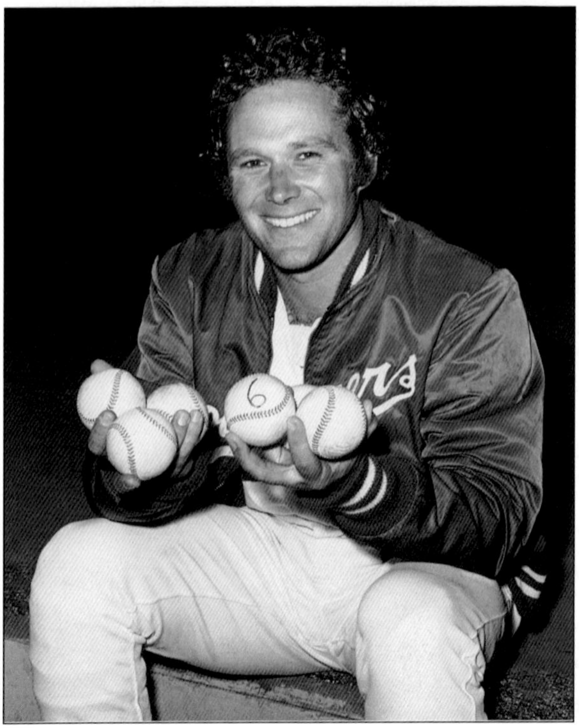

DANDY ANDY. Right-hander Andy Messersmith set a Dodger record when he struck out the first six Philadelphia Phillies' batters he faced on May 28, 1973. Acquired from the California Angels after the 1972 season, Messersmith won 53 games with Los Angeles from 1973 to 1975. Messersmith became one of baseball's first free agents prior to the 1976 season, but he later returned to the Dodgers and finished his career with Los Angeles in 1979.

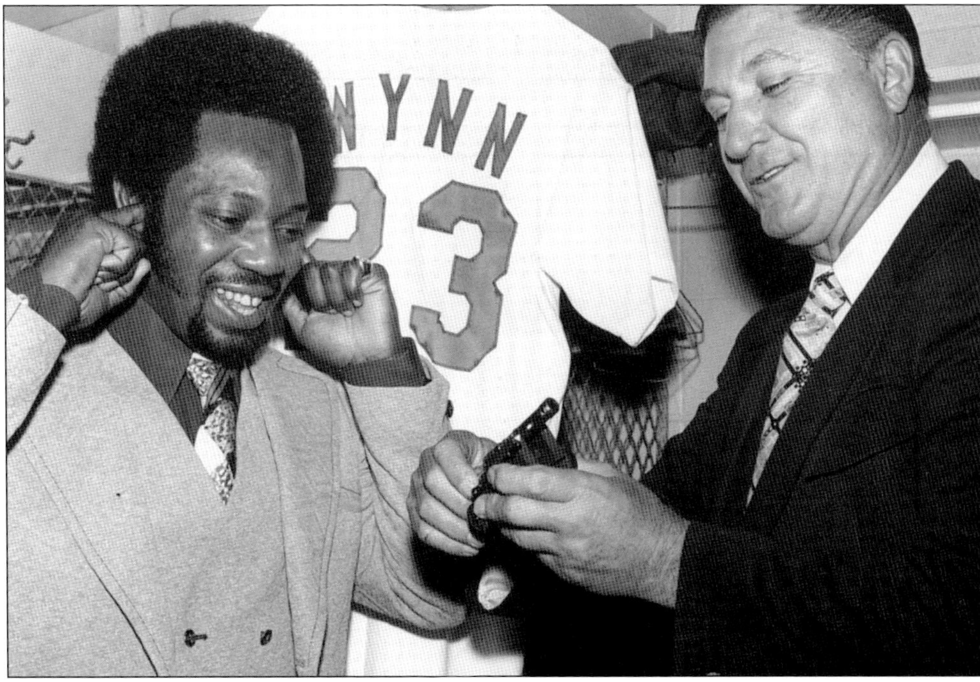

The Toy Cannon. One of the major trades in Los Angeles history sent pitcher Claude Osteen to Houston in exchange for outfielder Jimmy Wynn, the 5-foot-9, 170-pound slugger who was the Astros' career home run leader. In his first season with the Dodgers, Wynn blasted 32 home runs in 1974 and the outfielder pavilions became "Cannon Country" in his honor.

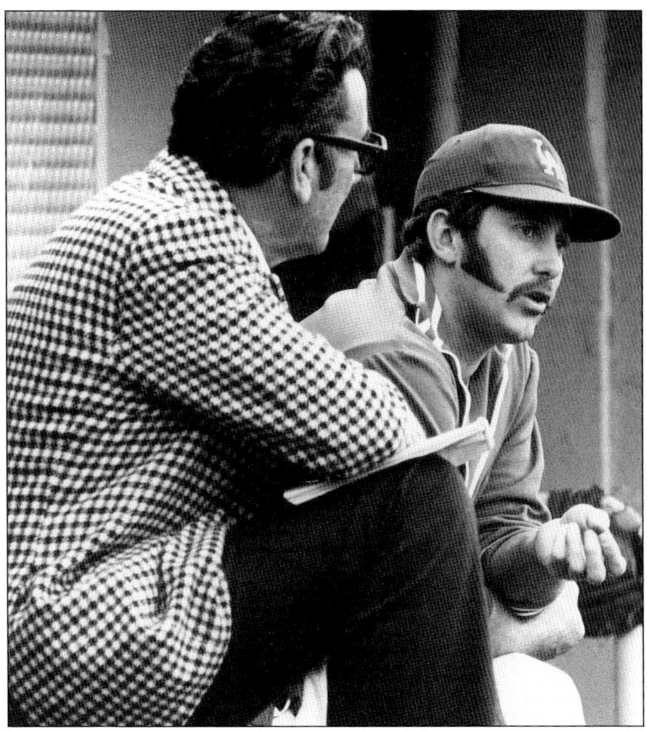

Iron Mike. *Los Angeles Times* sports columnist Jim Murray interviews right-hander Mike Marshall, who in 1974 became the first relief pitcher to win Cy Young Award honors. Marshall set a major league record with 106 appearances and 208 innings as he posted a 15-12 record and 2.42 ERA. Marshall, who also appeared in 13 consecutive games, and returned to his Michigan State alma mater during the winter to work toward his doctorate in physiological psychology. The Dodgers acquired Marshall after the 1973 season from Montreal in a trade for outfielder Willie Davis.

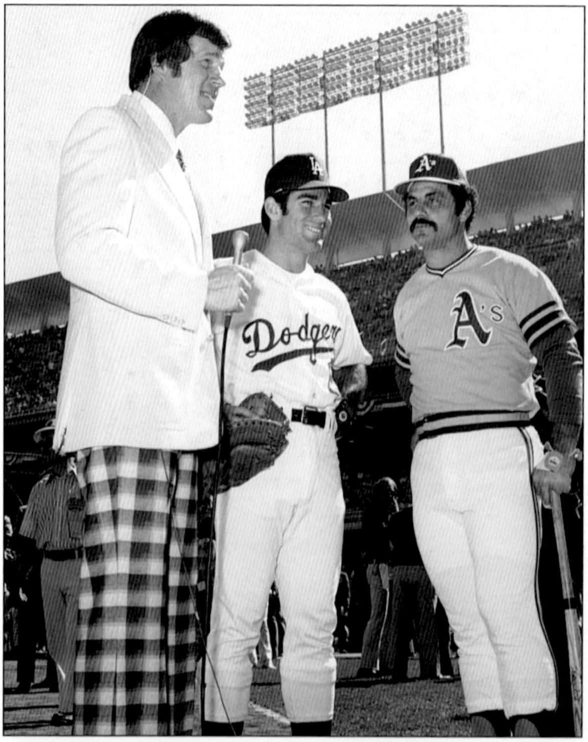

The California Series. NBC broadcaster Tony Kubek interviews first baseman Steve Garvey and Oakland A's third baseman Sal Bando prior to the 1974 World Series. It was quite a year for Garvey, the National League's MVP who earned a starting berth in the All-Star Game as a write-in candidate. Garvey batted .381 in the Fall Classic, but Oakland defeated Los Angeles in five games for its third consecutive championship.

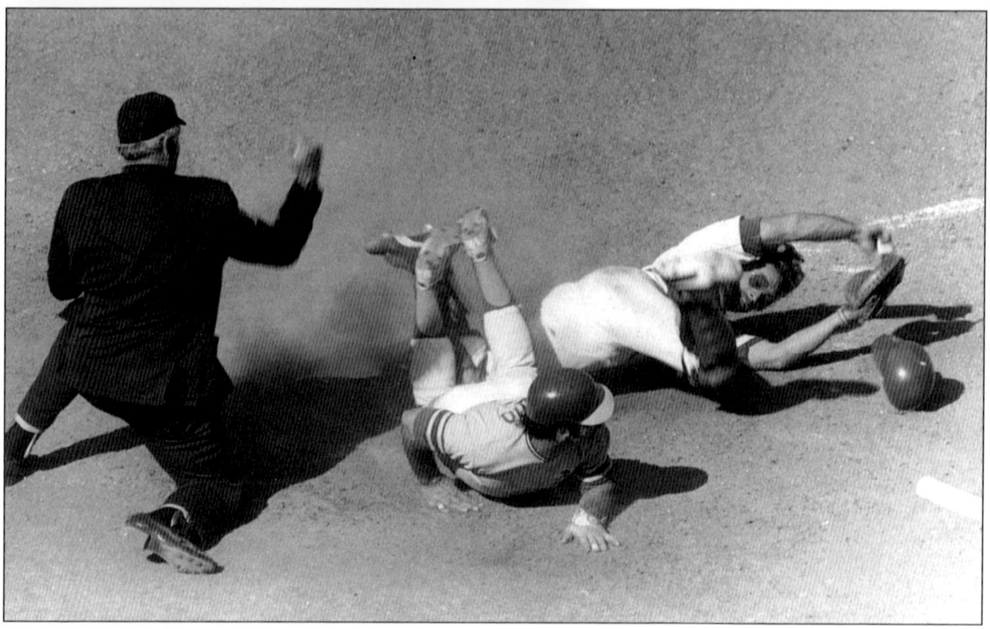

Out at Home. One of the most exciting plays in Dodger Stadium postseason history occurred in the eighth inning of Game 1 of the 1974 World Series when Oakland's Reggie Jackson lofted a fly ball to center field. Because of Jimmy Wynn's sore arm, Joe Ferguson charged over from his right-field position and stepped in front of Wynn at the last minute for the catch. Ferguson gunned a perfect throw on the fly to catcher Steve Yeager, who held onto the ball as Sal Bando tried to score. Umpire Tom Gorman calls out Bando.

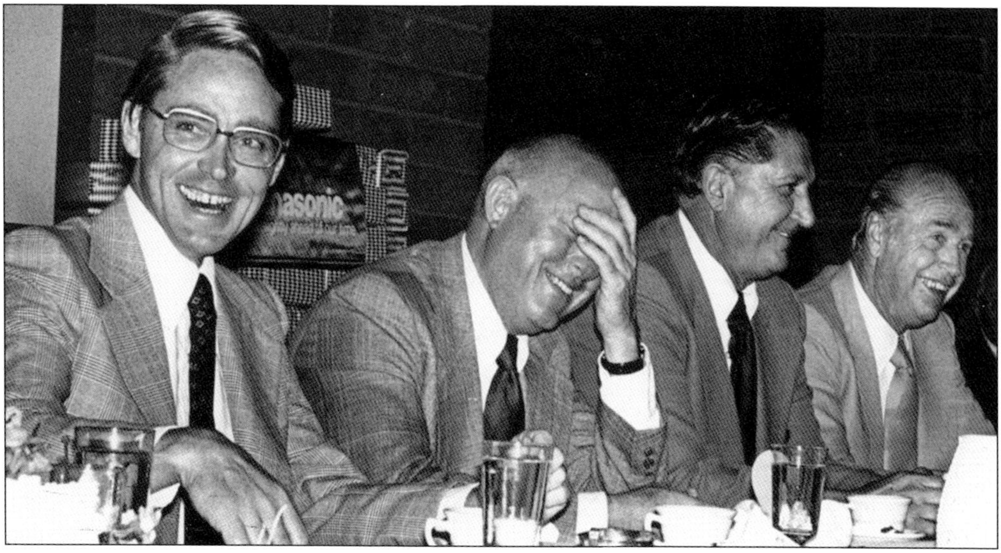

Oldtimers Day Luncheons. During the annual Oldtimers Day festivities from 1971 to 1995, the Dodgers held a luncheon hosted by Dodger President Peter O'Malley and his sister Terry Seidler. The event provided a forum for nostalgia and memories as the ballclub often celebrated the anniversaries of championship seasons. In this 1976 luncheon, a funny story cracks up members of the Dodger head table, including, from left to right, Vice President Fred Claire, Minor League Director Bill Schweppe, General Manager Al Campanis, and Manager Walter Alston.

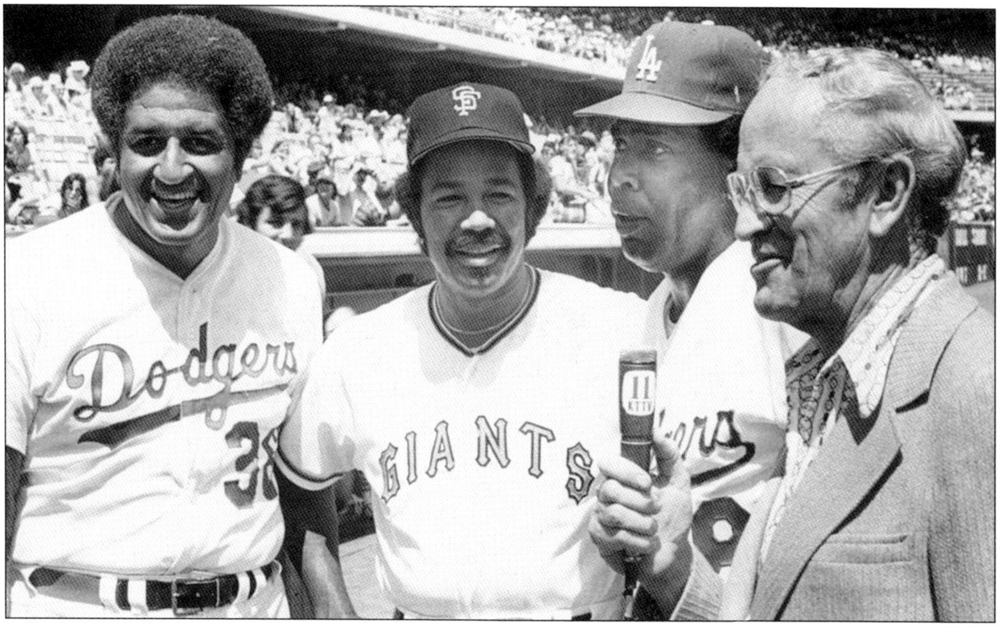

Bittersweet Reunion. Oldtimers Day 1975 at Dodger Stadium featured, from left to right, Don Newcombe, Juan Marichal, John Roseboro, and KTTV announcer Bill Welsh. With the Giants in 1965, Marichal attacked Roseboro with a bat at Candlestick Park and was suspended eight games by National League President Warren Giles. Marichal ended his playing career in Los Angeles, appearing in two games in April 1975. The two rivals eventually made their peace and Marichal was one of the speakers at Roseboro's funeral in 2002.

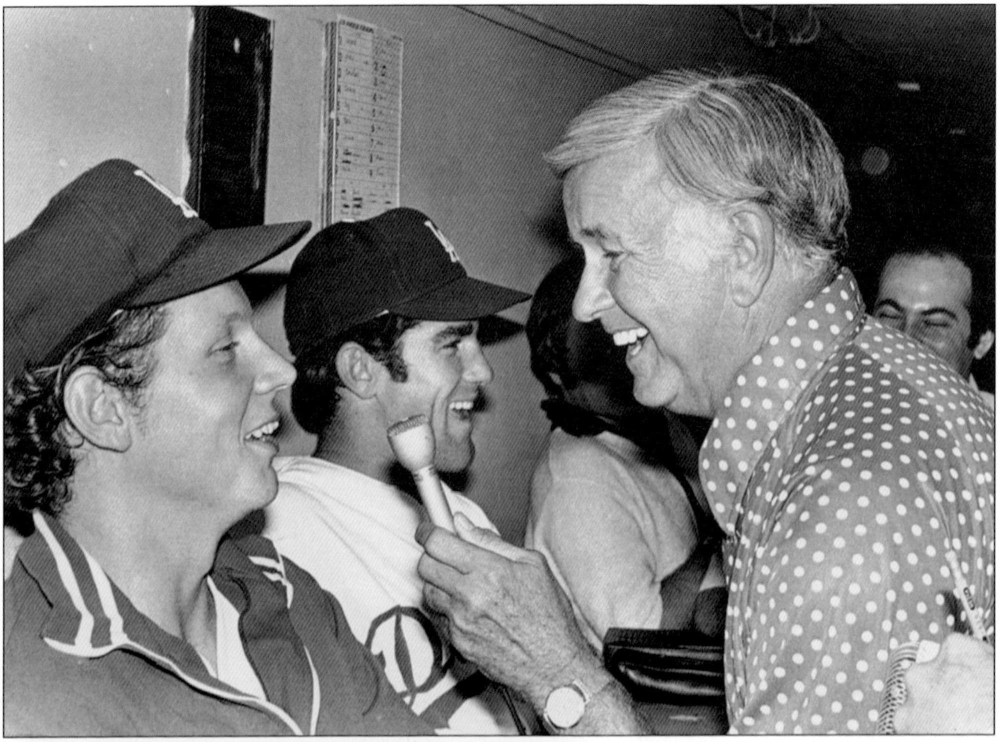

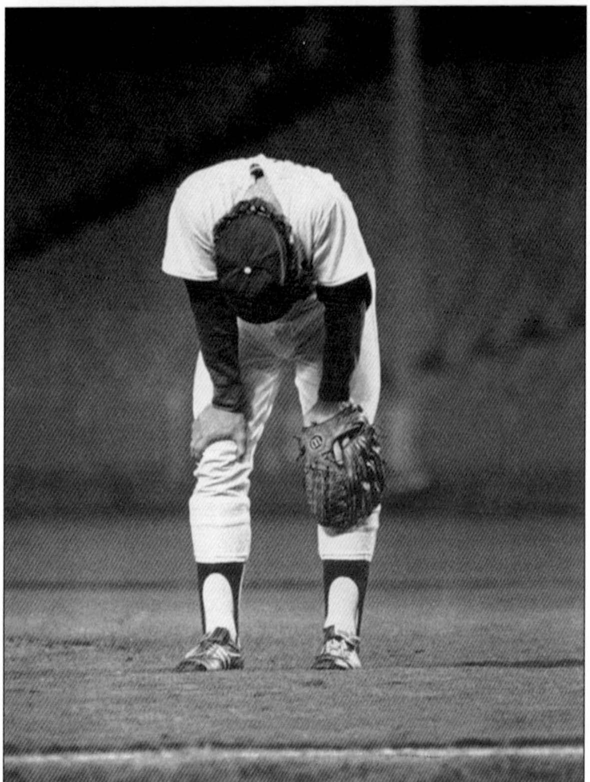

UNHAPPY TO HAPPY. Acquired in May 1975 from the Chicago Cubs, right-hander Burt Hooton set a Los Angeles record that season with 12 consecutive victories. When the former University of Texas star reported to Los Angeles, he was nicknamed "Happy" by Coach Tommy Lasorda because of the pitcher's low-key demeanor. Hooton's streak appeared in jeopardy (top photo) on September 26 against the Houston Astros after he fell behind 2-1 on a two-out, two-run home run by Cliff Johnson in the ninth inning. Steve Garvey's two-run home run in the bottom of the frame pulled out a 3-2 decision. Hooton, who finished with an 18-7 record, enjoyed a postgame interview with Garvey and broadcaster Jerry Doggett.

Elton John. On October 26, 1975, Elton John's musical performance at the ballpark included a unique Dodger uniform. Other concerts at Dodger Stadium have included KISS, the Rolling Stones, the Bee Gees, Michael Jackson, the Beatles, David Bowie, Genesis, U2, Eric Clapton, and the Dave Matthews Band.

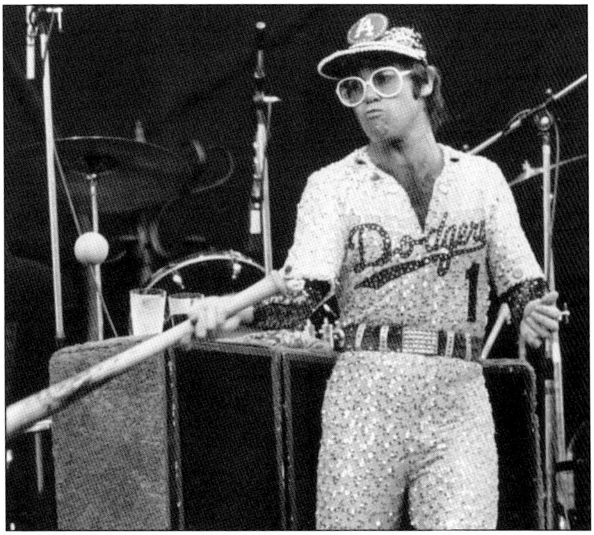

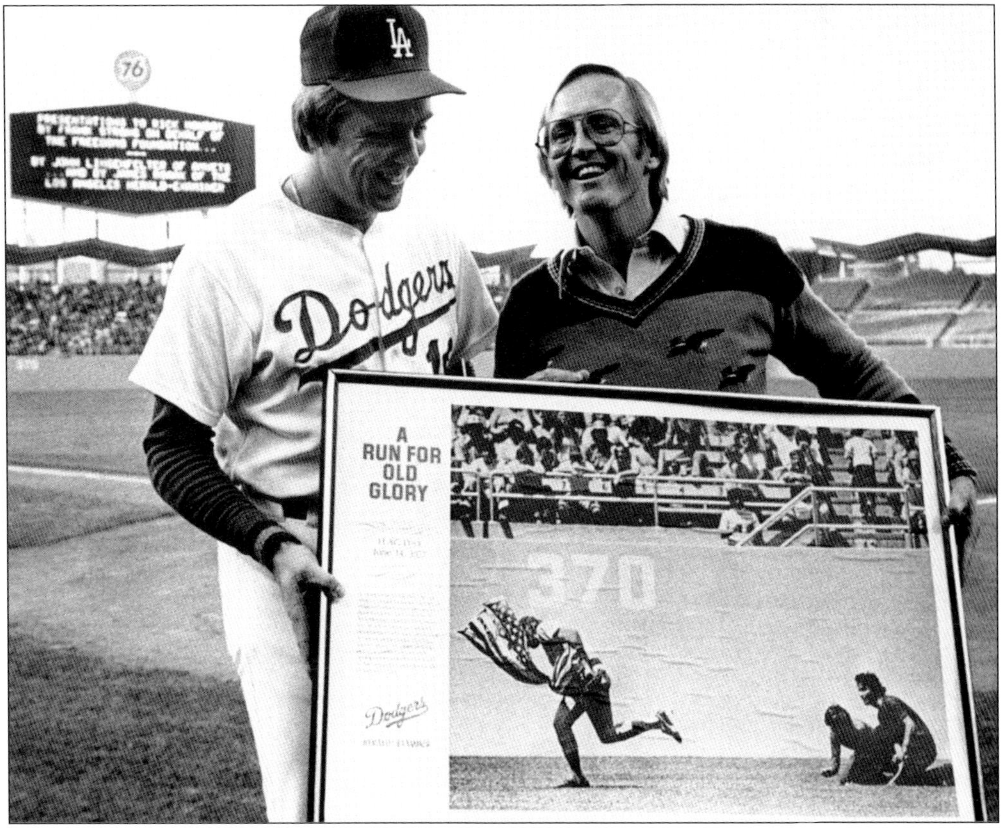

A Hero's Portrait. While playing for the Chicago Cubs at Dodger Stadium on April 25, 1976, outfielder Rick Monday saved an American flag from being burned by two protesters who ran onto the field during the game. The picture of Monday snatching the flag became a symbol of the country's bicentennial celebration that summer. Monday joined Los Angeles in 1977 and received a framed poster from *Los Angeles Herald-Examiner* photographer James Roarke, who captured the dramatic moment.

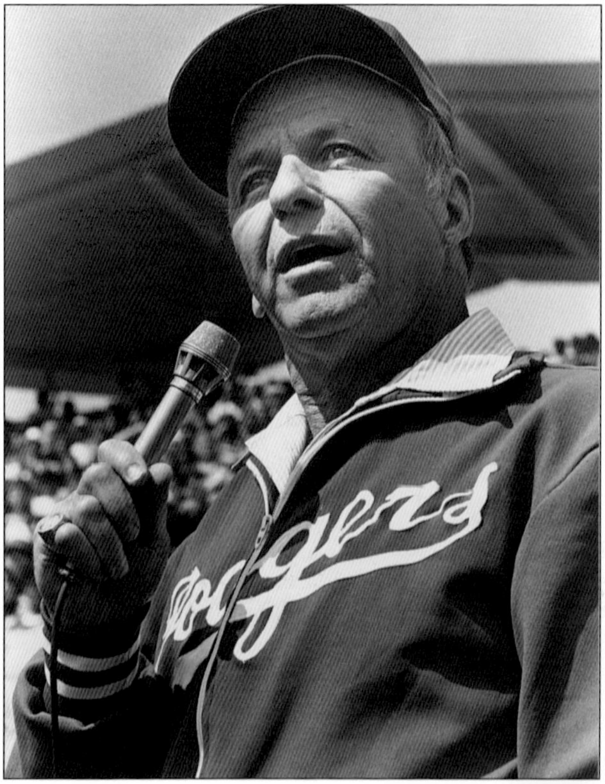

DODGER BLUE EYES. For Tommy Lasorda's first Opening Day as Dodger manager in 1977, legendary singer Frank Sinatra performed the National Anthem. Moments later, the San Francisco Giants stunned Lasorda when leadoff hitter Gary Thomasson deposited Don Sutton's inaugural pitch of the season into the bleachers for a home run. Sutton pitched a complete game five-hitter and the Dodgers posted a 5-1 victory in front of 51,022.

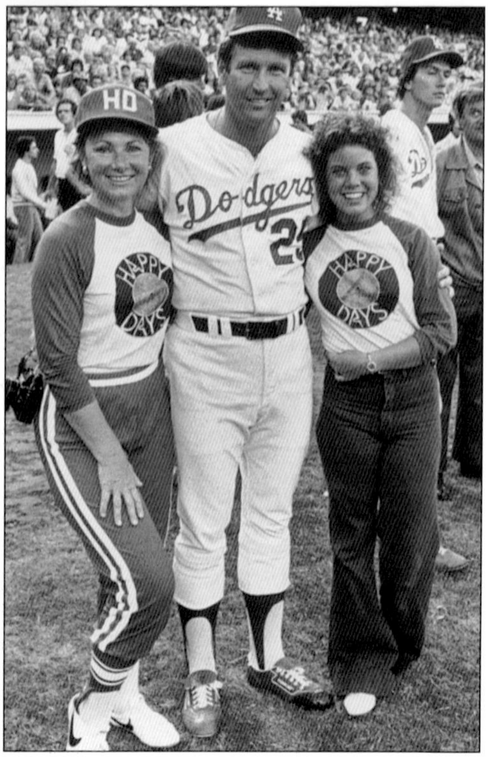

HAPPY DAYS. The popular television series inspired a series of yearly softball games featuring the show's cast members in the late 1970s. Marion Ross and Erin Moran pose with Tommy John, who was able to enjoy his own happy days again following historic surgery by team physician Dr. Frank Jobe. John suffered a ruptured ligament in his elbow on July 17, 1974 against Montreal. Two months later, Jobe reconstructed John's left elbow with a tendon from his right forearm. John returned to the Dodgers in 1976 and pitched in the majors until age 46, compiling a 288-231 record in 26 seasons,

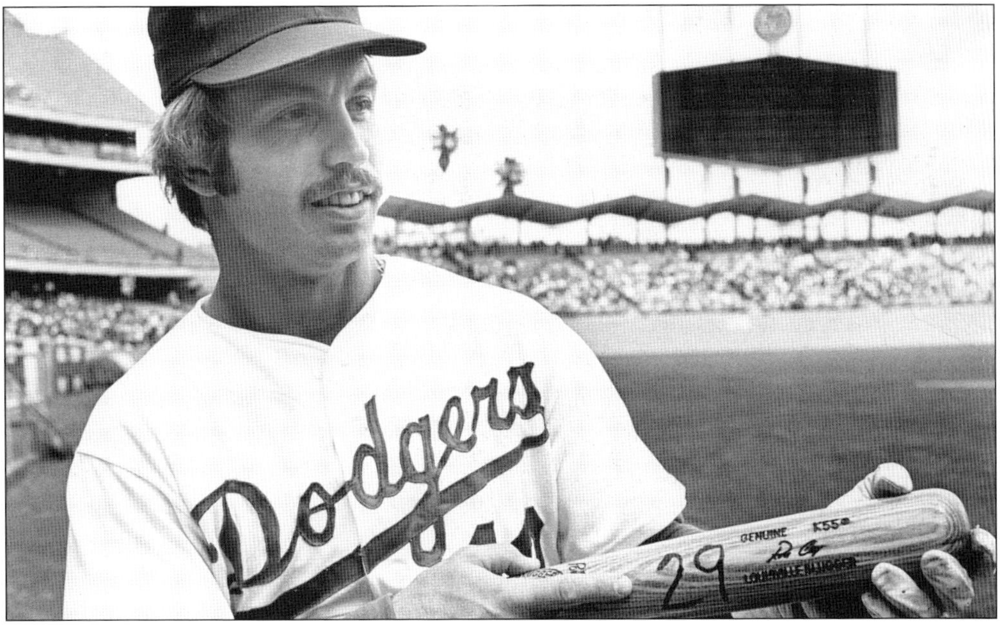

HOT PENGUIN. The Dodgers began the 1977 season with a 17-3 record as third baseman Ron Cey set a major league record with 29 RBI in April, including nine home runs and a .425 batting average. In 153 games, he registered 30 home runs and 110 RBI. The Washington native also hit three grand slams in 1977, two in the regular season and one in the first game of the National League Championship Series against the Phillies' Steve Carlton.

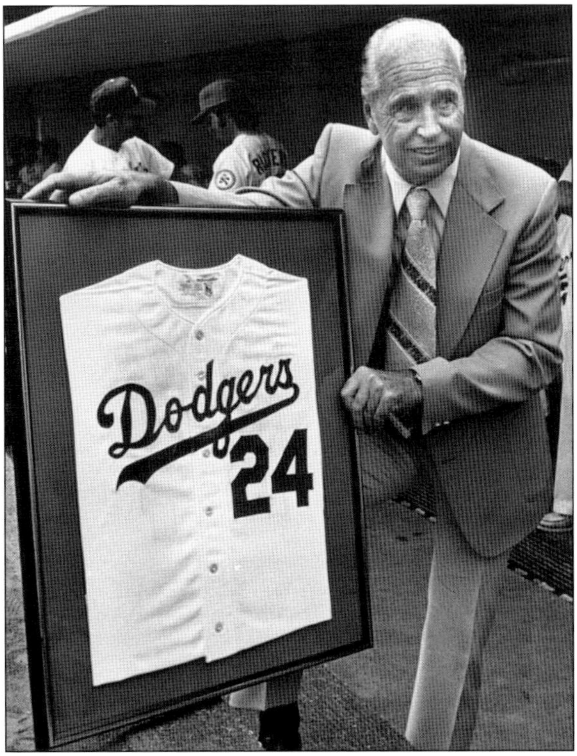

THE QUIET MAN. After 23 seasons in the Dodger dugout and 2,040 lifetime regular season victories, Manager Walter Alston stepped down on September 27, 1976. Alston, the first National League manager to win four World Series titles, was honored on Oldtimers Day 1977 as the club retired his uniform No. 24. He was elected to the Hall of Fame in 1983.

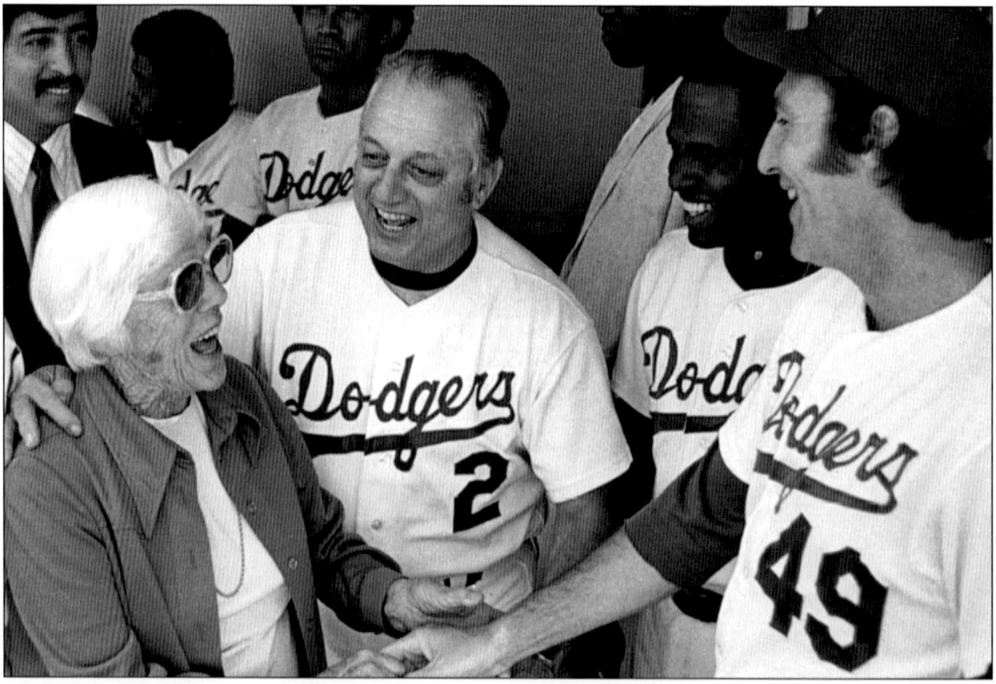

MISS LILLIAN. When Jimmy Carter was elected President of the United States in 1976, the Georgia peanut farmer had a family member loyal to the Dodgers. Lillian Carter, the President's mother who was a longtime nurse and at age 68 joined the Peace Corps for service in India, was invited to Dodger Stadium to enjoy the playoffs. She was greeted in the dugout by Manager Tommy Lasorda and sat in the owner's box during the game.

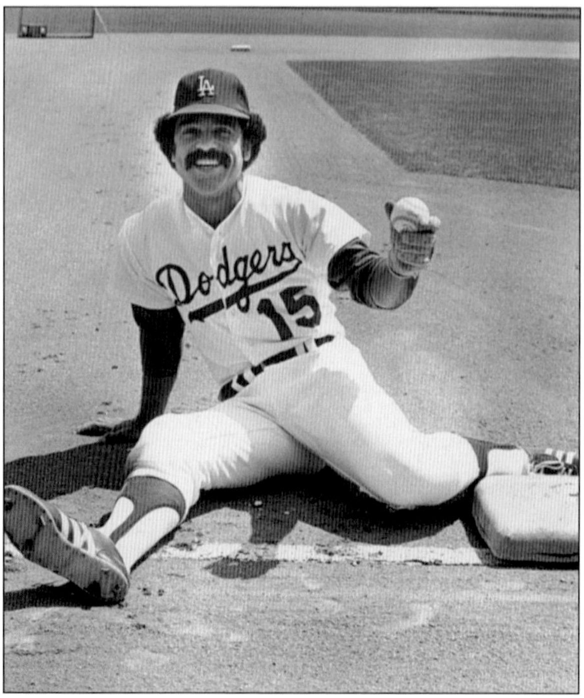

DAVEY LOPES. During his tenure with the Dodgers from 1972 to 1981, Davey Lopes twice led the National League in stolen bases, swiping 77 in 1975 and 63 in 1976. He tied a National League record in 1974 with five steals in one game and set another mark in 1975 with 38 consecutive stolen bases without being caught.

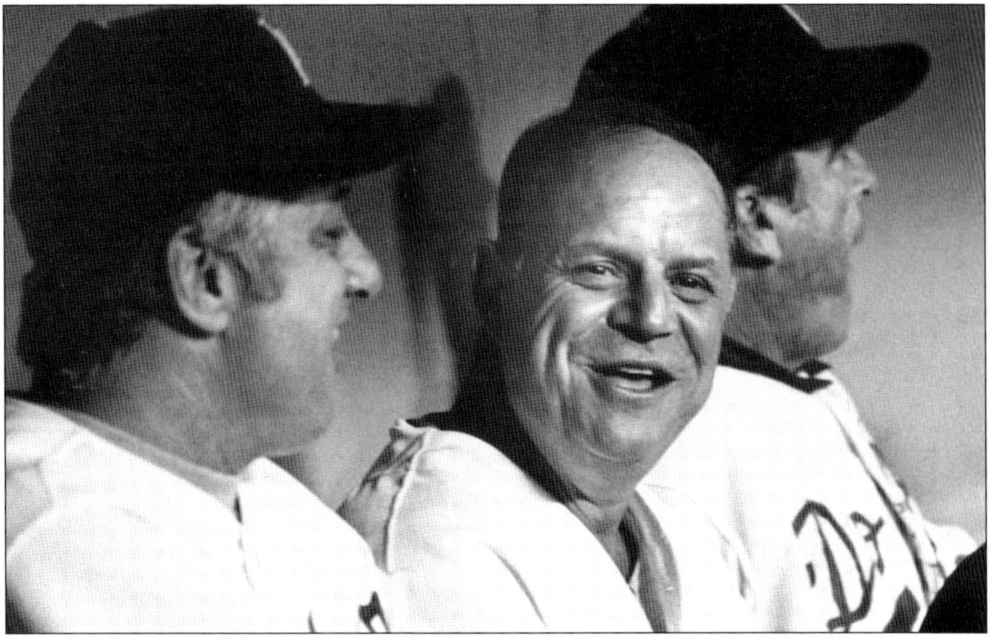

Comedy Hour. Sitting on an 11½-game lead in the National League West and on his way to the divisional title, Manager Tommy Lasorda invited entertainer Don Rickles to sit in the Dodger dugout during a game on September 17, 1977. The actor even made a trip to the pitcher's mound in the ninth inning with the Dodgers ahead by four runs, but things didn't quite follow the script. Reliever Elias Sosa spoke Spanish and wasn't sure of Rickles' identity. Wearing number 40 but no name on the back of his Dodger uniform, the entertainer grew nervous when umpires joined the confused conference. But the crisis passed when one of the arbiters asked Rickles for tickets to an upcoming Las Vegas performance. Rickles obliged, returned to the dugout, and Sosa closed out a 7-3 victory.

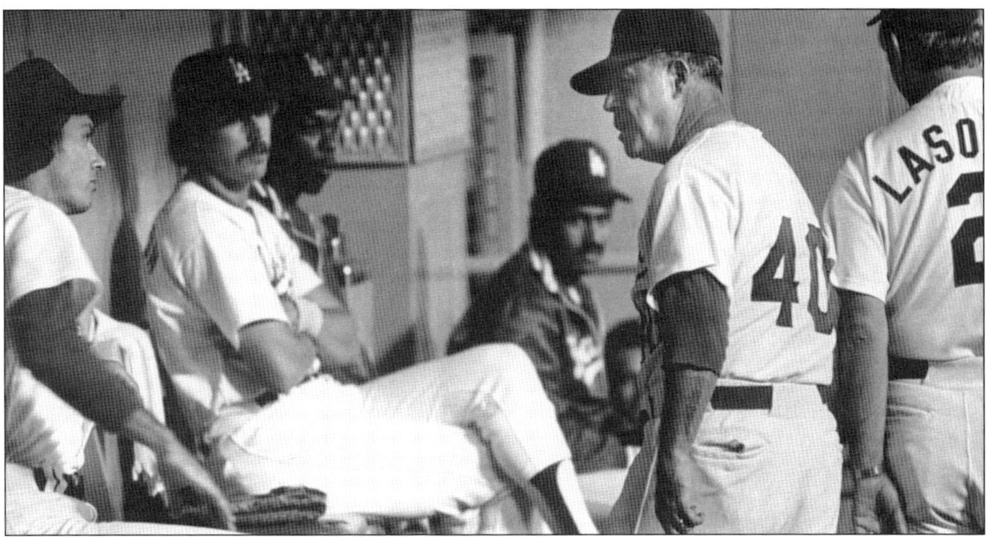

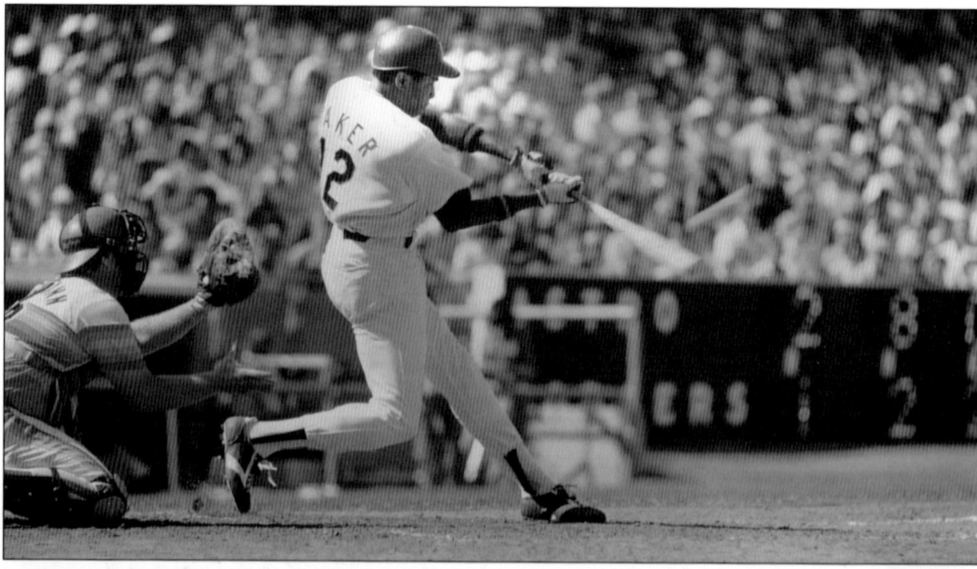

Joining the Club. On the final day of the 1977 season, Dusty Baker needed a home run to join teammates Steve Garvey, Reggie Smith, and Ron Cey as the first quartet in major league history to each hit at least 30 home runs for one team in the same season. Facing Houston's J.R. Richard, Baker blasted a home run in the sixth inning to set off a wild scene at Dodger Stadium.

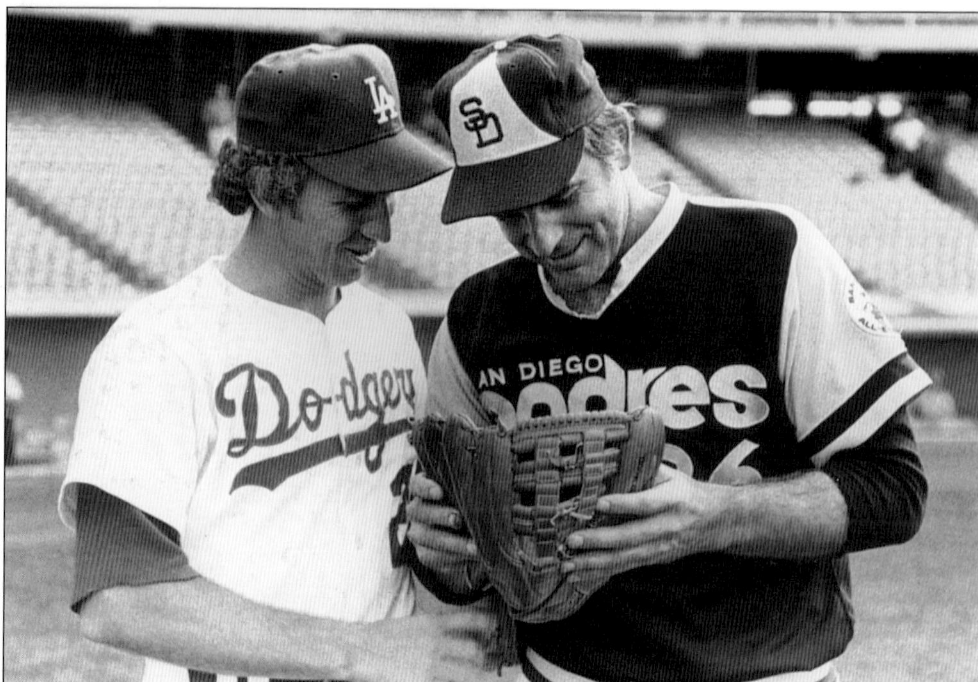

Check the Glove. Gaylord Perry, San Diego Padres pitcher and noted spitball artist, compares gloves with veteran pitcher Don Sutton at Dodger Stadium on May 31, 1978. Perry won the Cy Young Award that season at age 40 with a 21-6 record. Sutton was ejected in a game at Dodger Stadium in 1978 for defacing a baseball. Both Perry and Sutton would become members of the Baseball Hall of Fame after combining for 638 career victories.

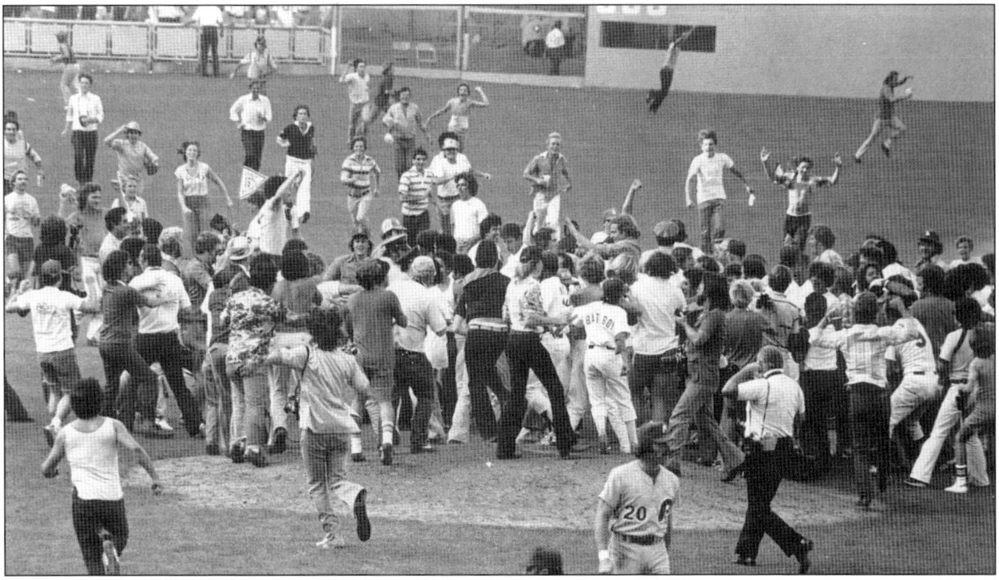

PENNANT CELEBRATION. After winning the 1977 pennant in the rain at Philadelphia's Veterans Stadium, the Dodgers again defeated the Phillies in the 1978 League Championship Series. Fans in Los Angeles stormed the field after Bill Russell's tenth-inning single against reliever Tug McGraw was bobbled by center fielder Garry Maddox, allowing Ron Cey to score from second base and cap a 4-3 victory.

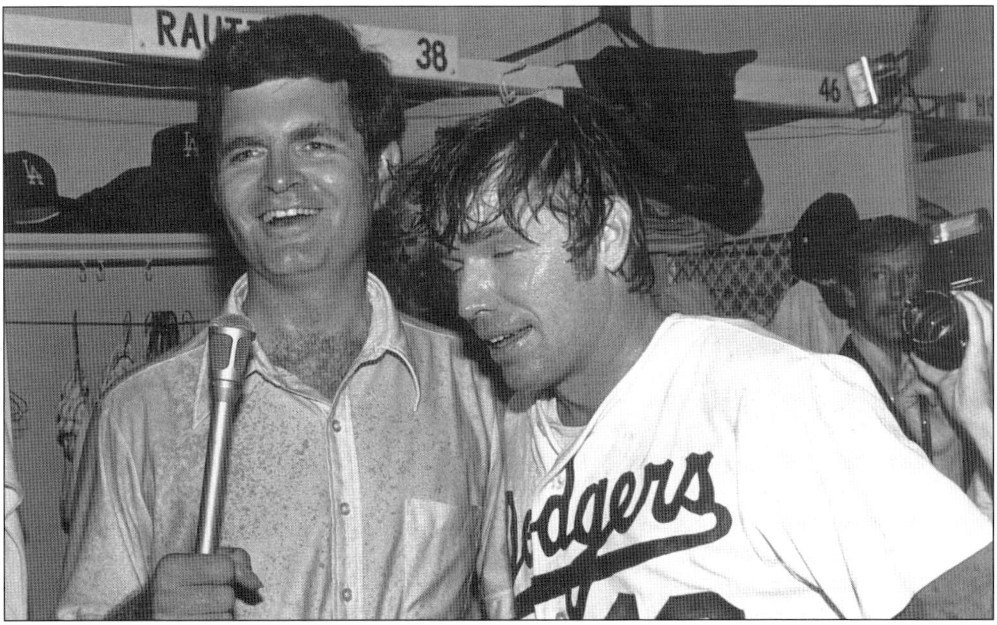

CHAMPAGNE PARTY. In the victorious Dodger clubhouse, broadcaster Ross Porter interviews shortstop Bill Russell following Game 4 of the 1978 League Championship Series. Porter joined the Dodgers in 1977 following a distinguished reporting career at KNBC Channel 4 in Los Angeles. When Porter called the play-by-play for Southern California high school basketball "Game of the Week," his first color commentator was former Dodger pitcher Sandy Koufax, a standout basketball player at the University of Cincinnati.

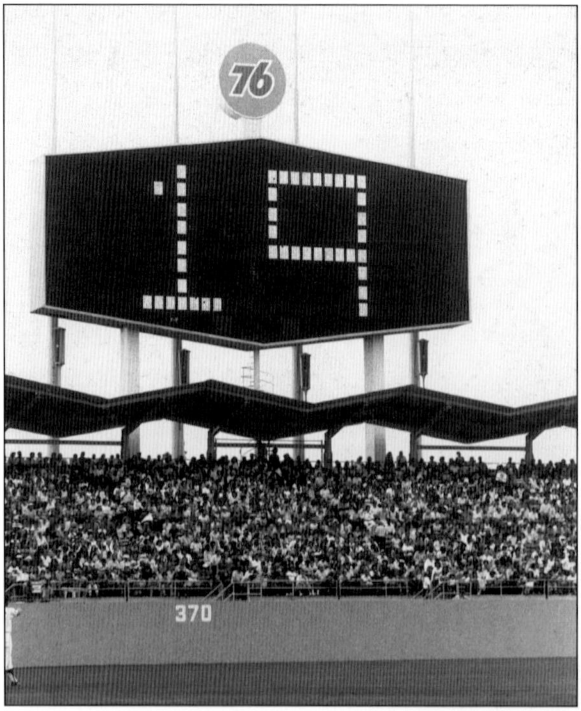

SILENT TRIBUTE. The celebration of the Dodgers' 1978 pennant was muted by the passing of Jim Gilliam, the longtime player and coach who suffered a cerebral hemorrhage on his way to the ballpark in mid-September. Gilliam won the National League Rookie of the Year award with the Brooklyn Dodgers in 1953 and spent his entire major league career in a Dodger uniform, batting .265 in 1,956 games. The Dodgers retired his uniform No. 19 on October 10, 1978 and wore a commemorative patch on their sleeve in his honor during the World Series.

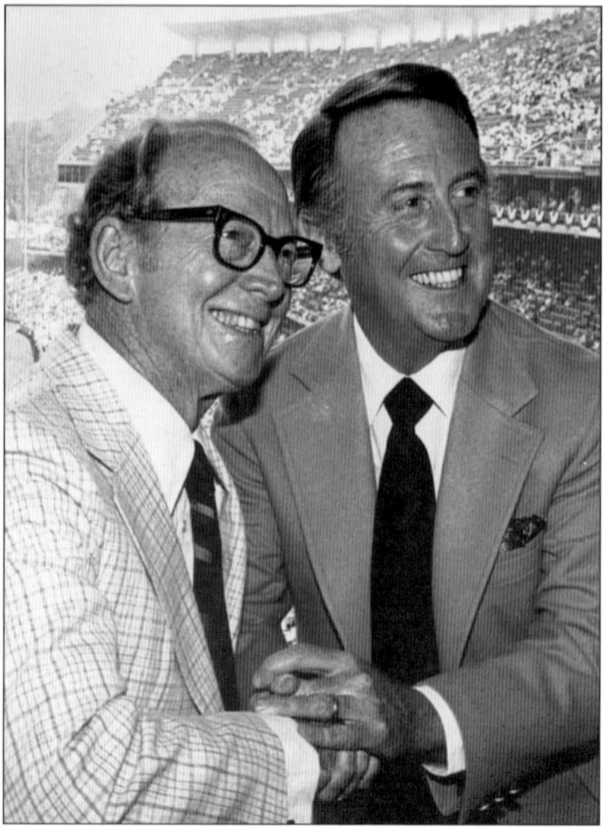

RED AND VIN. Hall of Fame broadcaster Walter Lanier "Red" Barber threw out the ceremonial first pitch at Dodger Stadium prior to the second game of the 1978 World Series. Barber, who anchored "the catbird seat" at Brooklyn's Ebbets Field from 1939 to 1953, recommended in 1950 to team president Branch Rickey that the Dodgers should hire a Fordham University product as the team's No. 3 announcer. Barber served as a mentor to Vin Scully and warned him not to copy the style of other famous announcers, challenging him to use his unique qualities over the airwaves. Scully followed in Barber's footsteps as a Dodger icon and became the most revered personality in Dodger Stadium history. In 2000, Scully was named "Sportscaster of the Century" by the American Sportscasters Association.

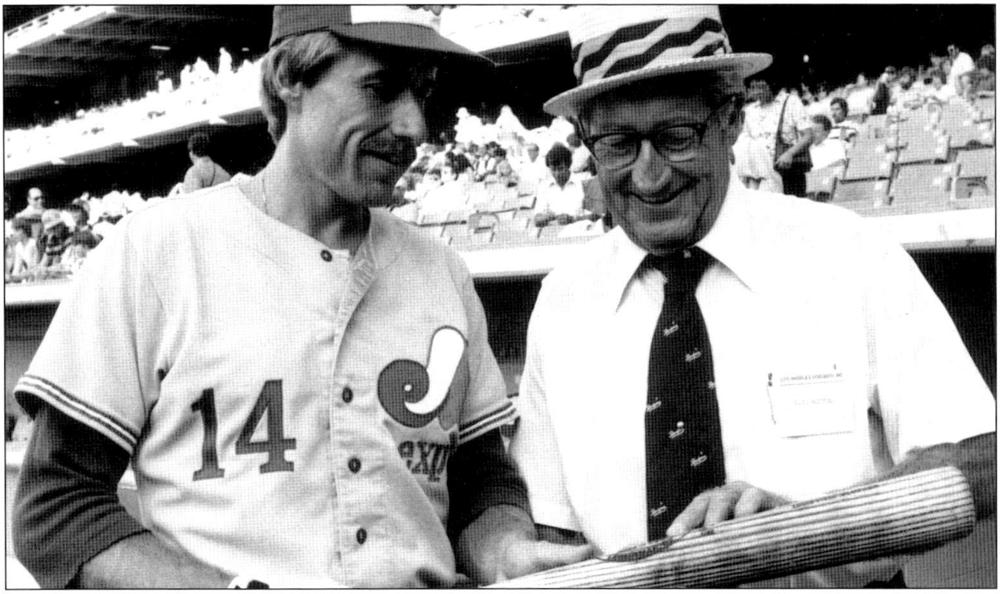

THE HUTTON FAMILY. Tommy Hutton, a first baseman from nearby South Pasadena High School, was signed by Dodger scout Tommy Lasorda in 1964. Hutton spent most of his time with the Dodgers at the Triple-A level as a backup to Gold Glove infielder Wes Parker. Hutton was later traded after the 1971 season and would compile a lifetime .248 batting average in 952 games with the Dodgers, Phillies, Blue Jays, and Expo before embarking on a successful broadcasting career. His father, George Hutton, was a popular fixture at Dodger Stadium as an usher behind home plate on the dugout level.

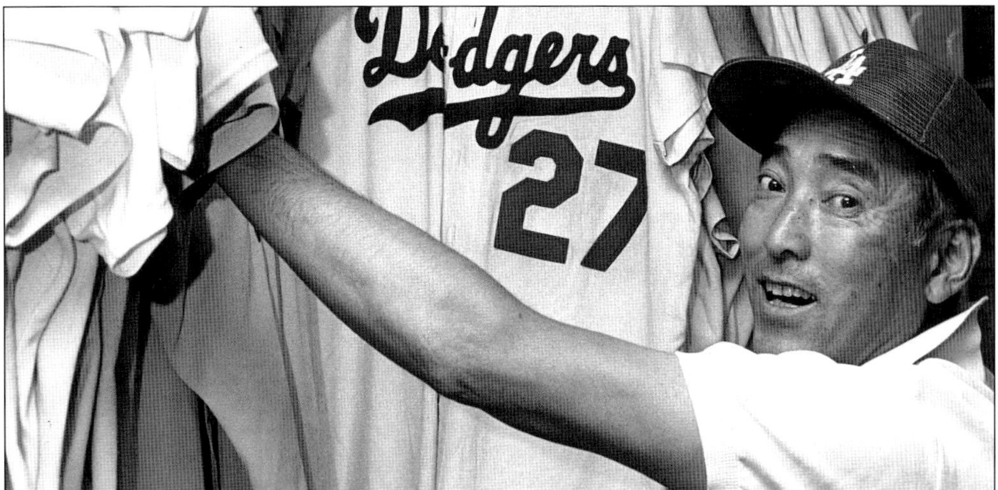

NOBE KAWANO. A longtime member of the Los Angeles organization was Nobe Kawano, a former Pacific Coast League clubhouse attendant who joined Los Angeles in 1964. In her 2002 biography on Sandy Koufax, author Jane Leavy described how the pitcher wanted to quit following the 1960 season and Kawano rescued his equipment from the trash can, perhaps because he knew Koufax might give baseball another chance. Asked later about the book's passage, Kawano smiled and said, "Actually, it's tough to get size 12 baseball shoes." Nobe's brother, Yosh Kawano, has spent more than six decades with the Chicago Cubs in the home and visitor's clubhouse.

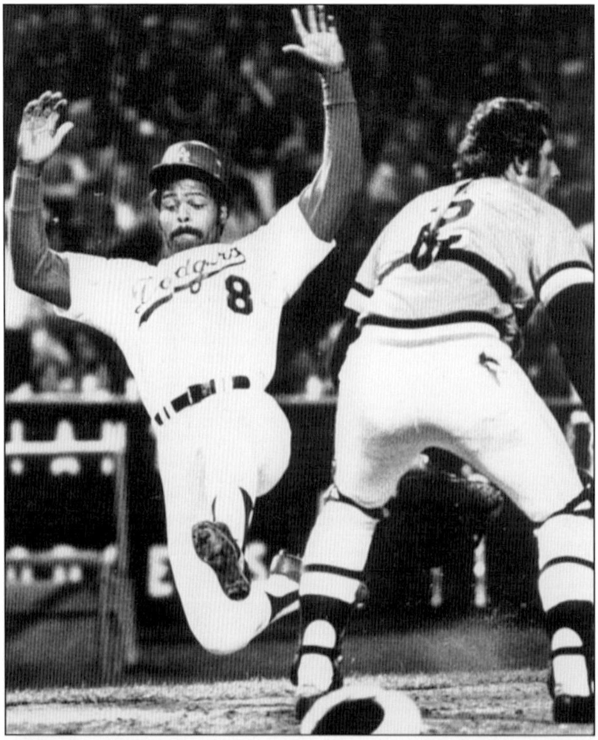

Reggie Smith. The Dodgers made a key acquisition in June 1976, acquiring outfielder Reggie Smith from the St. Louis Cardinals in exchange for catcher Joe Ferguson. Smith became a catalyst to the offense and leader in the clubhouse. In 1977, he joined Steve Garvey, Ron Cey, and Dusty Baker as the first quartet in major league history to each hit at least 30 home runs for the same team in one season. The Southern California native first stepped on the field at Dodger Stadium during a tryout with the Houston Colt .45s in 1963.

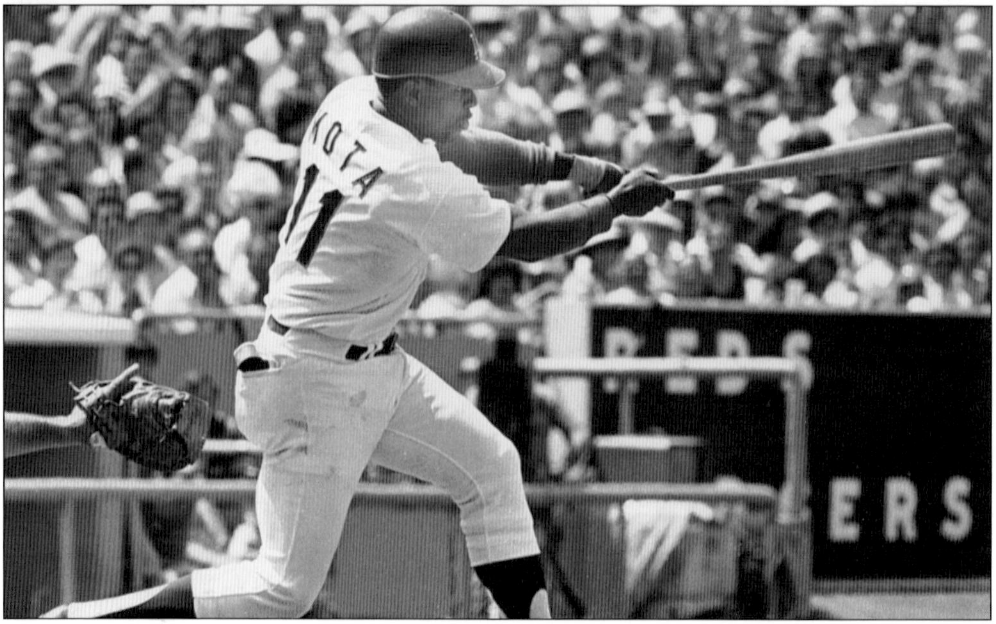

In a Pinch. Veteran Manny Mota set a major league record on September 2, 1979 with his 145th career pinch hit at Dodger Stadium against Chicago Cubs' pitcher Lynn McGlothlin. Mota retired as an active player to become a coach following the 1980 season, although he came back for one more at-bat in 1982. He compiled a .304 lifetime batting average in 20 seasons. Mota's career pinch-hit record was surpassed in 2001 by the New York Mets' Lenny Harris, who played with Los Angeles from 1989 to 1993.

FOUR

1980s

Dodger Stadium was the center of the major league spotlight in 1980 when the sport's Mid-Summer Classic was staged on July 8. In this, the only All-Star Game staged at Dodger Stadium the National League defeated the American League, 4-2. Dignitaries from across the country converged as the Dodgers hosted All-Star events and retired the uniform No. 4 of Hall of Famer Duke Snider during Oldtimers Day ceremonies.

In 1981, "Fernandomania" hit Dodger Stadium when a 20-year-old rookie pitcher from Mexico pitched a shutout on Opening Day and began the season with an 8-0 record, 0.50 ERA, and five shutouts. With his signature screwball, Fernando Valenzuela delighted sellout crowds at Dodger Stadium and packed opposing National League ballparks in one of the most memorable chapters in Dodger history. Valenzuela led the Dodgers to a World Series title and became the only pitcher to win both the Rookie of the Year and Cy Young Awards in the same season.

"Fernando came at a time when baseball needed a hero," said Dodger Hall of Fame broadcaster Jaime Jarrin, who served as Valenzuela's interpreter at press conferences during the 1981 season. "I have seen superstars like Roberto Clemente, Sandy Koufax, Maury Wills, and Don Drysdale, but we will never see in Los Angeles a player do what Fernando did in 1981. He was a phenomenon, not only in sports but in the social field."

The Dodgers won another championship in 1988 as pitcher Orel Hershiser authored 59 scoreless innings en route to 23 victories and the Cy Young Award. Outfielder Kirk Gibson captured league MVP honors despite modest statistics during the regular season—a .276 batting average with 25 home runs and 76 RBI in 150 games.

The intangibles of leadership and determination that garnered the MVP honor for Gibson were on display in Game 1 of the 1988 World Series at Dodger Stadium. Gibson was unable to start due to knee and hamstring injuries. He was sitting in the trainers' room in the ninth inning when he heard broadcaster Vin Scully lament the Dodgers wouldn't have their catalyst available.

Gibson grabbed a uniform and began hitting baseballs off a batting tee with the assistance of clubhouse attendant Mitch Poole. Trailing 4-3, the Dodgers' hopes were still alive when Mike Davis drew a two-out walk against Oakland Athletics reliever Dennis Eckersley. Gibson hobbled to the plate as a pinch-hitter. It was a desperate roll of the dice by Manager Tommy Lasorda because Gibson could barely run, which made any type of infielder grounder a sure out. Gibson fouled off several pitches and Davis stole second base. On a full count, Gibson remembered advice from Dodger scout Mel Didier, who said Eckersley usually threw a backdoor slider on a 3-and-2 count. Gibson climbed back into the batter's box and deposited the predicted pitch into the Right Field Pavilion. The home run gave the Dodgers a 5-4 victory and momentum to defeat the favored Athletics in five games. Gibson's home run remains the popular choice for the most memorable moment in Dodger Stadium history.

During the 1980s, Dodger Stadium also became a central figure within the international baseball community as the team hosted international exchanges and promoted the game almost everywhere the sport was played. Many languages were spoken at the second annual International Baseball Association World All-Star Game hosted by the Dodgers in August 1991. The finest amateur baseball stars from around the world displayed their skills. Forty-four players from 28 countries participated in the historic event.

The road to an Olympic baseball tournament began in 1979 when Peter O'Malley hosted international baseball leaders in Los Angeles at the International Association of Amateur Baseball (AINBA) Congress. From those meetings came a plan to give baseball a visible role in the 1984 Olympic Games in Los Angeles. In previous years, a handful of dedicated individuals kept the hope of Olympic baseball alive and formed groups as early as 1932 that would be forerunners to the AINBA and United States Baseball Federation. And the Olympics used baseball only as a "demonstration game" at Stockholm in 1912; Berlin in 1936; at Helsinki in 1952, Melbourne in 1956 and Tokyo in 1964. But in almost every case, baseball was played on a field more suited for football.

The tremendous success of the exhibition baseball tournament at Dodger Stadium during the 1984 Olympic Games turned out to be the single-most important factor in the International Olympic Committee's vote on October 12, 1986 to include baseball as a medal sport, which began in 1992. "Since the AINBA Congress in 1979, virtually everything that has been done in the area of international baseball has the fingerprints of the Dodger organization," said Dr. Robert Smith, past president of the International Baseball Association. "I believe that Peter O'Malley is probably the single-most important person in getting baseball into the Olympics." Smith in 1996 said the worldwide exposure to the sport triggered a groundswell of interest that caused the number of nations with baseball programs to skyrocket from 39 to more than 80 during a 16-year period. He also predicted the Olympic exposure could result in the addition of as many as five countries per year actively taking up the sport.

"I really have a deep feeling for Dodger Stadium," said Rod Dedeaux, the former University of Southern California and 1984 United States Olympic baseball coach and a longtime supporter of international baseball. "I obviously saw it go up and become a beautiful edifice. One of the biggest thrills is bringing people here. I've entertained people from across the country and from all over the world through certain contacts. But for me to walk up the aisles and show the people the certain spotlessness of it, how kitchen-clean it is and how everyone is so polite to the people they meet, to me it's like home. I can truly say that for me and the people who visit here, it's not a ballpark—it's part of their home."

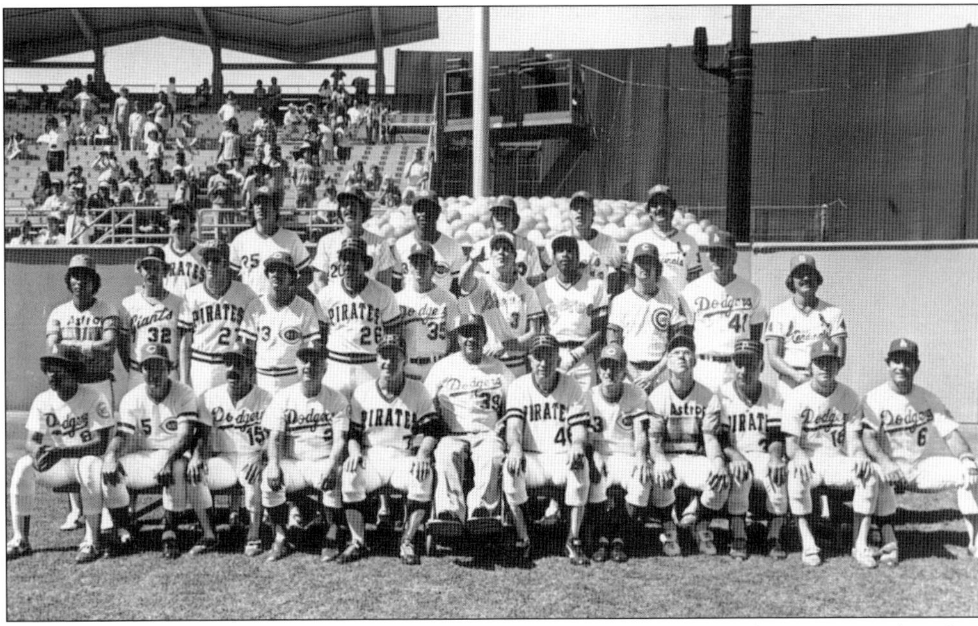

THE ALL-STAR GAME. The only All-Star Game in Dodger Stadium history was played on July 8, 1980. A workout was held on July 7 with free admission and parking. The All-Star luncheon was held at the Los Angeles Biltmore Hotel, and the 5:30 p.m. game was televised nationally by ABC-TV and locally on KTTV Channel 11. The previous All-Star Game in Los Angeles was played in 1959 at the Los Angeles Memorial Coliseum.

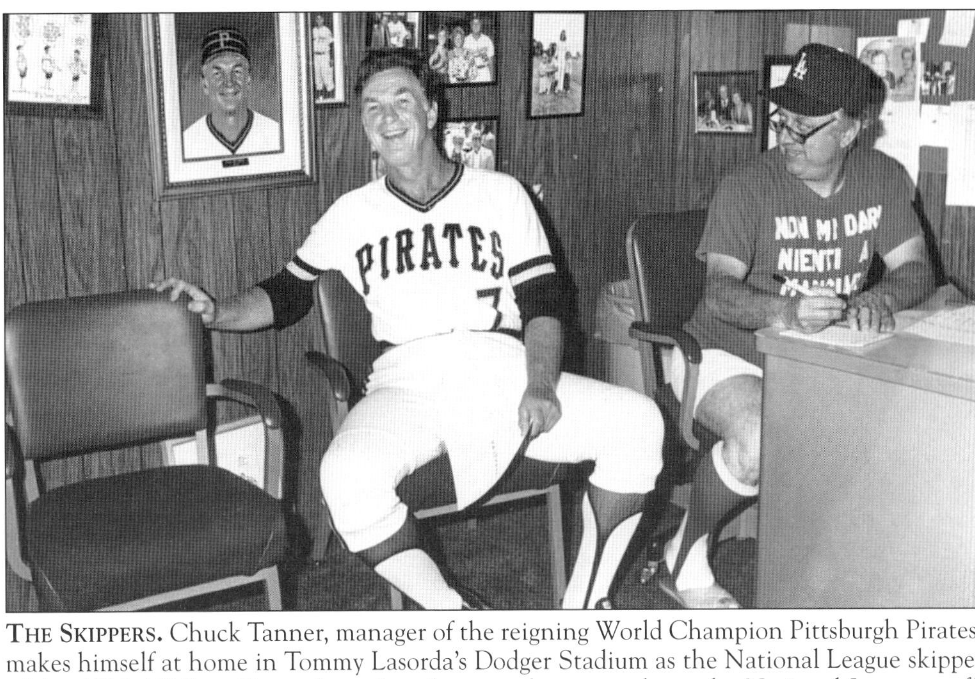

THE SKIPPERS. Chuck Tanner, manager of the reigning World Champion Pittsburgh Pirates, makes himself at home in Tommy Lasorda's Dodger Stadium as the National League skipper of the 1980 All-Star Game. Lasorda, who served as a coach on the National League staff, placed Tanner's All-Star portrait on his wall alongside the collection of movie stars and other well-known personalities.

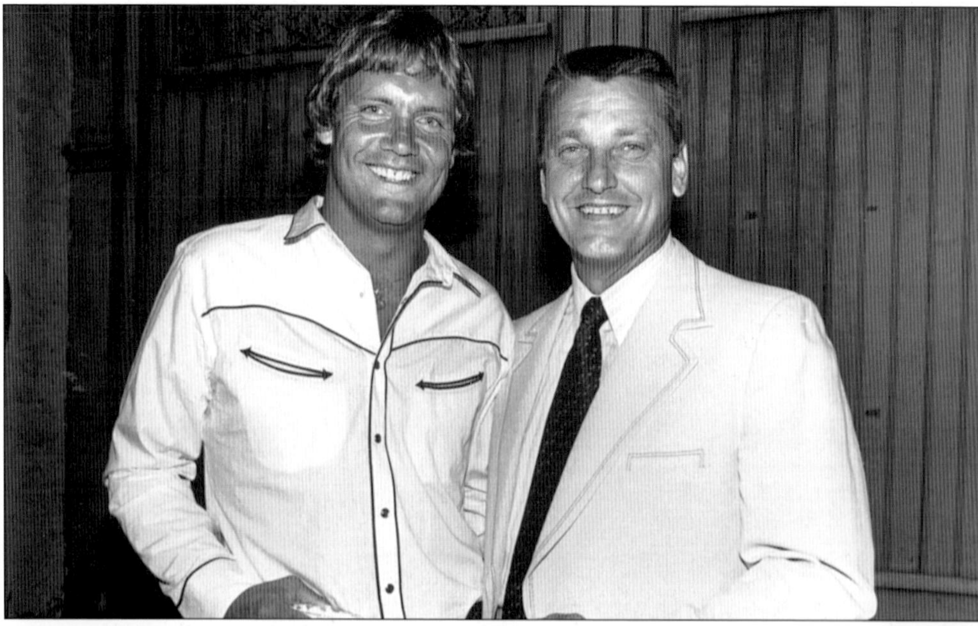

ALL-STAR CELEBRATION. Kansas City Royals third baseman George Brett, a Southern California native, made his only Dodger Stadium appearance as a major leaguer during the 1980 All-Star Game. At the All-Star Game reception, Brett shared a laugh with former outfielder Roger Maris, the two-time American League MVP who played at Dodger Stadium as a member of the New York Yankees (1963) and St. Louis Cardinals (1967–1968).

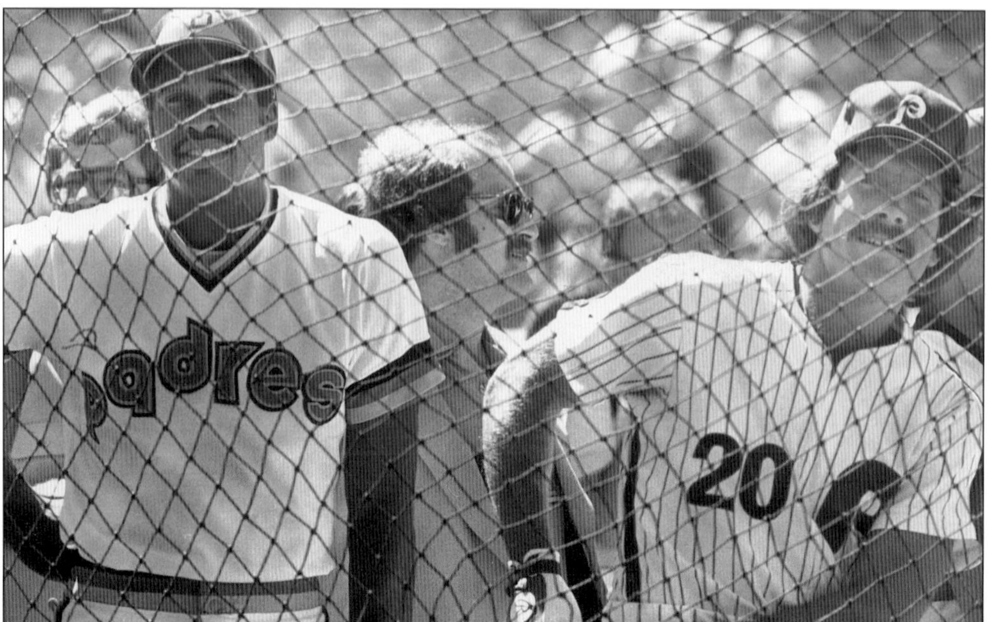

POWER AT THE PLATE. Sluggers Dave Winfield (San Diego) and Mike Schmidt (Philadelphia) played in the 1980 All-Star Game at Dodger Stadium. Others in the National League's starting lineup included Dodgers Davey Lopes, Bill Russell, Steve Garvey, and Reggie Smith. Pitchers Jerry Reuss and Bob Welch also made the National League squad.

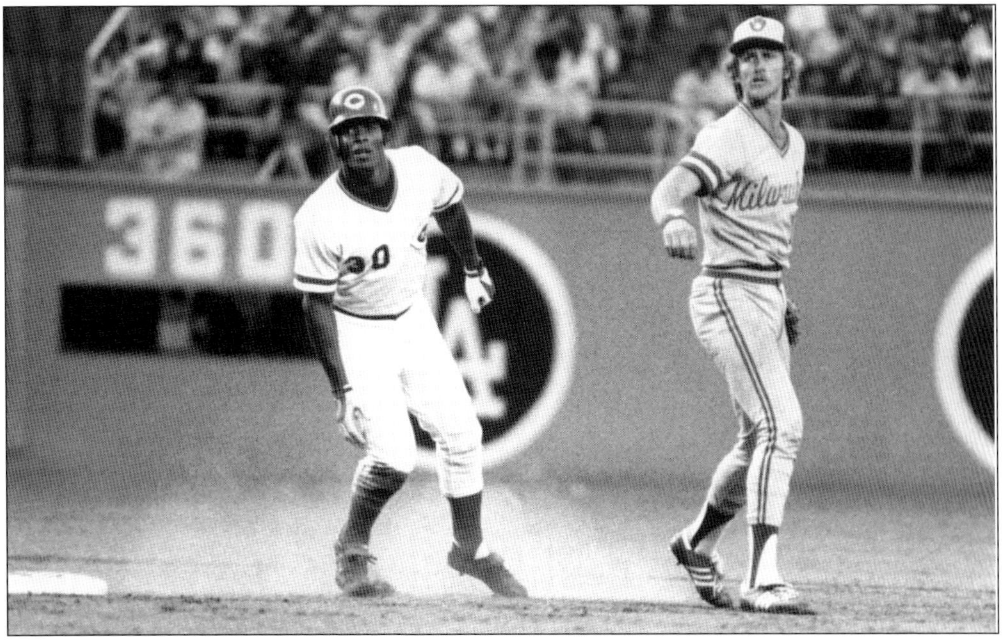

Robin Yount. The future Hall of Famer was a local product from Taft High School in Woodland Hills who made his major league debut at age 18 for the Milwaukee Brewers in 1974. The 1980 All-Star Game would be his only appearance at Dodger Stadium as an active player. Yount, who went 0-for-2, fields a throw from second baseman Bobby Grich to retire Cincinnati's Ken Griffey, who won game MVP honors in the National League's 4-2 victory.

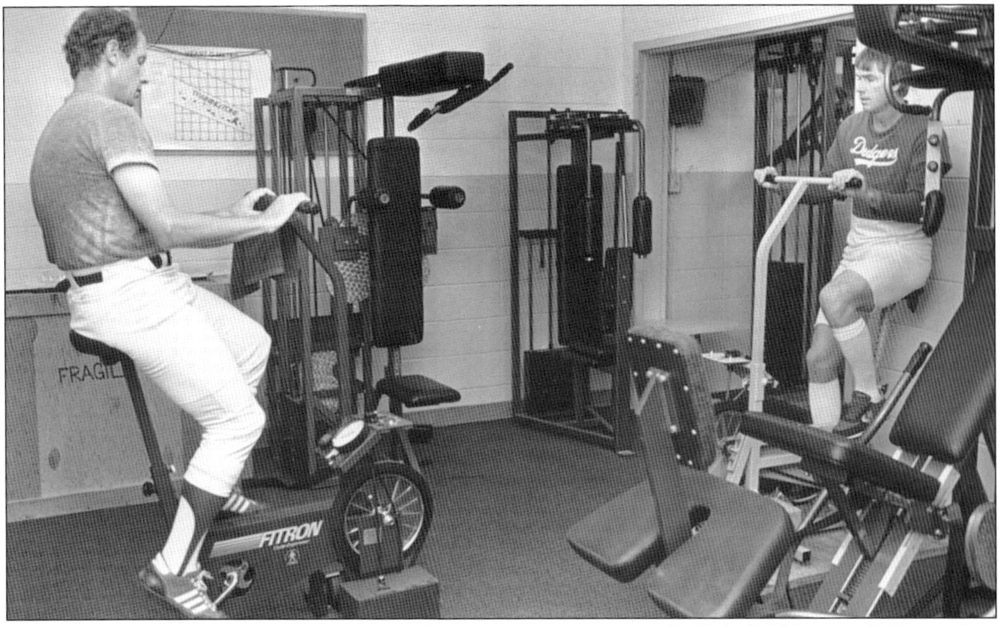

Off the Field. Located between the indoor batting cage along the left-field line and the Dodger clubhouse is a workout room for players and staff. The furnishings have been improved over the years along with the machines featuring the latest technology in physical fitness. Away from the spotlight, pitcher Burt Hooton and shortstop Bill Russell quietly exercise on stationary bicycles.

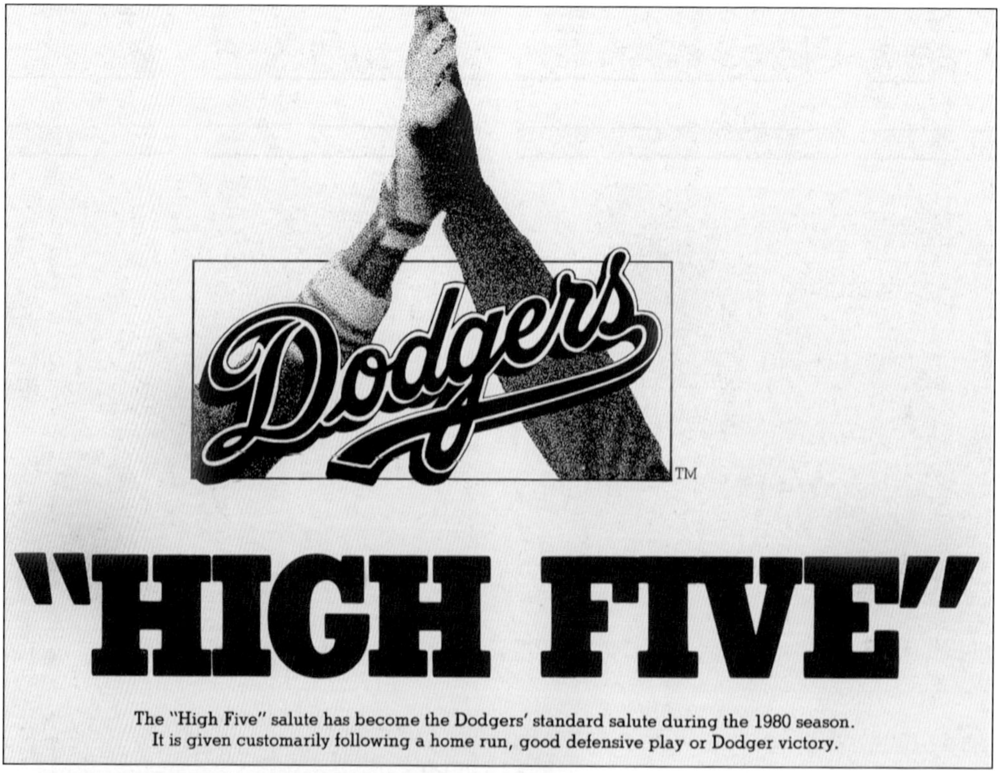

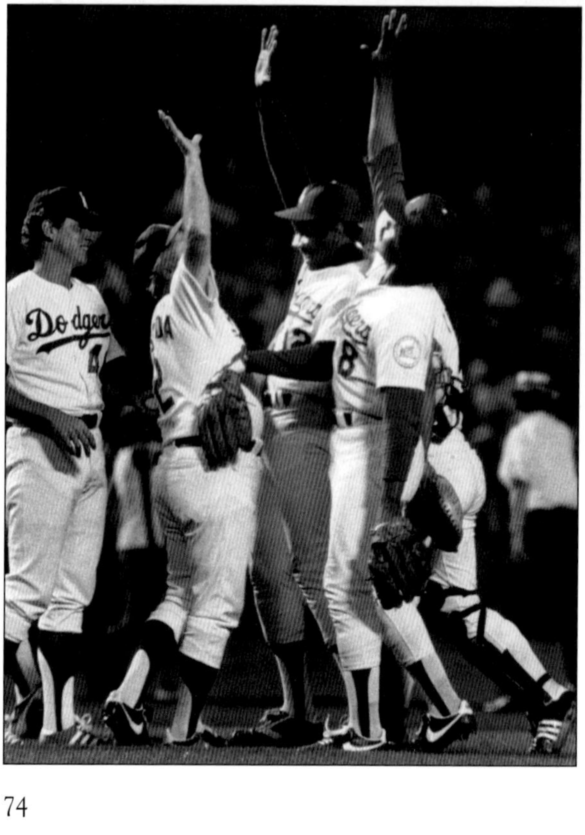

HIGH FIVE. During the late 1970s, an above-the-head handshake simply became known as a "High Five." The Dodgers used this as a rally cry during a second-half surge in 1980 in which Los Angeles sported a 55-27 record at home, surpassing the previous mark for most victories at Dodger Stadium by the 1962 and 1978 teams. The 1980 Dodgers finished the season with a 92-71 record and won 24 games in their final at-bat.

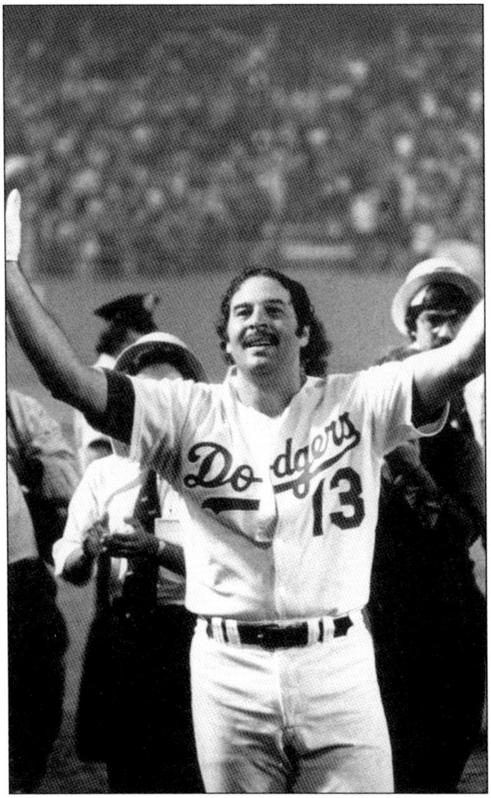

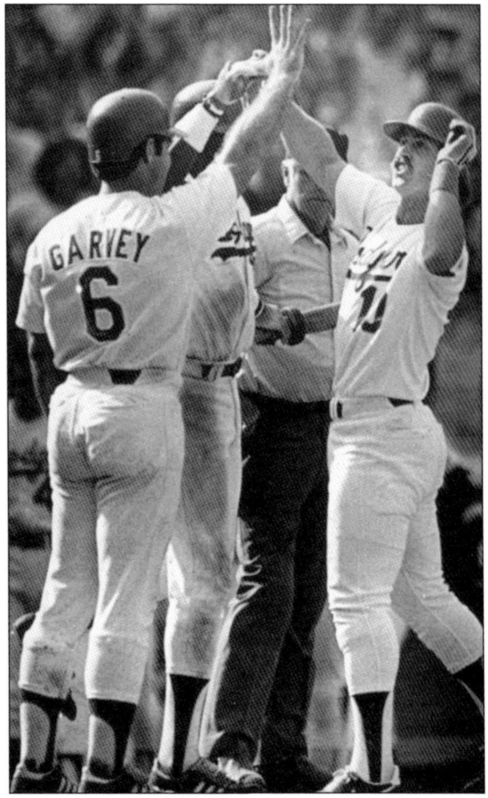

THE BIG SWEEP. The Dodgers swept the Houston Astros on the final weekend of the 1980 season at Dodger Stadium to force a one-game playoff in the National League West. When Joe Ferguson's home run in the 10th inning (above) gave Los Angeles a 3-2 victory on October 3, the catcher flipped his batting helmet toward the dugout while rounding third base and picked up Manager Tommy Lasorda at home plate. Jerry Reuss outdueled Nolan Ryan in a 2-1 victory on October 4. Ron Cey's two-run home run in the seventh inning off reliever Frank LaCorte on October 5 gave Los Angeles a 4-3 lead and veteran Don Sutton came out of the bullpen for the save. Cey, who fouled a pitch off his foot earlier in the game, couldn't play the following day as Houston defeated Los Angeles, 7-1, in a one-game playoff.

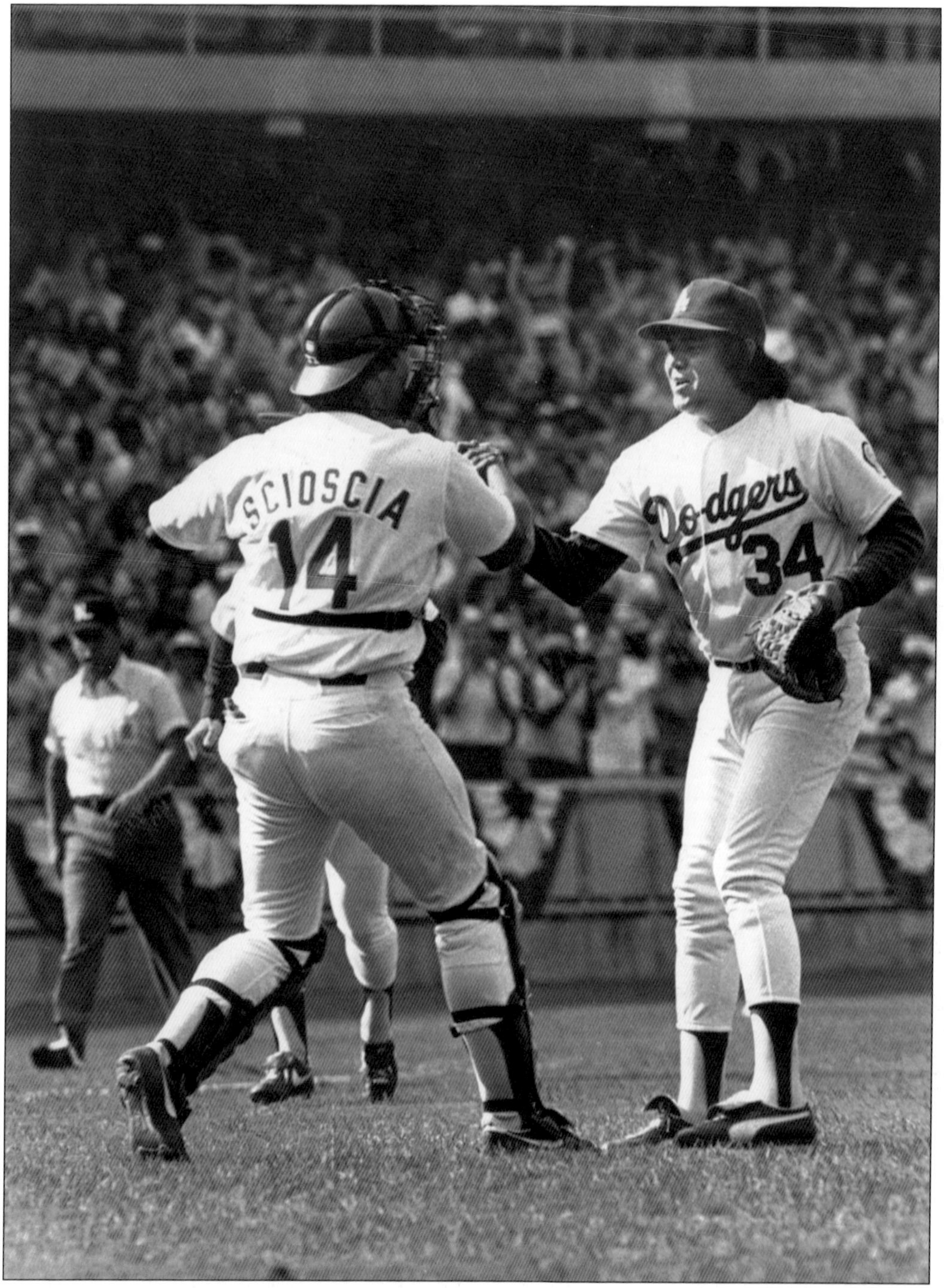

FERNANDOMANIA. Injuries to Jerry Reuss and Burt Hooton forced Tommy Lasorda to call on pitcher Fernando Valenzuela for the Opening Day assignment in 1981. In his first major league start, the 20-year-old blanked the Houston Astros on five hits in a 2-0 victory. Valenzuela, who became a household name in Southern California and a legend in his native Mexico, began the season with an 8-0 record, 0.50 ERA, and five shutouts in his first eight starts. He is the only pitcher to win both the Cy Young and Rookie of the Year Awards in the same season.

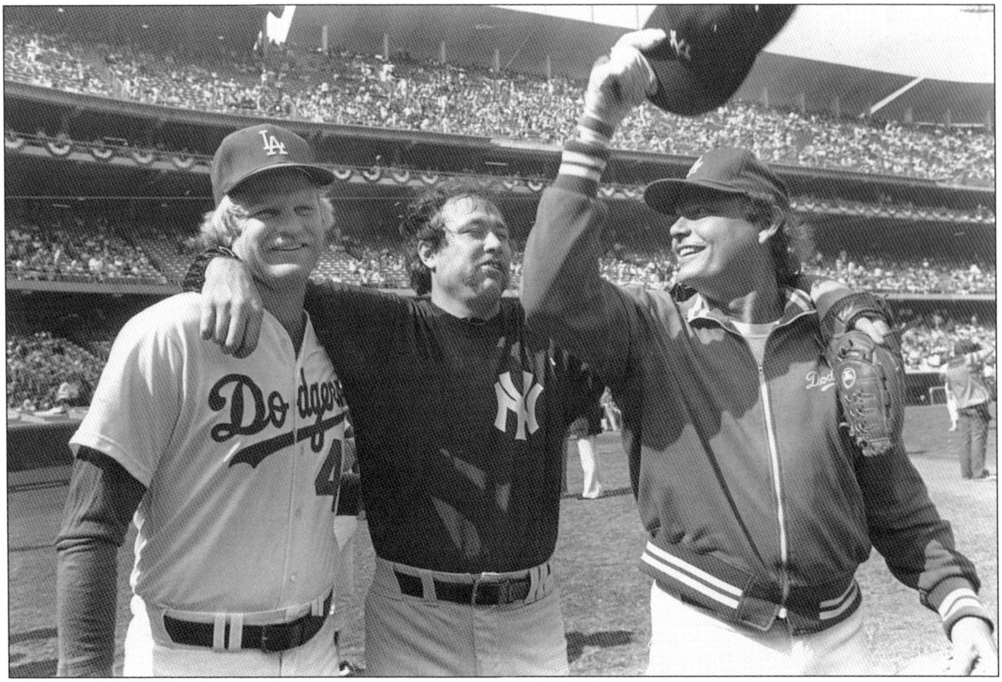

WORLD SERIES REUNION. The Dodgers lost the first two games of the 1981 World Series at Yankee Stadium, but appeared relaxed during the first workout at Dodger Stadium prior to Game 3. Pitchers Jerry Reuss and Terry Forster flank New York bullpen ace Rich "Goose" Gossage, who was a teammate of Forster for six seasons on the Chicago White Sox (1972–1976) and Pittsburgh Pirates (1977). Reuss also pitched for the Pirates from 1974 to 1978 before he was traded to Los Angeles in 1979 for pitcher Rick Rhoden.

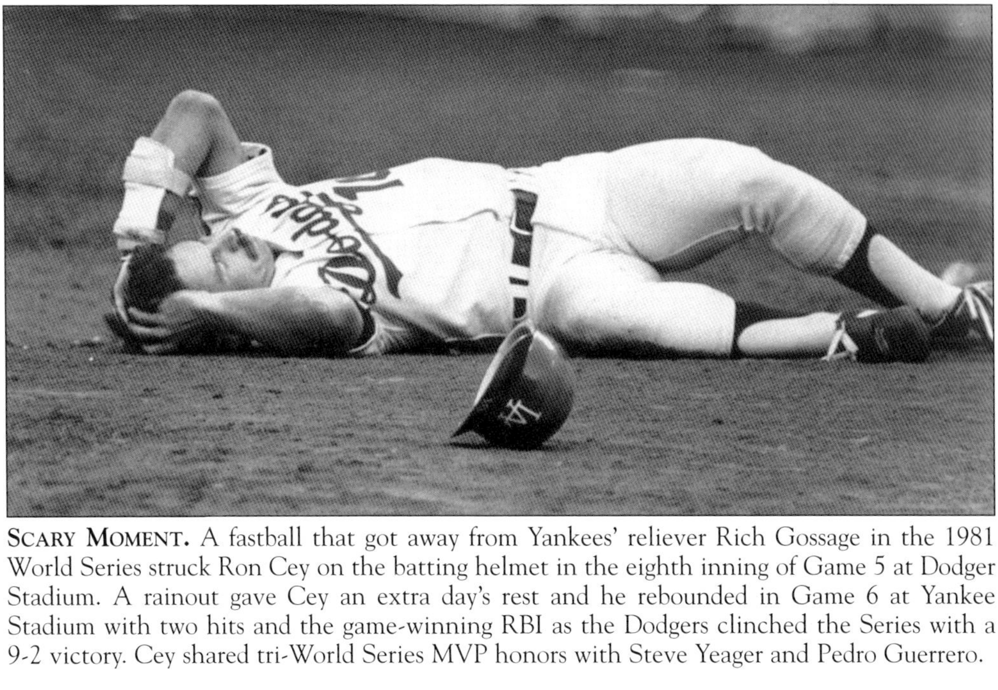

SCARY MOMENT. A fastball that got away from Yankees' reliever Rich Gossage in the 1981 World Series struck Ron Cey on the batting helmet in the eighth inning of Game 5 at Dodger Stadium. A rainout gave Cey an extra day's rest and he rebounded in Game 6 at Yankee Stadium with two hits and the game-winning RBI as the Dodgers clinched the Series with a 9-2 victory. Cey shared tri-World Series MVP honors with Steve Yeager and Pedro Guerrero.

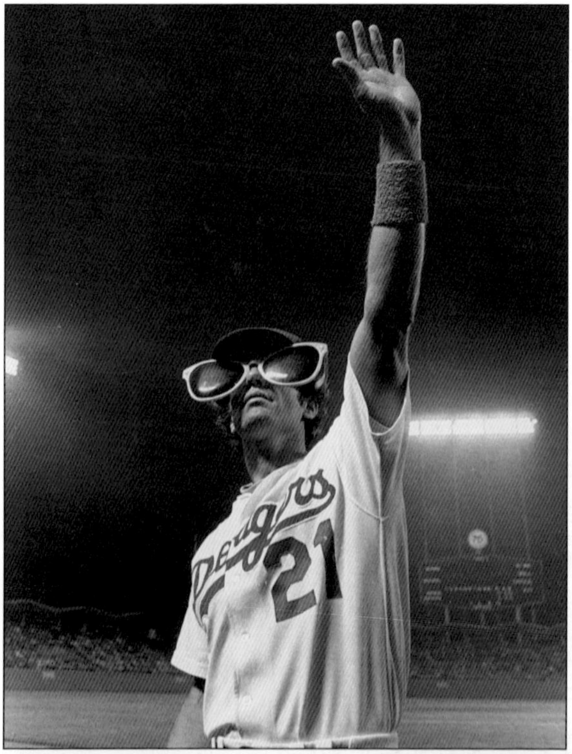

PRANKSTER. Outfielder Jay Johnstone was known for his colorful personality during his career with the Dodgers. But one of his biggest hits occurred during the 1981 World Series. His pinch-hit, two-run home run in Game 4 of the World Series at Dodger Stadium launched a comeback from a 6-3 deficit and was a turning point in the Series.

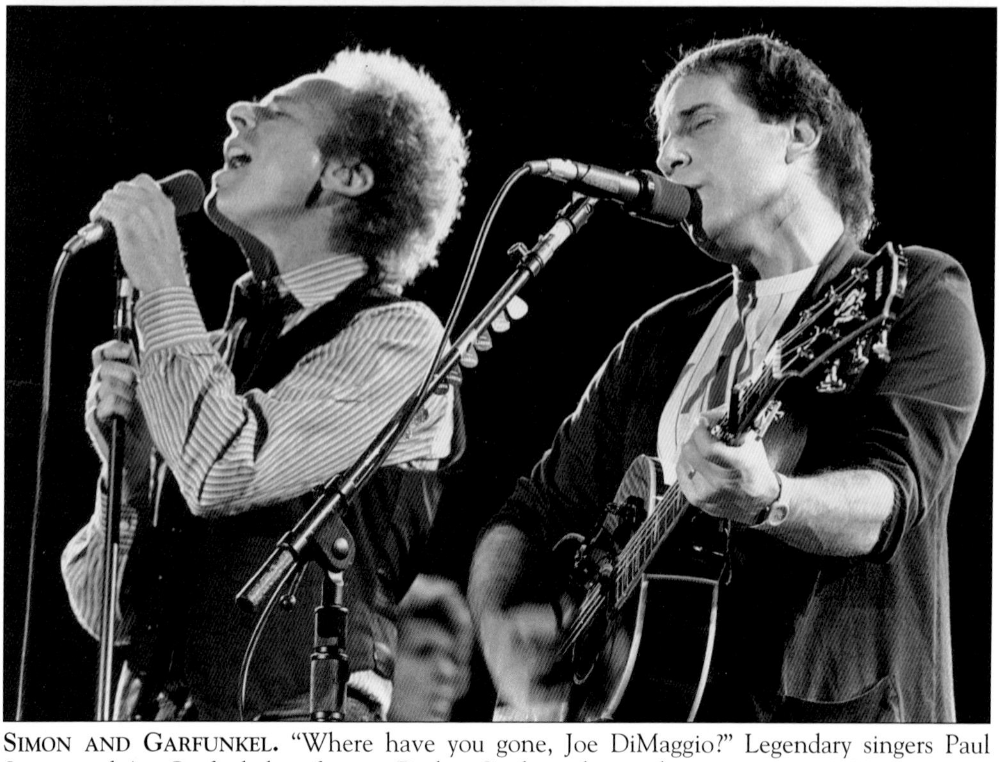

SIMON AND GARFUNKEL. "Where have you gone, Joe DiMaggio?" Legendary singers Paul Simon and Art Garfunkel perform at Dodger Stadium during their concert in 1983.

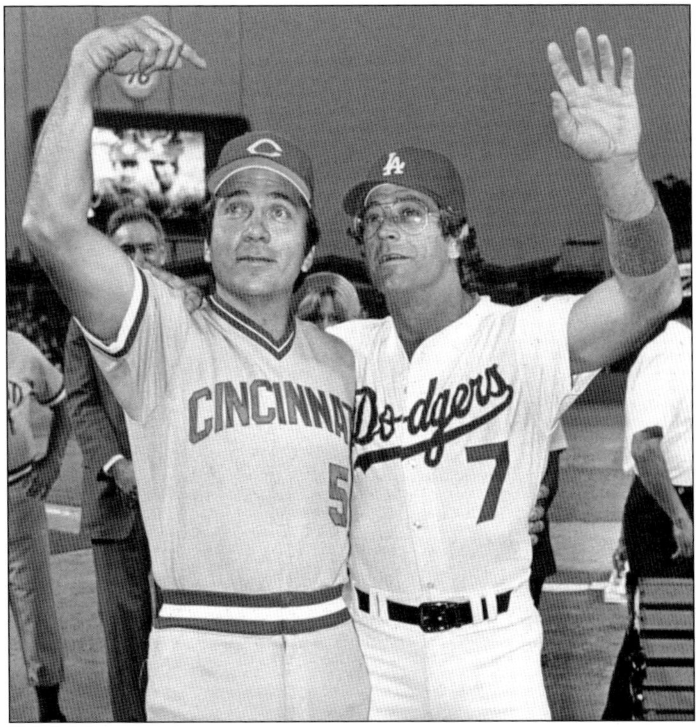

Johnny Bench Night. The Dodgers honored the Cincinnati Reds' Hall of Fame receiver upon his retirement in 1983. Bench and the Dodgers' Steve Yeager were considered among the top defensive catchers in baseball during the 1970s and they combined to appear in seven World Series in the decade.

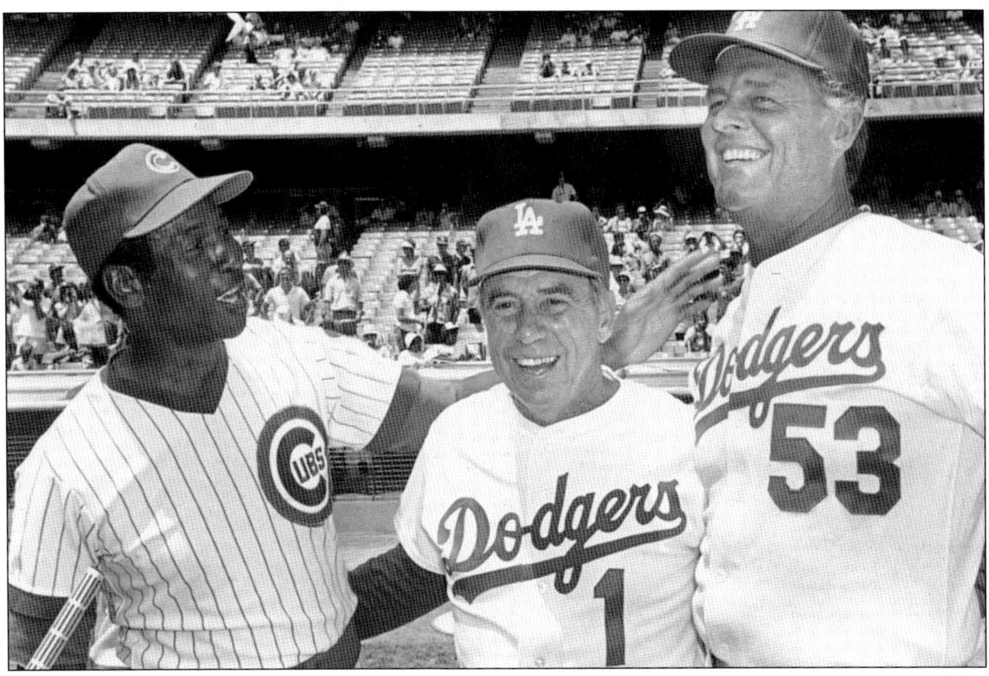

Heading to Cooperstown. During 1984 Oldtimers Day ceremonies, the Dodgers retired the uniform numbers of shortstop Pee Wee Reese (1) and Don Drysdale (53), who were teammates in Brooklyn and Los Angeles from 1956 to 1958 and both inducted into the Hall of Fame that summer. Joining Reese and Drysdale is fellow Hall of Famer Ernie Banks, who hit 512 home runs with the Chicago Cubs from 1953 to 1971.

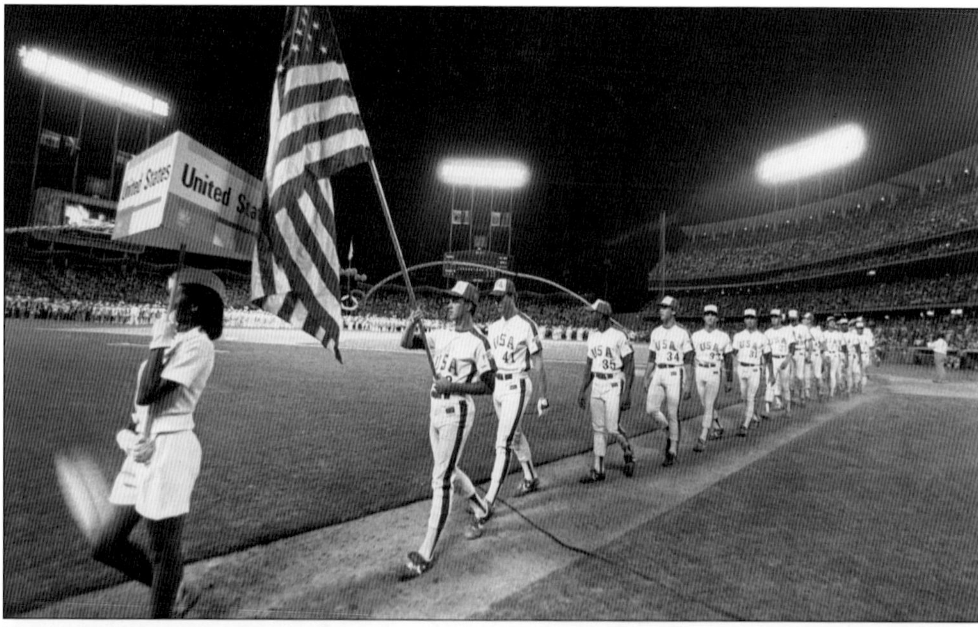

THE 1984 OLYMPICS. Baseball made its Olympic tournament debut as a demonstration sport during the eight-team competition at Dodger Stadium. The United States roster included future major leaguers Mark McGwire, Will Clark, Barry Larkin, and Randy Johnson. The Dominican Republic's team featured pitcher Ramon Martinez, who recorded 123 victories with Los Angeles from 1988 to 1998.

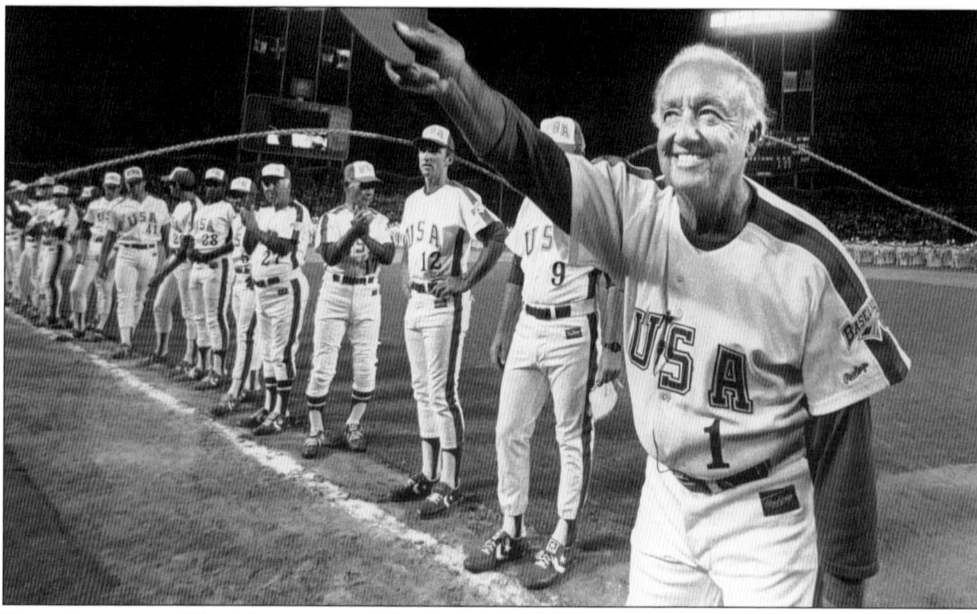

ROD DEDEAUX. The University of Southern California baseball coach brought a wealth of international experience to the 1984 Olympics. A former member of the 1935 Brooklyn Dodgers, Dedeaux worked as an usher during the 1932 Olympics at the Los Angeles Coliseum and later was a pioneer in starting the USA-Japan Collegiate Series. Dedeaux also coached the U.S. team in a 6-2 victory over Japan in an Olympic Baseball demonstration game in Tokyo in 1964.

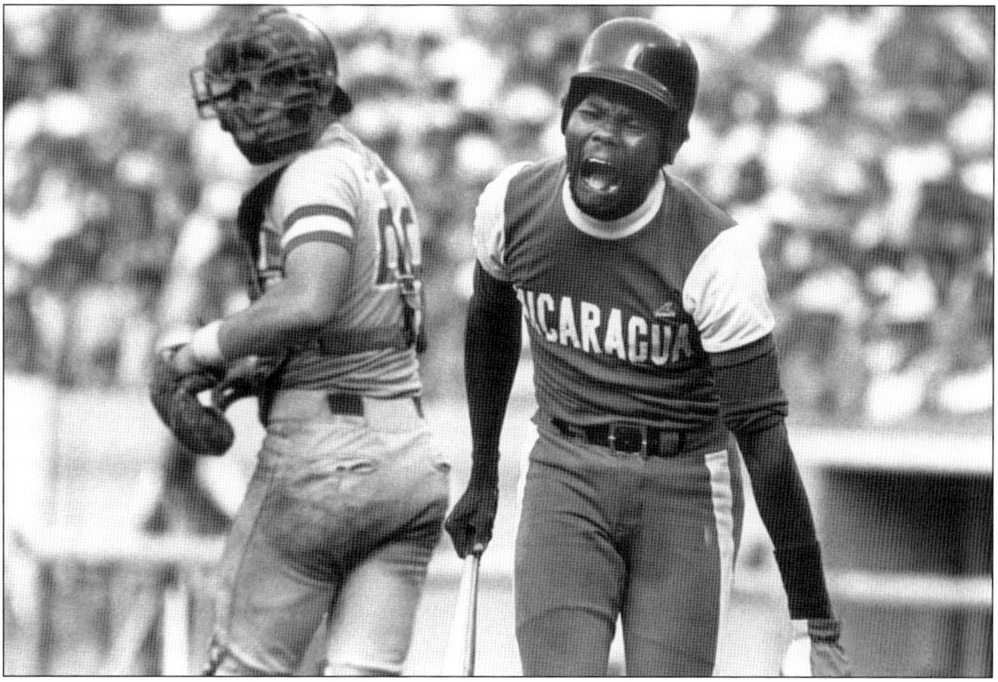

OUCH. A Nicaraguan player winces in pain after being hit by a pitch in a game against Canada during the 1984 Olympic baseball tournament at Dodger Stadium. Other participating teams included the United States, Japan, Dominican Republic, Italy, Chinese Taipei, and Korea.

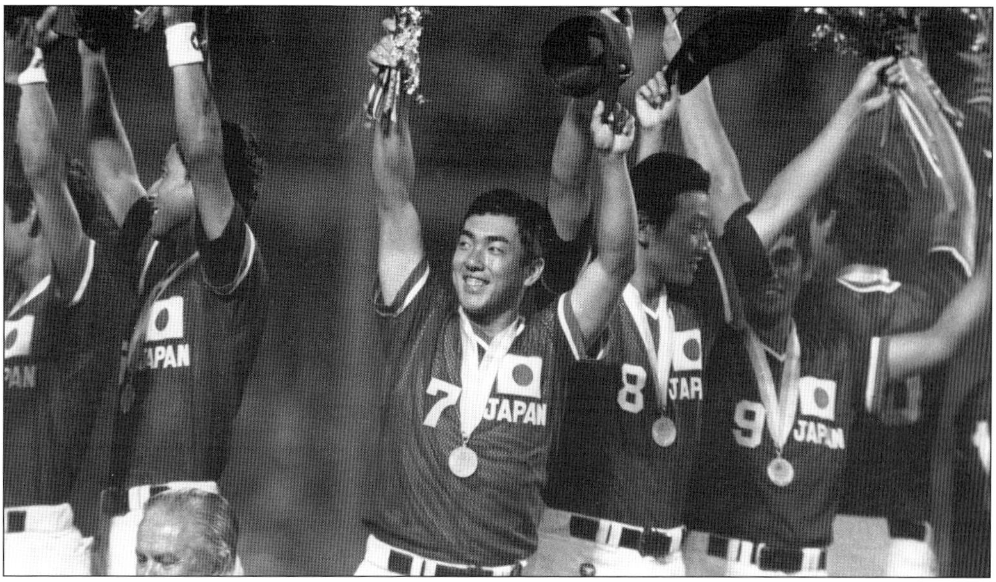

JAPAN STRIKES GOLD. A 6-3 victory over the United States gave Japan the gold medal in the 1984 Olympics in Los Angeles. The eight-team tournament at Dodger Stadium was a far cry from the initial Olympic baseball game when a group of United States servicemen faced Australia for a demonstration game at Melbourne in 1956. The U.S. team won that game, 11-5, in front of a crowd that started with only a few thousand and swelled to 100,000 at the game's conclusion because a track competition was scheduled on the same field later in the day.

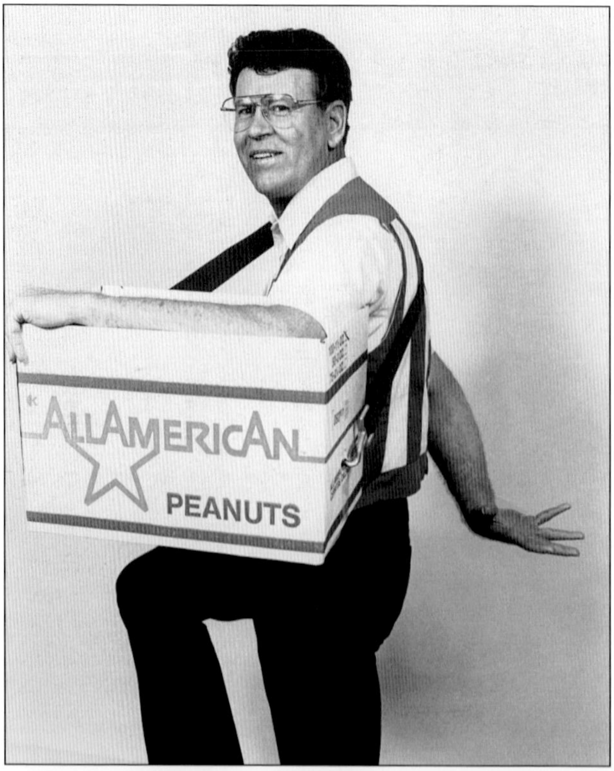

THE PEANUT MAN. Roger Owens began selling at the Los Angeles Coliseum and later became one of the most popular peanut vendors in sports history. Owens has appeared on *The Tonight Show* and has tossed an estimated 2 million peanut bags during his days at Dodger Stadium from every direction, including under the legs and around the back. Owens threw peanuts at President Carter's inaugural party in 1977 and sold a record 2,400 peanut bags during a Dallas Cowboys' playoff game in 1976.

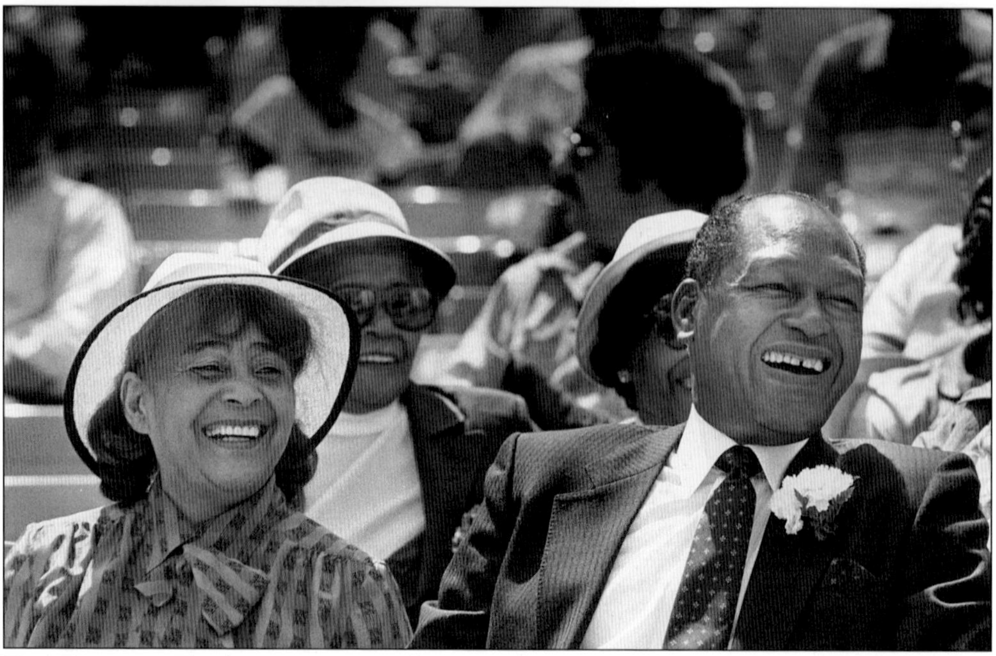

TOM BRADLEY. The five-term mayor of Los Angeles was a frequent visitor to Dodger Stadium, including this Opening Day 1984 game with his wife, Ethel. The former Los Angeles police officer was a member of the City Council in 1965 when he participated in a City Hall ceremony honoring World Series hero Lou Johnson.

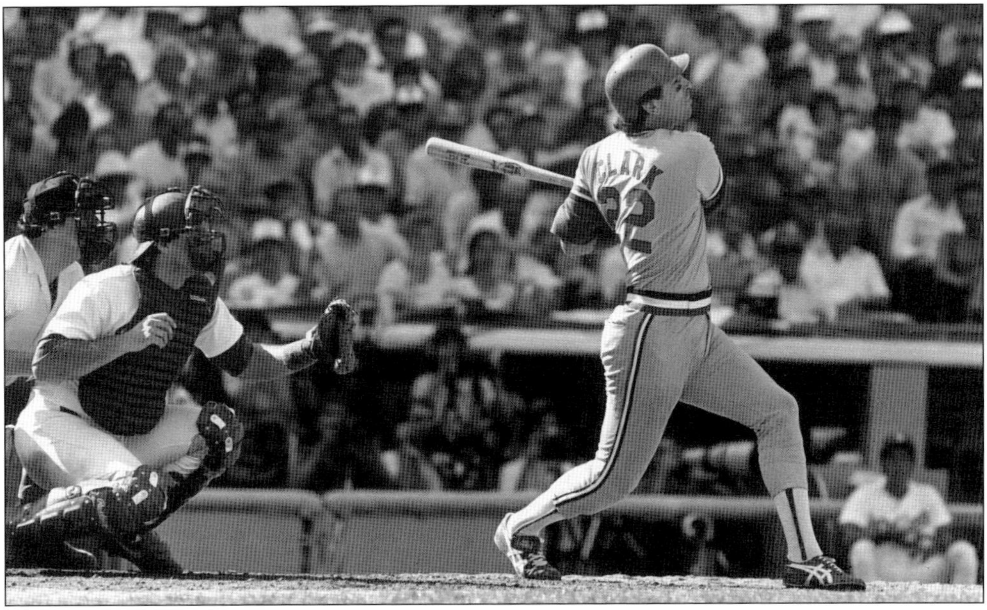

JACK CLARK. One of the most famous opponent home runs in Dodger Stadium history was Jack Clark's three-run blast off reliever Tom Niedenfuer in Game 6 of the 1985 National League Championship Series. The home run gave the St. Louis Cardinals a berth in the World Series. Clark later served as the Dodgers' batting coach from 2001 to 2003, joining Sal Maglie, Juan Marichal, and others as a famous nemesis who later wore a Dodger uniform.

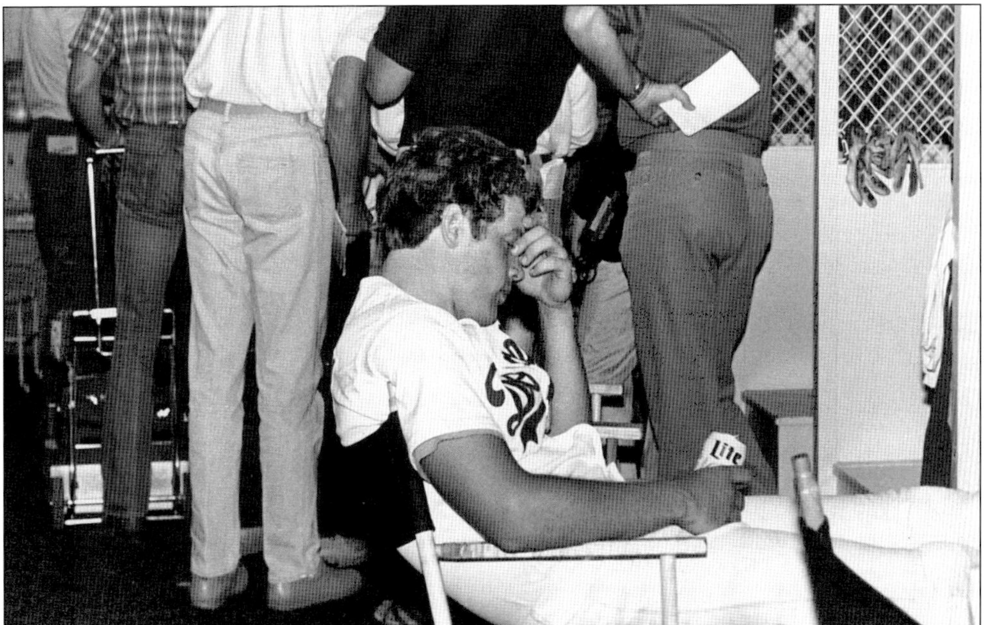

WAIT 'TIL NEXT YEAR. First baseman Greg Brock ponders the sudden end to the Dodgers' 1985 season after Jack Clark's home run knocked Los Angeles out of the playoffs. The Dodgers took a 5-4 lead into the ninth inning. It was the first time the Dodgers were eliminated at home from a multi-game postseason series since losing to San Francisco in 1962.

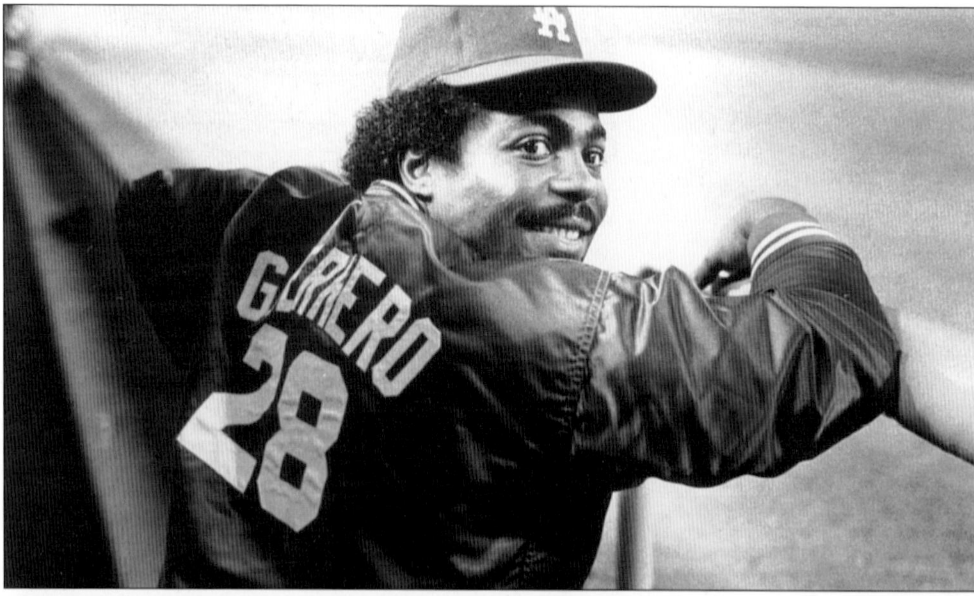

PEDRO GUERRERO. The Dodgers purchased the outfielder from the Cleveland Indians on April 4, 1974 and sold pitcher Bruce Ellingsen in the same deal. Guerrero blossomed into a dangerous hitter and after earning tri-World Series MVP honors in 1981 with Ron Cey and Steve Yeager, he posted consecutive seasons with at least 30 home runs and 100 RBI in 1982 and 1983. He tied a major league record with 15 home runs in June 1985.

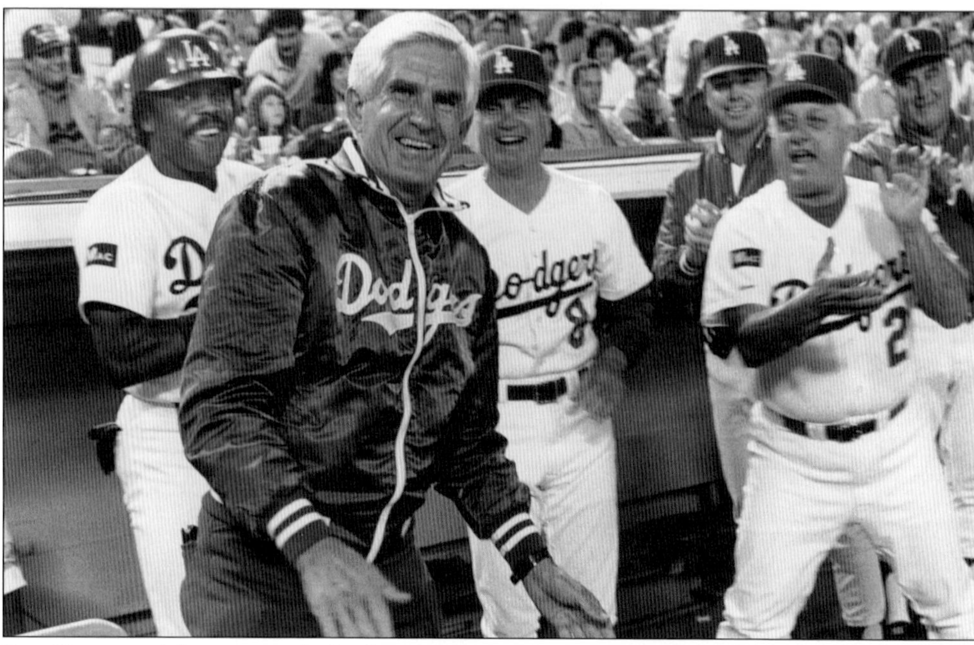

BILL BUHLER. After joining the Dodgers as a minor league trainer in 1952, Valparaiso University graduate Bill Buhler was appointed assistant trainer for the Brooklyn Dodgers in 1957 and the head trainer for Los Angeles in 1960. During his 43-year tenure with the Dodgers, Buhler brought many new ideas to the game, including the "Steve Yeager Throat Guard" in 1977 after the Dodger catcher was injured by pieces of a broken bat while standing in the on-deck circle.

THE VOICE. A fixture on the Southern California sports scene was John Ramsey, who was the public address announcer for the Dodgers at the Los Angeles Coliseum and at Dodger Stadium until 1986. His first professional sports job was announcing the 1957 Los Angeles Angels of the Pacific Coast League, and he received his biggest break in 1958 when Tex Rickard, the Dodgers' public address announcer in Brooklyn, declined to move to Los Angeles. The El Camino College and USC graduate also became the voice of USC football and basketball, the Rams, Raiders, Lakers, Angels, and Kings.

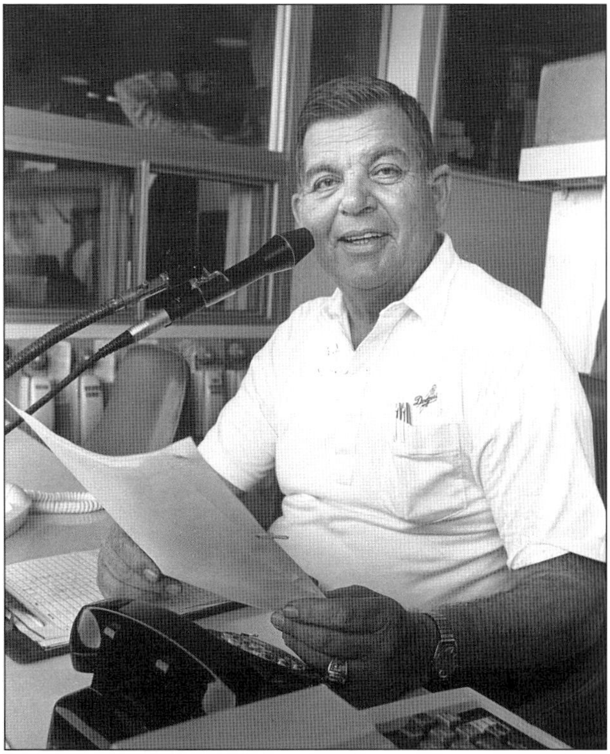

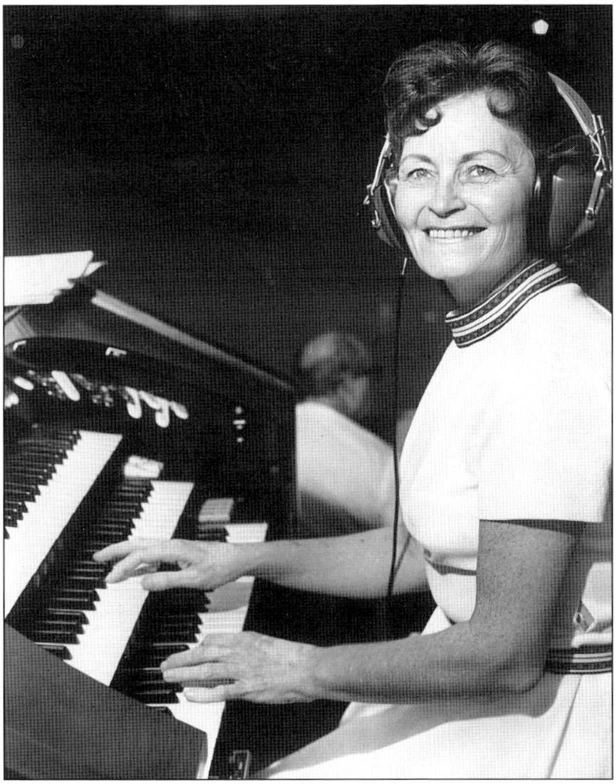

MUSIC, MUSIC, MUSIC. As a student at Whittier College, Helen Dell was the only woman to play the accordion. She was already a Dodger fan in 1972 when Dodger Vice President Red Patterson sent word to an organ company that the team needed an organist. "I played the national anthem for Red and that seemed to be a critical point with him," Dell recalled upon her 1987 retirement ceremonies at Dodger Stadium. "I got about three or four measures into it and Red said, 'That's the way it's supposed to sound,' which made me feel good."

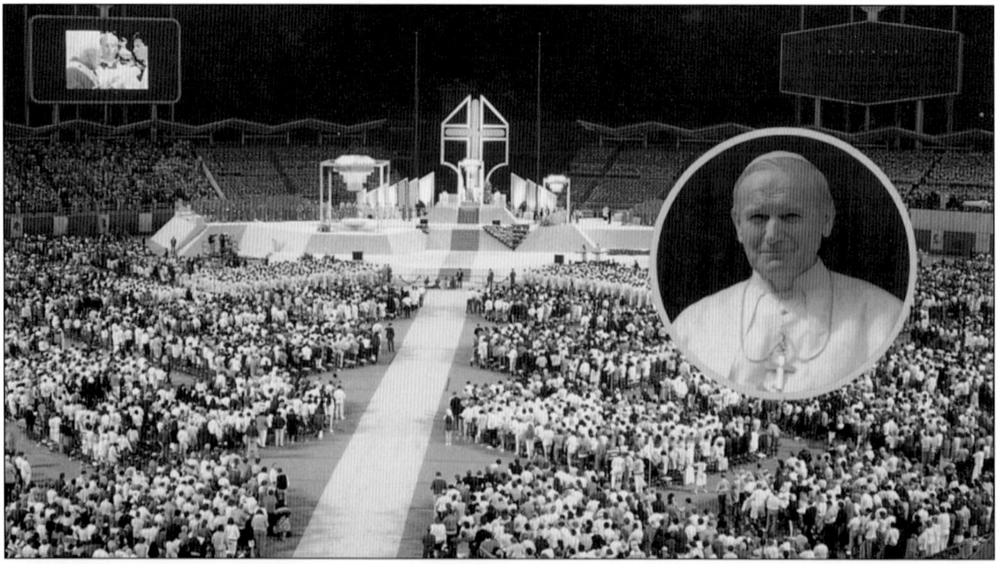

PAPAL VISIT. Pope John Paul II celebrated a Mass at Dodger Stadium on September 16, 1987, during his visit to Los Angeles. This is the Dodgers' holiday greeting card with the message from His Holiness: "Bless the children of this generation and let them grow up in a world of peace, justice and fraternal love."

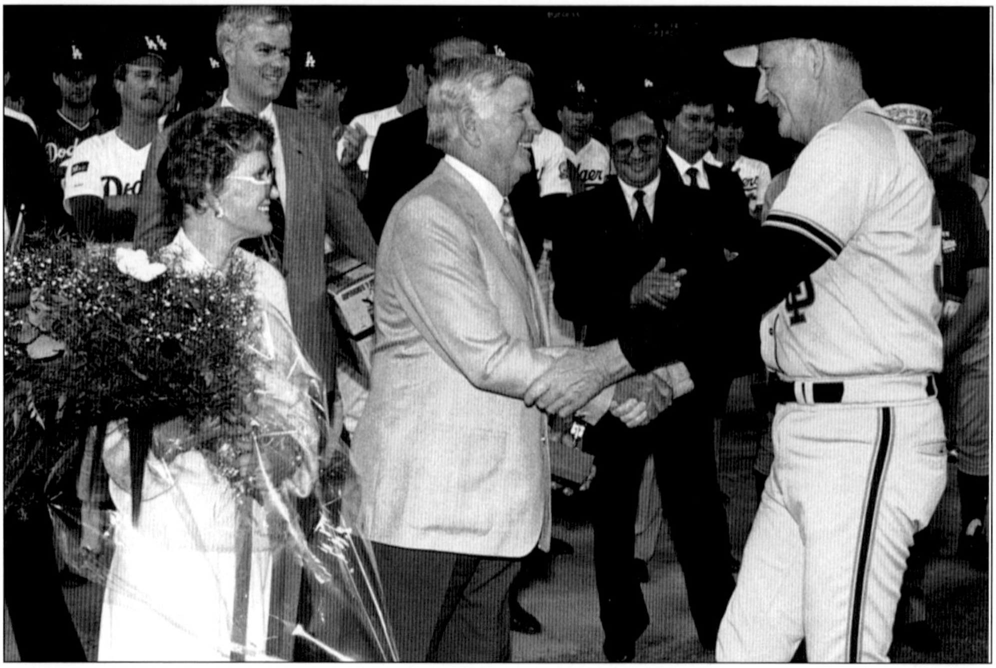

JERRY DOGGETT NIGHT. Texas native Jerry Doggett was the broadcasting partner of Vin Scully for 32 seasons, the longest tenure by a duo behind the microphone in major league history. Doggett joined the Brooklyn Dodgers on Labor Day 1956 and moved to the West Coast with the ballclub in 1958. Giants Manager Roger Craig, a Dodger pitcher from 1955 to 1961, greets Doggett and his wife, Jody, during pre-game ceremonies on October 1, 1987. In his first 31 years with the Dodgers, Doggett missed only one game to attend the high school graduation of his daughter Sandra.

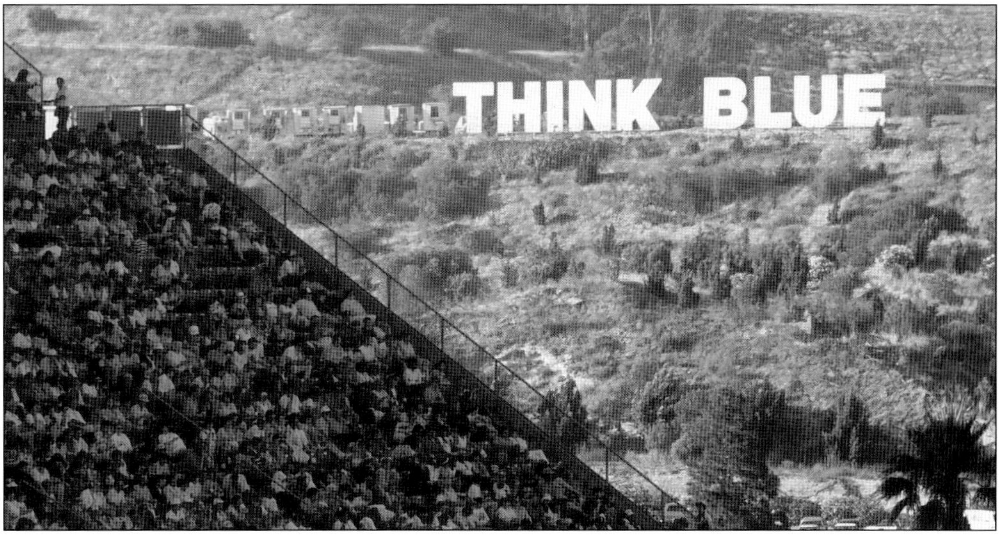

THINK BLUE. Beginning in 1987, Think Blue Week at Dodger Stadium gives fans the opportunity to live out their baseball dreams. Participant write letters in hopes of being selected for one of several categories, which include being a member of the grounds crew, throwing out the ceremonial first pitch, and singing the national anthem.

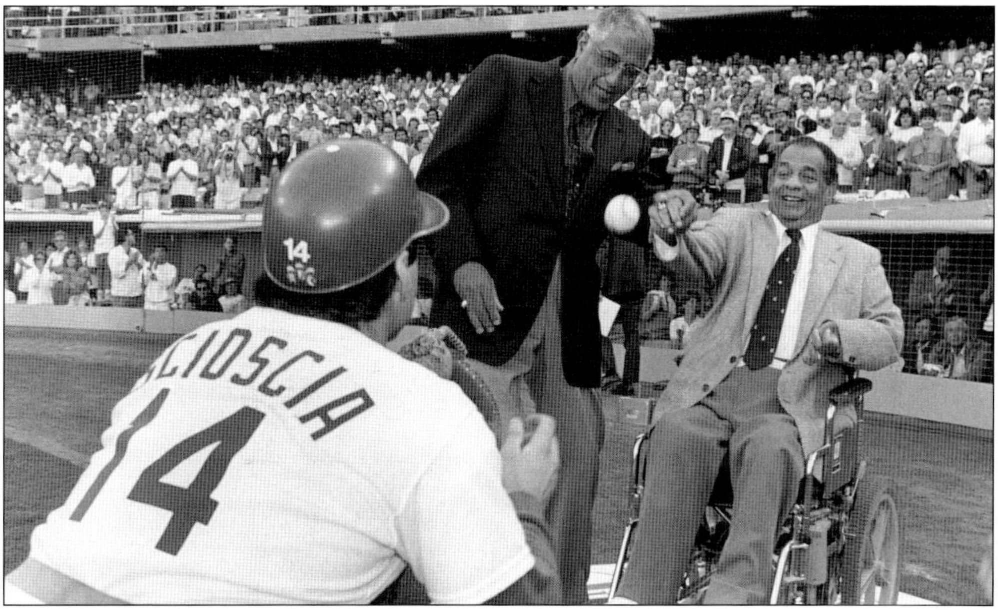

PASSING THE TORCH. Prior to the 1988 League Championship Series at Dodger Stadium, former Dodger pitcher Don Newcombe watched as Roy Campanella threw out the ceremonial first pitch to Mike Scioscia. The Hall of Famer was a catching instructor who mentored Scioscia as a minor leaguer during spring training. Scioscia caught a team-record 1,395 games with Los Angeles from 1980 to 1992. Scioscia was known for his skills at blocking the incoming runner on close plays at home plate. He was a member of two World Series teams with the Dodgers in 1981 and 1988 and managed the Anaheim Angels to a championship in 2002.

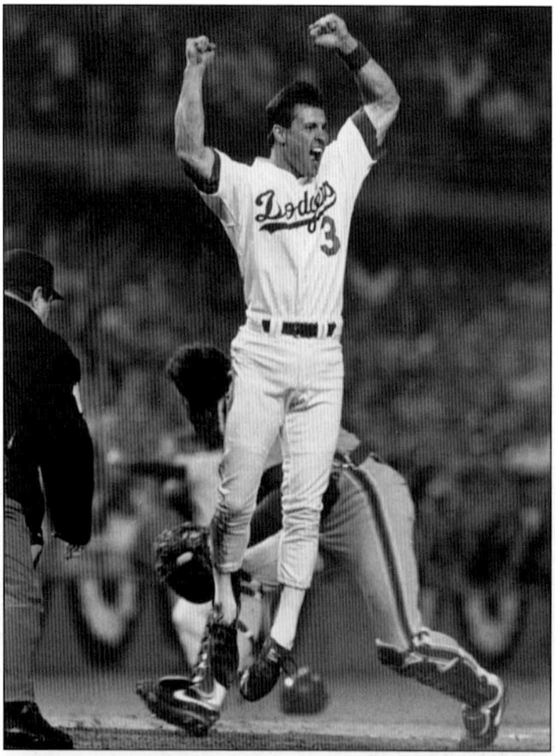

Steve Sax. The second baseman crosses the plate with joy during a 6-0 victory over the New York Mets in the final game of the 1988 National League Championship Series. It was the first Game 7 in the history of Dodger Stadium and it gave Los Angeles a berth in the World Series against the Oakland Athletics.

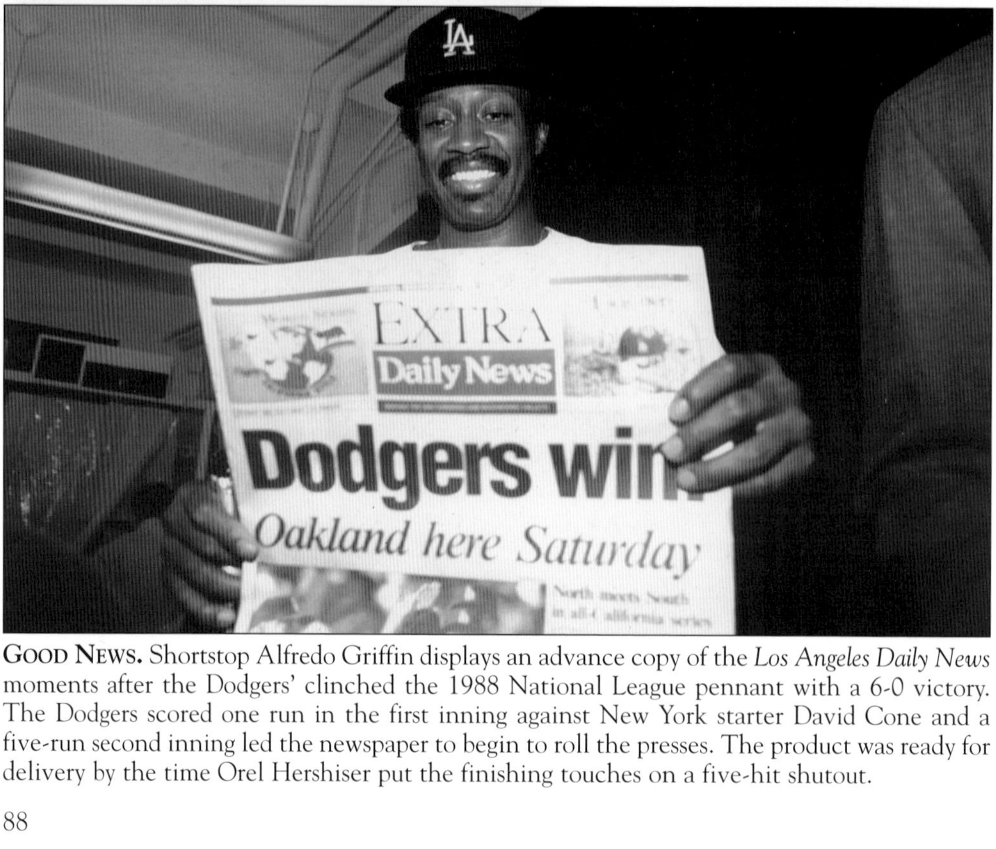

Good News. Shortstop Alfredo Griffin displays an advance copy of the *Los Angeles Daily News* moments after the Dodgers' clinched the 1988 National League pennant with a 6-0 victory. The Dodgers scored one run in the first inning against New York starter David Cone and a five-run second inning led the newspaper to begin to roll the presses. The product was ready for delivery by the time Orel Hershiser put the finishing touches on a five-hit shutout.

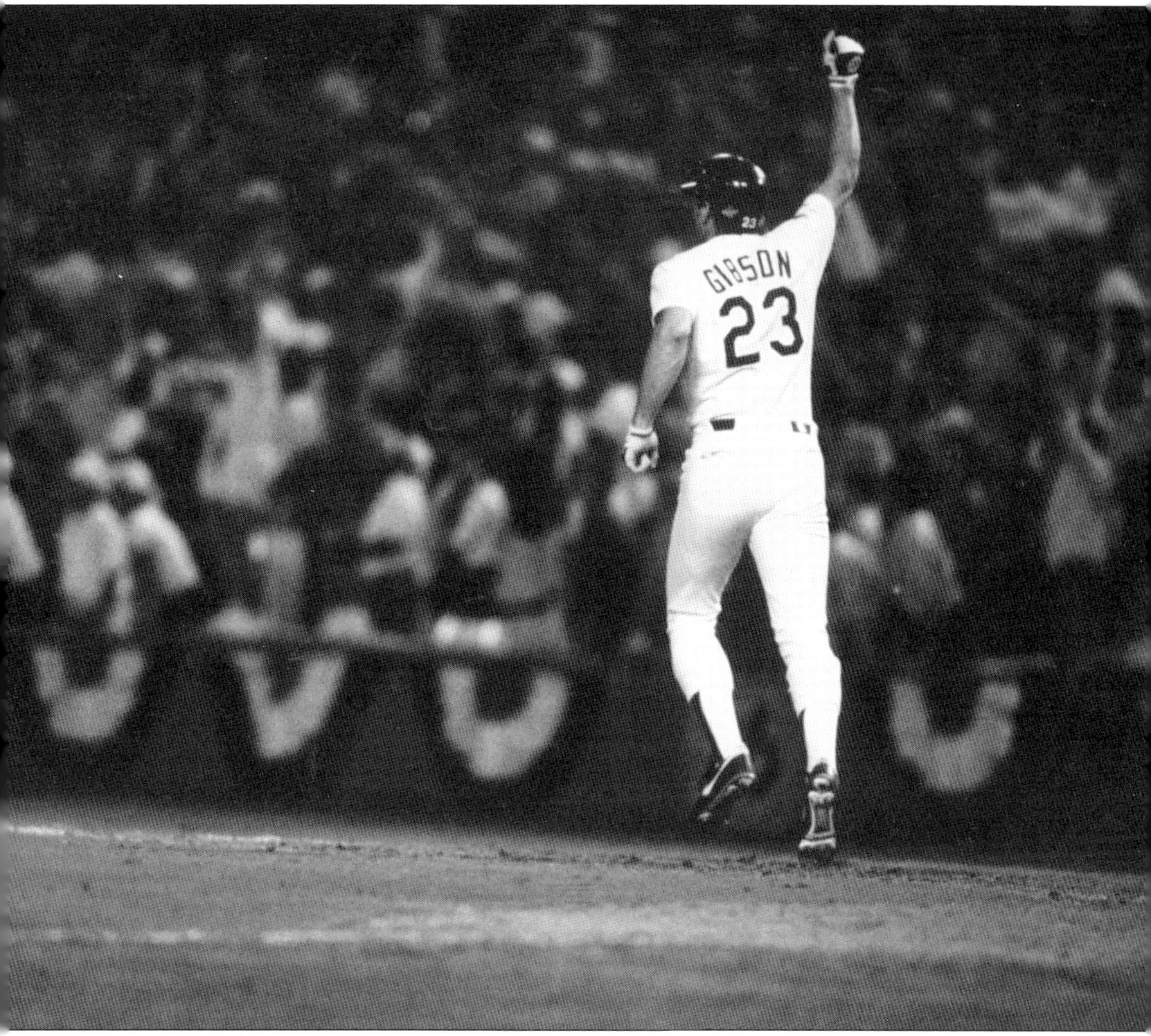

KIRK GIBSON'S HOME RUN. It would be later proclaimed "The Greatest Moment in Southern California Sports History." The Dodgers trailed, 4-3, in the bottom of the ninth inning in Game 1 of the 1988 World Series against the Oakland Athletics. Unable to start the game because of knee and hamstring injuries, Gibson hobbled to home plate as a pinch-hitter against relief ace Dennis Eckersley with two outs and a runner on first base. Gibson eventually worked Eckersley to a full count and looked for a "backdoor slider" as predicted by Los Angeles scout Mel Didler. Unable to generate power from his legs, Gibson muscled a swing with his forearms while standing on his front foot. The ball arched into the evening sky and disappeared into the Right Field Pavilion.

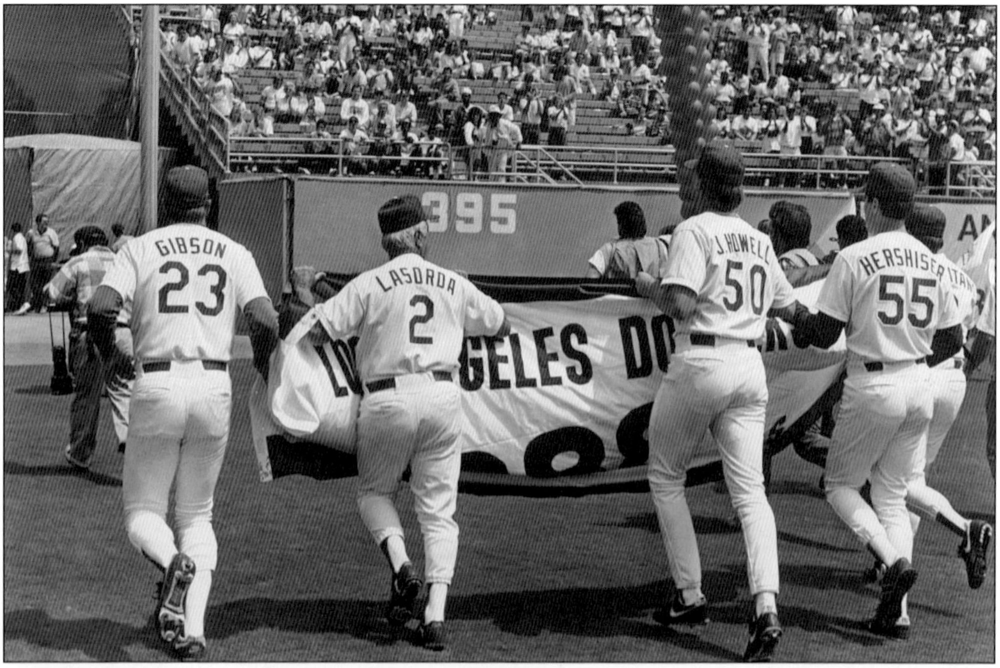

RAISING THE FLAG. Kirk Gibson, Tommy Lasorda, Jay Howell, and Orel Hershiser carry the World Championship flag toward the center field pole on Opening Day 1989.

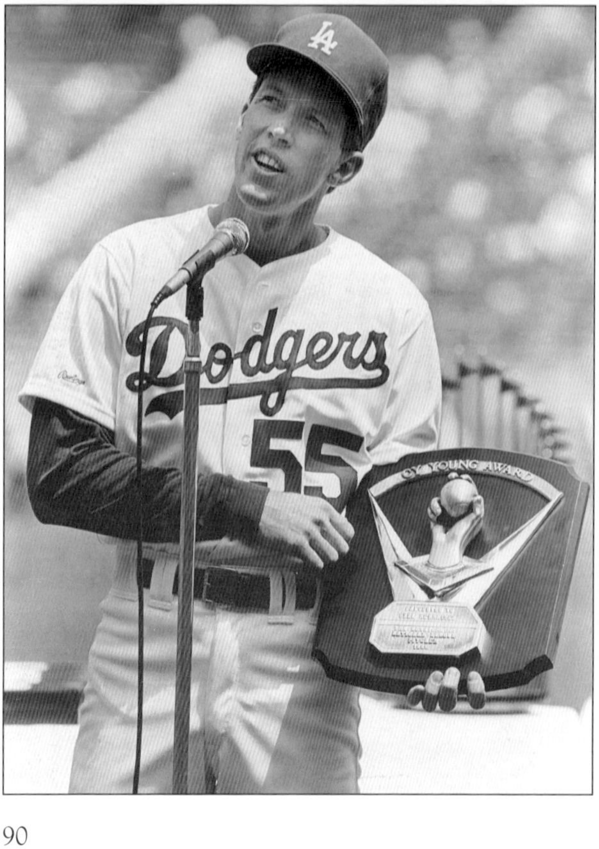

THE BULLDOG. Don Drysdale rejoined the Dodgers as a broadcaster in 1988 and the organization that summer honored the 20th anniversary of his 58 2/3 scoreless innings streak with a pre-game ceremony involving pitcher Orel Hershiser. Little did anyone realize Hershiser would surpass Drysdale's record with 59 consecutive scoreless innings at the end of the season, finishing with a 23-8 mark and 2.26 ERA. Hershiser won the Cy Young Award and MVP honors in the League Championship Series and World Series.

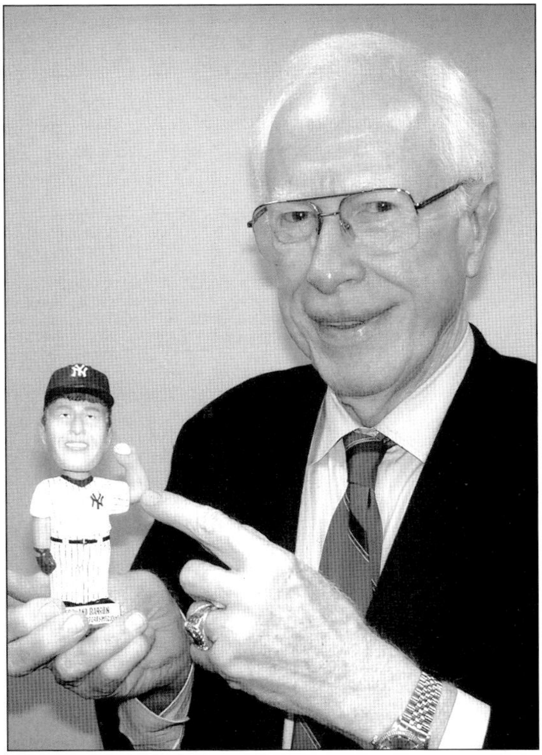

Tommy John Surgery. Dodger team physician Dr. Frank Jobe wasn't thinking of making medical history when he performed an elbow ligament replacement surgery in 1974 on an injured Dodger pitcher. But the surgery was a success and 28 years later there was a "bobble arm" doll saluting Tommy John's career. And Jobe used the left-hander's name when deciding what to call the operation. "When you say it, everyone knows what you mean," Jobe said. "Reconstruction of the ulnar collateral ligament with the palmaris longus tendon is a mouthful."

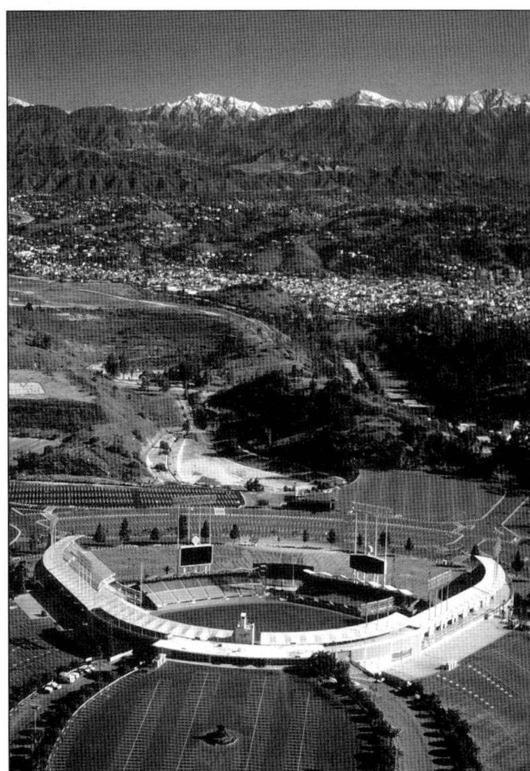

Let it Snow. The unique climates in Southern California can sometimes provide snow-capped mountains in the background of a sunny ballpark. But fans don't have to worry about packing snowshoes to the ballpark. There have been only 17 rainouts in Dodger Stadium history since 1962 and 9 occurred in the month of April.

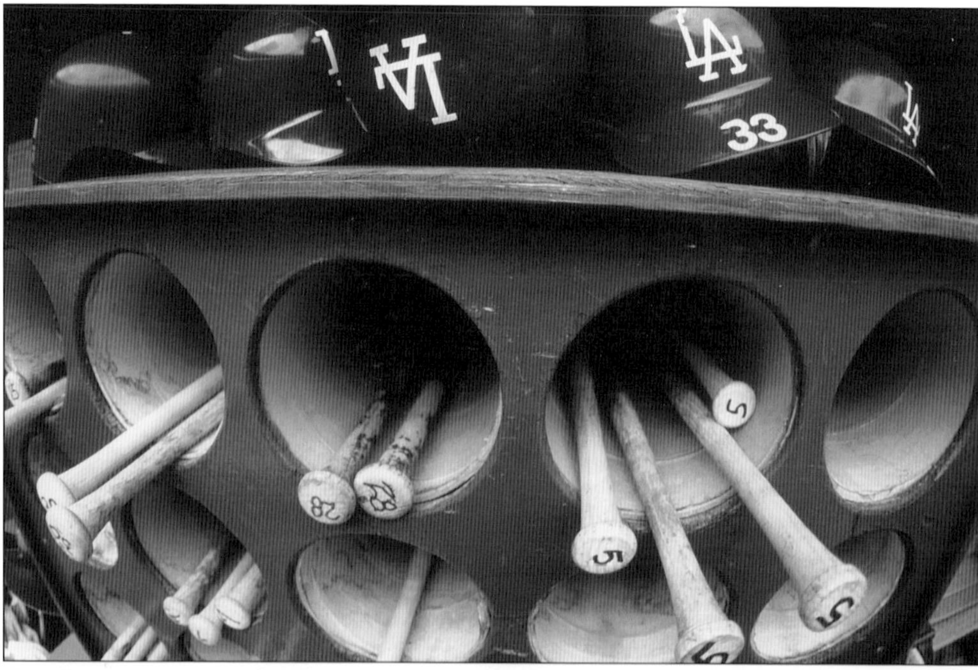

The Bat Rack. Located at the end of the Dodger dugout toward home plate, the valet is made of wood and stocked by a clubhouse attendant prior to batting practice. An average player keeps six bats in the rack in the event of a cracked handle during a plate appearance. The bats are stored in the clubhouse after the games and packed in large duffle bags for road trips.

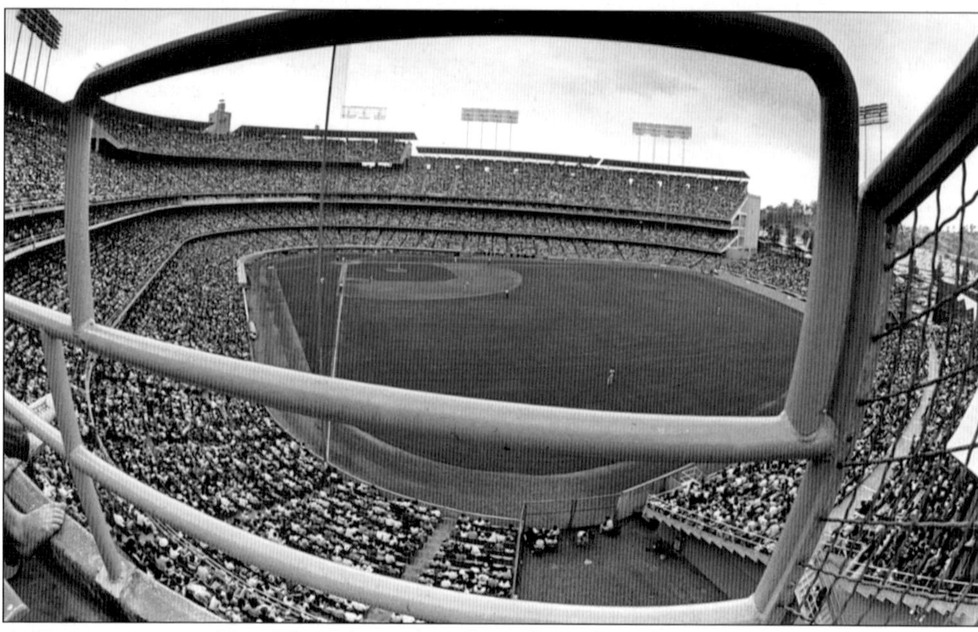

A View from the Top. The fish-eye lens from the right field corner of the Reserved Level provides a unique angle of a Dodger ballgame. These seats are located just above the Stadium Club restaurant. Fans with tickets along the far railing in Aisle 60 can watch the proceedings in the visitor's bullpen.

Five

1990s

The Dodgers celebrated the 100th anniversary as members of the National League in 1990. The centennial season began a unique decade in team history as the natural evolution of the sport—and the stadium as a multi-purpose facility—would unfold in the subsequent years.

The dramatic major league debut of right-hander Hideo Nomo with Los Angeles in 1995 became one of the most important events in baseball history. When Nomo decided he wanted to play in the United States, there was much speculation whether the he could even compete in the major leagues, let alone duplicate his success from his stellar career with the Kintetsu Buffaloes from 1990 to 1994.

Most U.S. fans had never heard of Nomo, nicknamed "The Tornado" in Japan because of his unorthodox pitching motion, which included turning his back to the batter in the middle of the windup. Nomo also had the weight of an entire country on his shoulders as the first player from a Japanese professional team to appear in the majors since Masanori Murakami, who pitched for the San Francisco Giants from 1964 to 1965 before returning to his homeland under pressure for the balance of his career.

Nomo would prove his skeptics wrong, winning the Rookie of the Year honors and later becoming one of only four pitchers in history to author a no-hitter in both the American and National Leagues. Nomo helped the Dodgers reach the playoffs in 1995 and 1996 and his success opened the door for other Japanese players such as Ichiro Suzuki, who won American League MVP honors as a rookie with the Seattle Mariners in 2001.

Dave Hansen, who spent most of the 1990s with the Dodgers as a reserve infielder, had a better appreciation for Nomo's rookie season with Los Angeles after he spent one season in Japan with the Hanshin Tigers in 1998.

"I appreciated Nomo, but I didn't know how fully I should have appreciated him. I did learn a lot from him. I know he must have been taught really well to control his emotions. What he brought to the table was awesome for our club that year. I didn't get a chance until I went to Japan to really fully understand how difficult and how important it was."

Nomo pitched for the Dodgers from 1995 to 1998 and returned as a free agent in 2002. The scrutiny was off Nomo the second time around and he didn't mind when Japanese camera crews paid more attention in spring training to left-hander Kazuhisa Ishii.

"Even if I had not come, I think there were a lot of players who wanted to come over here," Nomo said in 2002. "I just happened to be the first. Now, it's normal for a Japanese player to play in the major leagues."

Another change on the horizon occurred in March 1998 when Major League Baseball owners approved the sale of the Dodgers from the O'Malley family to the FOX Group. In October 1998, the Dodgers were named "the most successful organization in Major League Baseball during the 20th century" in a study conducted by Street and Smith's *SportsBusiness Journal*. Los Angeles finished first with a century performance index of 7.63 on a 10-point scale based on a rating formula that evaluated the on-field and ticket window success of each of the 35 major league teams that played at least 10 seasons from 1901 to 1998. The Brooklyn Dodgers finished ninth with a 5.38 century performance index rating.

In January 1999, the Dodgers announced a program of investment and limited renovation of Dodger Stadium to help make it more economically competitive with other ballparks across the nation. By the following season, the Dodgers would add new field level seats down the foul lines beyond the dugouts and a new expanded dugout section with an adjacent club area. In addition, suites were added on the Club Level to provide amenities available in every other major league ballpark.

During the O'Malley years, the only visible stadium advertising in the 1960s and 1970s was for Unocal 76, an original sponsor whose 20-year agreement with the Dodgers helped finance the new ballpark. When advertising appeared on the outfield wall for the first time in 1998, it was blended with great moments in Dodger Stadium history as part of a large mural. And outside the perimeter of the ballpark, large colorful banners featured action photos of the current players.

Despite the improvements and changes to the stadium's appearance, one of the cornerstones that remained in place was the Dodgers' work away from the ballpark. The Dodgers' relationships within the surrounding communities, which began during their first season on the West Coast in 1958, continued to flourish on a year-round basis.

The Dodgers Dream Foundation, founded in 1998, was created to provide educational, athletic, and recreational opportunities for the youth of the Greater Los Angeles community. Other community programs sponsored by the Dodgers included the Adopt-A-School program, Dodger Reading Dugout, a number of Dodger Wives fundraising events, player clinics, and visits to neighborhood schools and hospitals.

"I like doing clinics with these young kids and helping that way," said Glenn Hoffman, who has served the Dodgers as a player, coach, major league manager, and minor league instructor. "I also like the Christmas programs because you see the school and the dreams of the young people who hope to come to Dodger Stadium, not only as a player, but just to visit and say they've come with their parents. The only reason we're playing ball is for the people in the community and for them to come watch us. Any way we can support them, I think it's outstanding. When they come to the stadium, they can feel comfortable and put a face with somebody who has been to their school or helped out with a program."

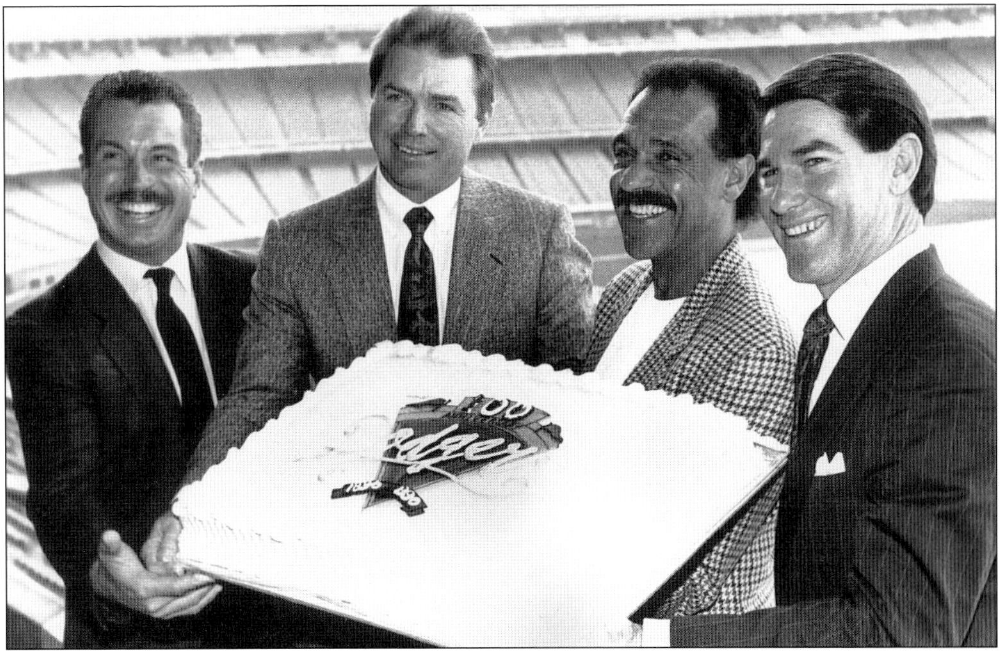

100TH ANNIVERSARY. The Dodgers celebrated their centennial season as members of the National League in 1990. Holding a special cake on the Club Level to kick off the year-long celebration was the Dodger infield, which spent a record $8^1/_2$ seasons together from 1973 to 1982: first baseman Steve Garvey, second baseman Davey Lopes, shortstop Bill Russell, and third baseman Ron Cey.

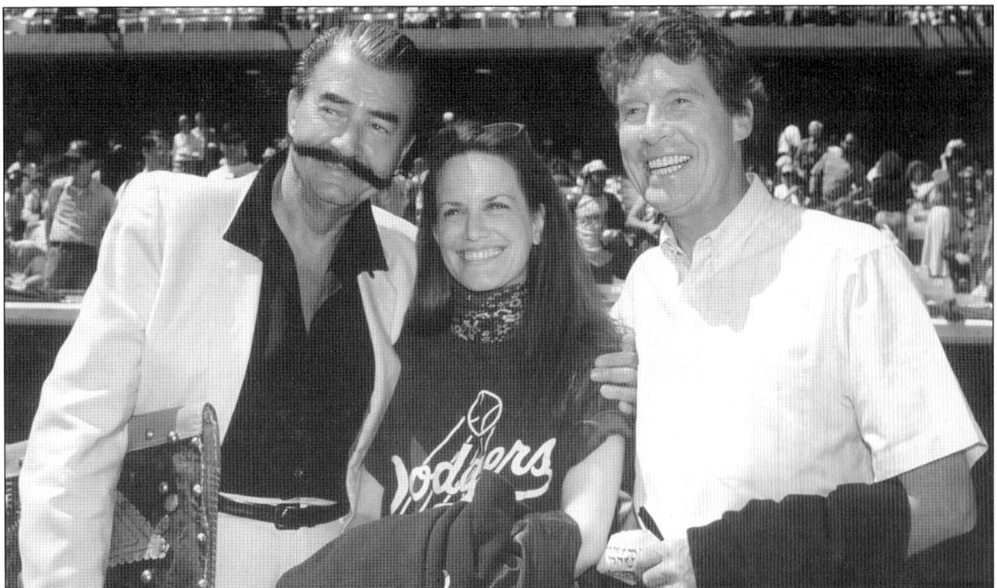

PAINTING HISTORY. Artist Leroy Neiman, who was commissioned by the Dodgers to create a commemorative painting for the 100th anniversary of Dodger baseball, meets *Phantom of the Opera* stars Dale Kristien and Michael Crawford on Opening Day 1990. Neiman's image was used for the cover of the 1990 Dodger Yearbook.

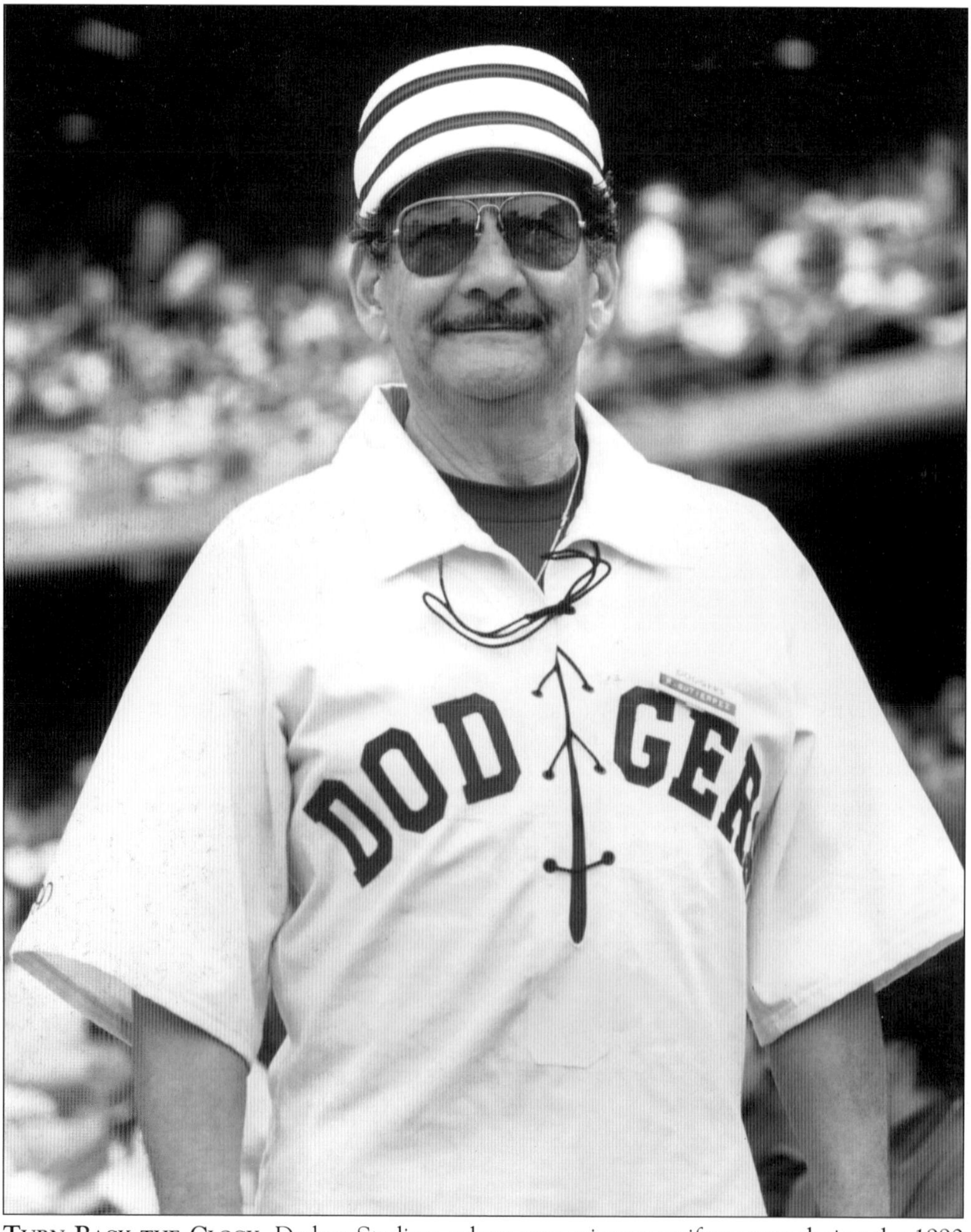

Turn Back the Clock. Dodger Stadium ushers wore vintage uniform tops during the 1990 centennial season. On April 21, the Dodgers celebrated the 100th anniversary of their first National League victory at Washington Park. The back cover of a special "playbill" program distributed at the turnstiles re-created the meeting of "Boston Beaneaters vs. Brooklyn Bridegrooms; April 21, 1890; Admit Gentlemen & Ladies." The Dodgers won 7-6, but the Brooklyn Eagle reported, "It was anything but a pleasant game or a good display of batting, as the hits were mostly flies to the outfield." The Bridegrooms were to undergo various name changes through the years, but the name that finally stuck was Dodgers. That moniker, which first surfaced in the 1880s, was derived from "Trolley Dodgers" because Brooklynites were supposedly adept at sidestepping trolley cars in a complicated maze that ran through the borough.

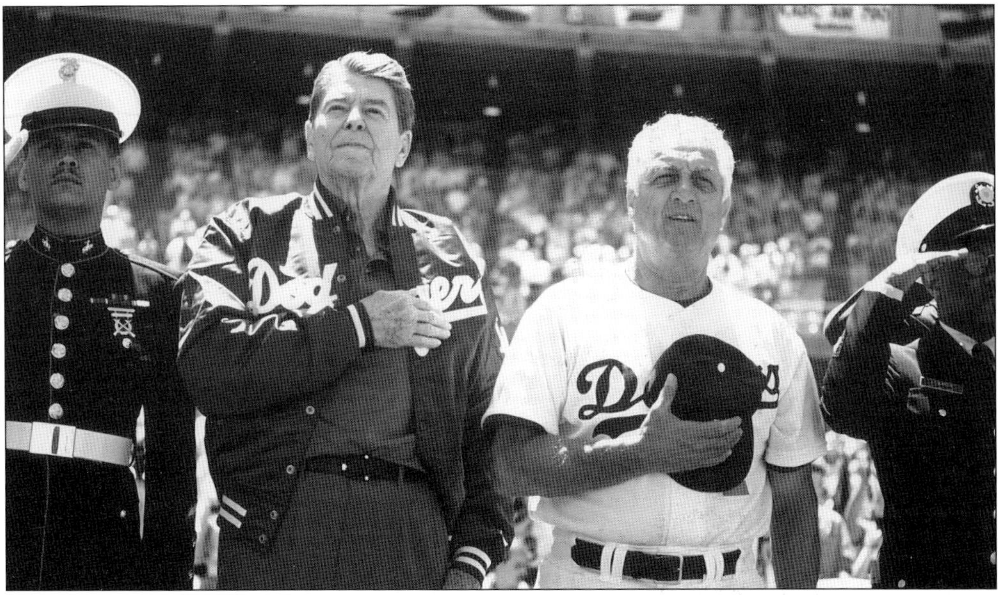

RONALD REAGAN. The former United States President threw out the ceremonial first pitch at Dodger Stadium on Opening Day 1991 and then stood alongside Manager Tommy Lasorda for the national anthem. Reagan's association with the Dodgers in Los Angeles began in 1959 when he was one of many Hollywood stars who were guests on a live, five-hour "Dodgerthon" on KTTV Channel 11 on the eve of the Proposition B ballot referendum. As California's former governor in 1971, Reagan made an appearance to kick off a recreational vehicle show in the parking lot at Dodger Stadium.

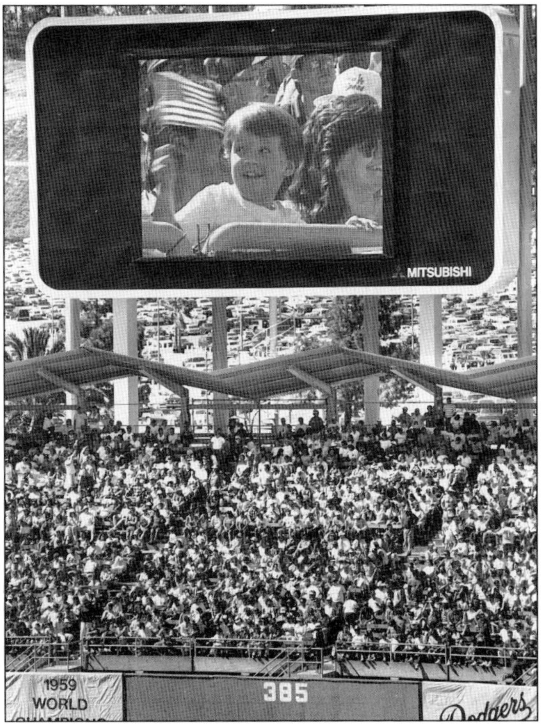

SUPER SCOREBOARD. When it made its debut for the 1980 All-Star Game, the Dodger Diamond Vision was the largest full-color matrix board in the world—35 feet wide and 25 feet high. The system worked on the same principle as a home color television set and was built by Mitsubishi Electronic Corporation of Japan. The original Diamond Vision consisted of 38,400 red, green, and blue lights, drawing only two watts per tube, or one-tenth of a comparable incandescent lamp. The Dodgers updated their video display system in 1991 and 2003.

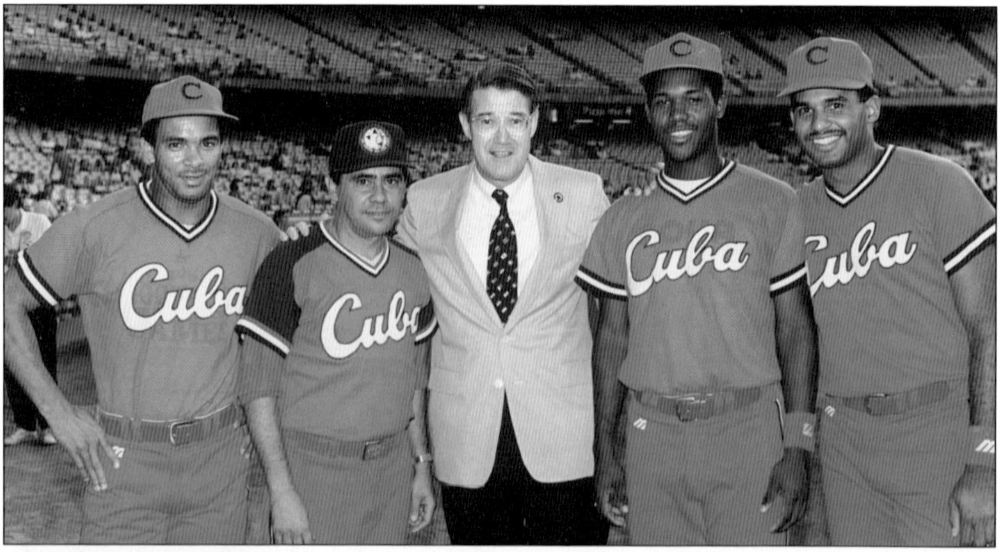

WORLDWIDE BASEBALL. On August 24, 1991, Dodger Stadium played host to the second annual International Baseball Association's World All-Star Game. The game, presented by the Dodgers, IBA, and the Los Angeles Sports Council, featured honorary coaches Sadaharu Oh for the East squad and former Dodgers Don Newcombe and Roy Campanella representing the West. Dodger President Peter O'Malley greets members from the Cuban team, from left to right, second baseman Antonio Pacheco, head coach Sergio Borges Suarez, third baseman Omar Linares, and catcher/outfielder Orestes Kindelan.

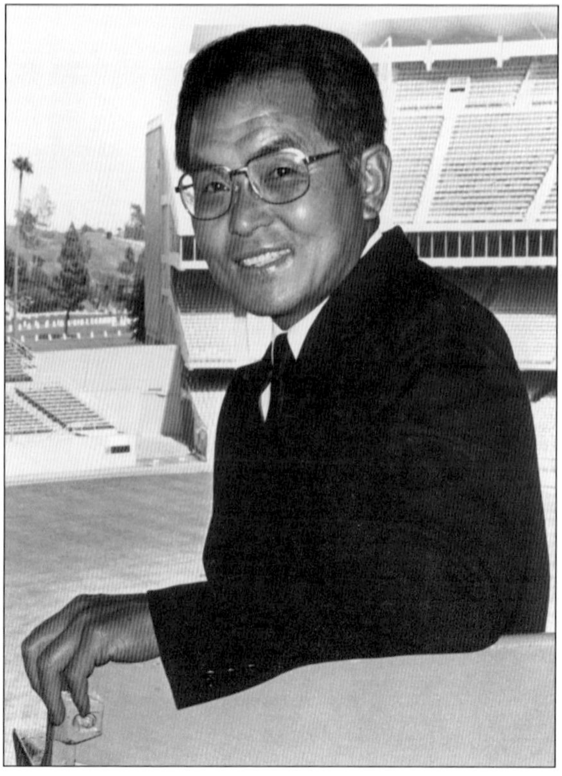

IKE IKUHARA. A letter of recommendation from Japanese baseball ambassador Sotaro Suzuki opened the door for Waseda University product Ike Ikuhara to join the Dodger organization in 1965. Ikuhara worked in many departments, including scouting, ticketing, and minor leagues. But it was his role as assistant to Dodger President Peter O'Malley and as a key figure within international baseball circles that led to Ikuhara's induction into the Japanese Baseball Hall of Fame in 2002. He also wrote two books published in Japan, *A Real Pro—Becoming a Major Leaguer* and *Dodger Way—A Winning Tradition.*

The Great One. Los Angeles Kings' star Wayne Gretzky received a hockey stick instead of a baseball bat at the annual Hollywood Stars game. Many other Southern California sports celebrities have participated, including the Lakers' Kareem Abdul-Jabbar.

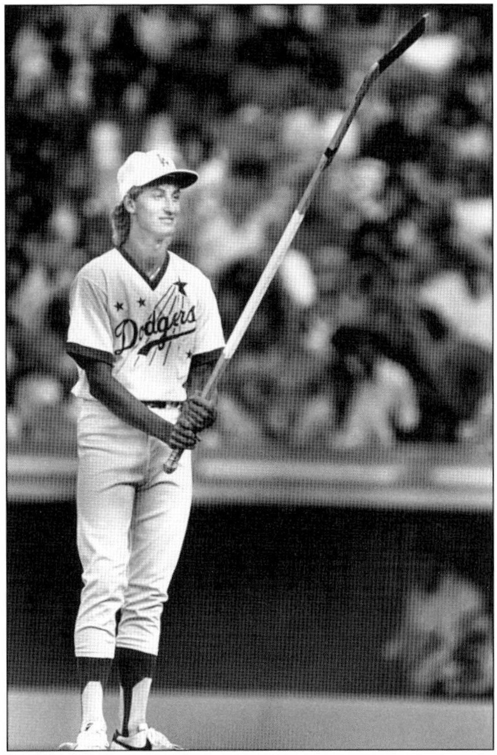

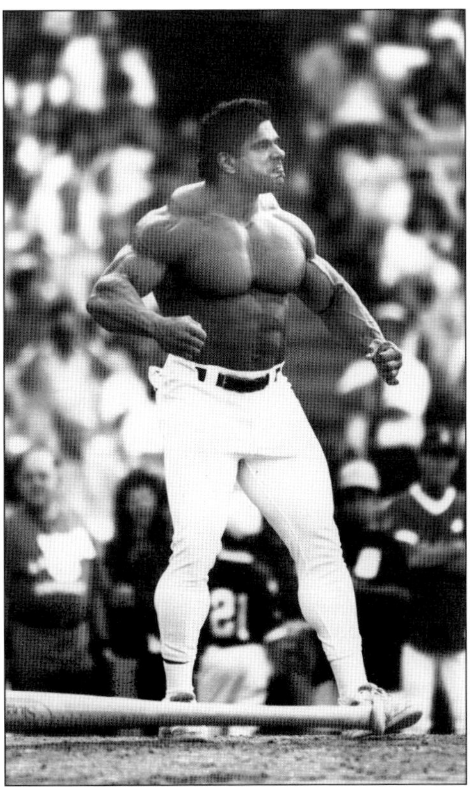

The Incredible Hulk. Actor Lou Ferrigno pretends to take exception to an inside pitch during the Hollywood Stars festivities. Note the giant-sized baseball bat at home plate, the perfect model for a muscular hitter.

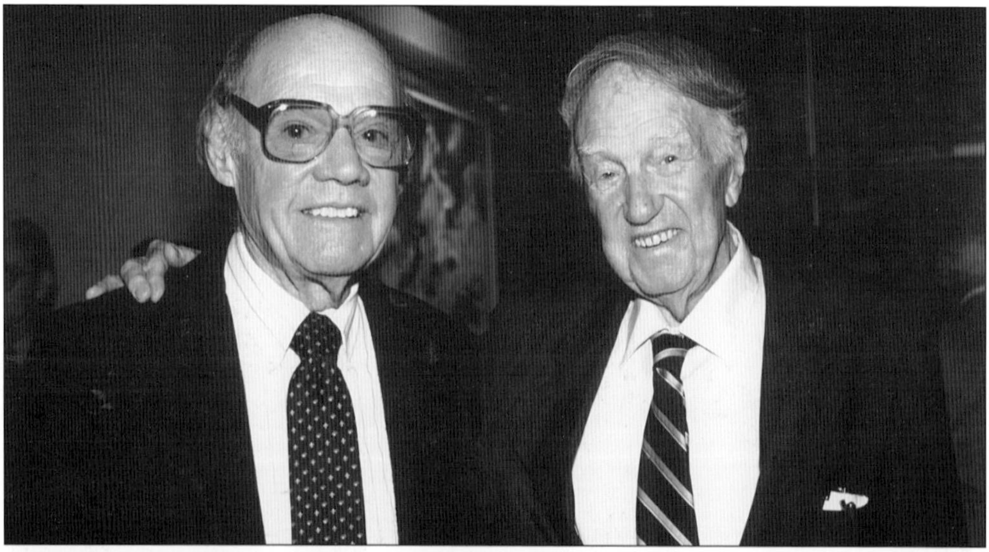

PRESS BOX LEGENDS. Bob Hunter (left) and Arthur E. "Red" Patterson devoted their lives to professional baseball. Both began their careers as sportswriters. Hunter covered the Pacific Coast League for the *Los Angeles Examiner* until the Dodgers moved to the West Coast in 1958. At the *New York Herald-Tribune*, Patterson broke stories about Lou Gehrig's retirement in 1941 and Branch Rickey becoming the new Dodger president in 1942. During his tenure in public relations with the Yankees from 1947 to 1953, Patterson was credited with numerous innovations, including Oldtimers Day and the "tape-measure home run."

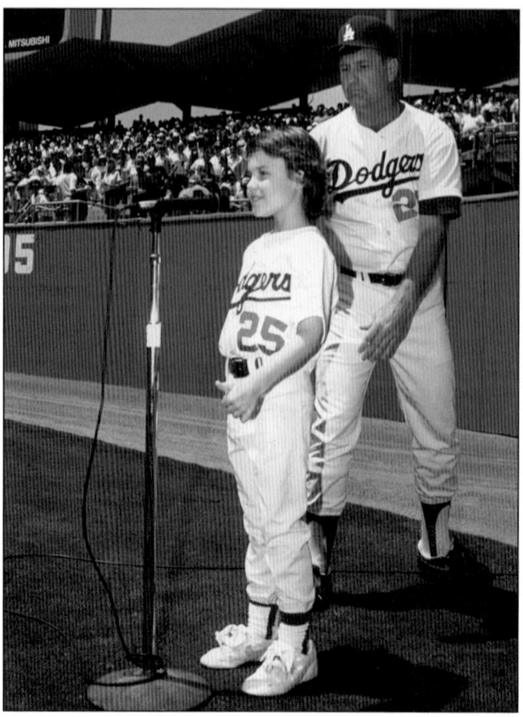

TOMMY AND TAYLOR JOHN. The youngest participant at the Dodgers' 1991 Oldtimers Day was Taylor John, the nine-year-old son of former Los Angeles pitcher Tommy John who performed the national anthem. Taylor John was a member of the Broadway musical *Les Miserables*, playing the orphaned street urchin Gavroche. One of Taylor's brothers, Travis, drew national attention at age two when he fell 26 feet from the upper floor of a New Jersey vacation home and lay in a coma for weeks. Travis John not only survived, but he made a complete recovery and threw out the "official first ball" at the 1981 playoffs escorted by his "best buddy," Yankees outfielder Reggie Jackson.

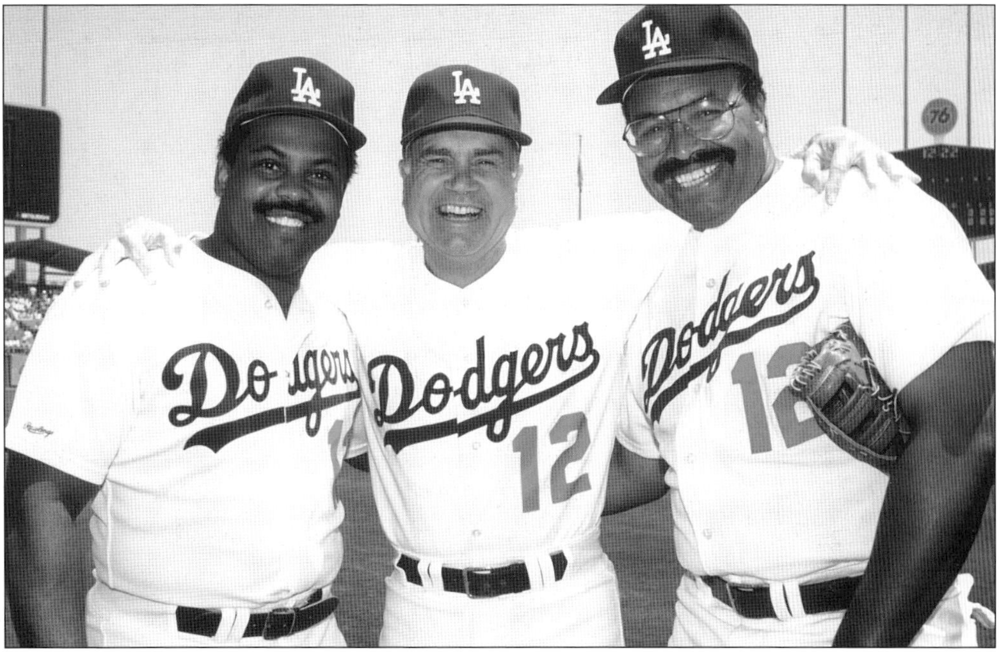

STROKE OF TWELVE. Sharing the same uniform number, former Dodgers Bill Madlock and Tommy Davis flank coach Joe Amalfitano during the 1991 Oldtimers Day festivities. The Dodgers acquired Madlock, a four-time National League batting champion, from the Pittsburgh Pirates for the pennant race in 1985. Madlock batted .360 in 34 games as Los Angeles captured the National League West title. In 1962–1963, Davis became the youngest player in National League history to win back-to-back hitting crowns. Amalfitano was a member of the Dodger coaching staff from 1983 to 1998.

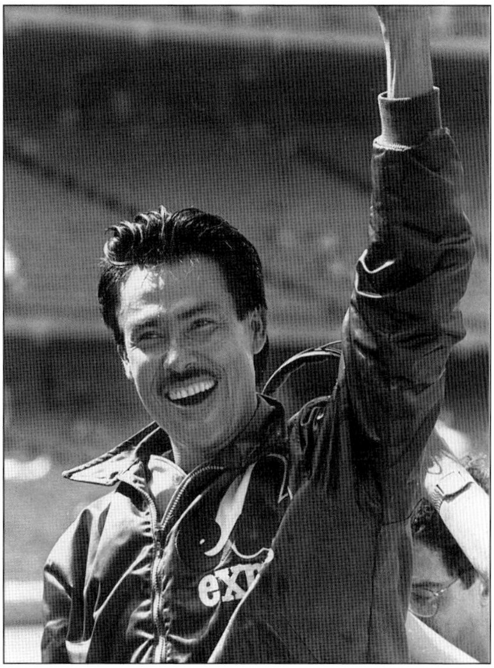

A PERFECT AFTERNOON. On July 28, 1991, Montreal Expos' right-hander Dennis Martinez retired all 27 batters he faced for a perfect game and 2-0 victory at Dodger Stadium. The Nicaraguan native struck out five and retired pinch-hitter Chris Gwynn on a flyout to center fielder Marquis Grissom to complete his gem. Two days earlier, Montreal's Mark Gardner pitched a no-hitter for nine innings but gave up a hit in the tenth inning and lost the game, 1-0. The first no-hitter in Dodger Stadium history was by the Los Angeles Angels' Bo Belinsky against the Baltimore Orioles on May 5, 1962. The only other no-hitter against the Dodgers in Los Angeles was on April 8, 1994 by Atlanta Braves' left-hander Kent Mercker during a 6-0 victory.

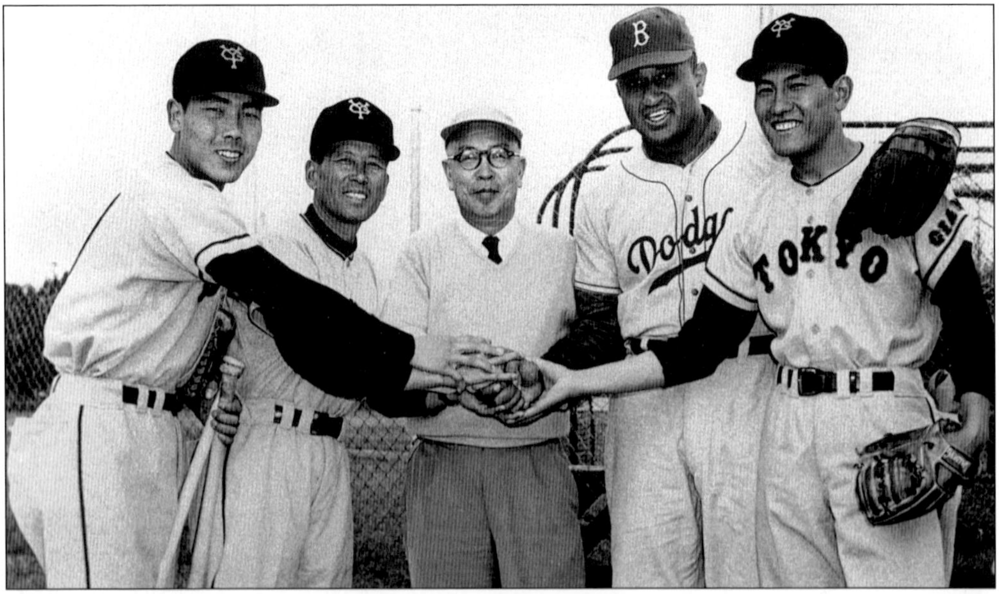

GOODWILL AMBASSADOR. When Dodger Stadium opened with a civic luncheon on April 9, 1962, one of the guests for the first game was the dean of Japanese sportswriters Sotaro Suzuki served as an interpreter between the United States and Japanese baseball officials, and he played a role in the Brooklyn Dodgers' trip to Japan in 1956. Sotaro traveled in 1957 to the Dodgers' training camp in Vero Beach, Florida. Here, he poses with, from left to right, Shigero Fujio, Shigeru Mizuhara, Don Newcombe, and Sho Horiuchi.

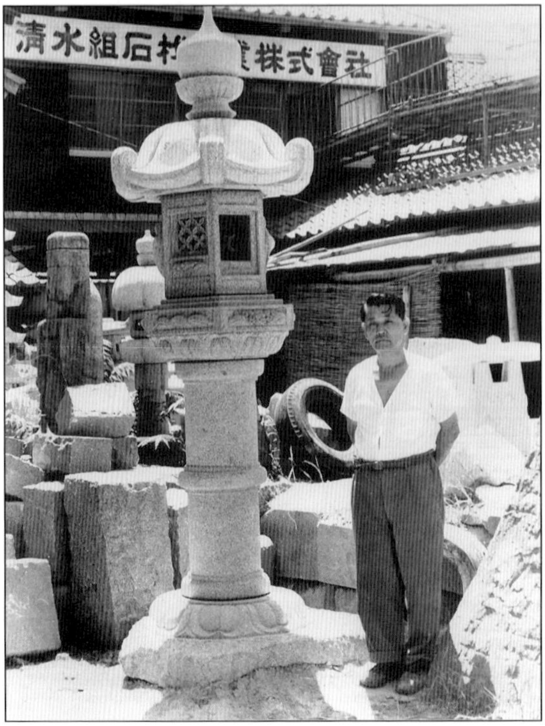

GIFT FROM JAPAN. Upon his return to Japan, Sotaro Suzuki decided to give Walter O'Malley and the Dodgers an ishi-doro (stone lantern). Suzuki said, "To commemorate the completion of Dodger Stadium, we need to present the Dodgers with a gift from Japan." The 3,921-pound, 10-foot-tall stone lantern arrived at Dodger Stadium in the winter of 1965. The stone lantern was built by Shimizugumi Stone Works Company, a famous stone-carving house in Aichi Prefecture.

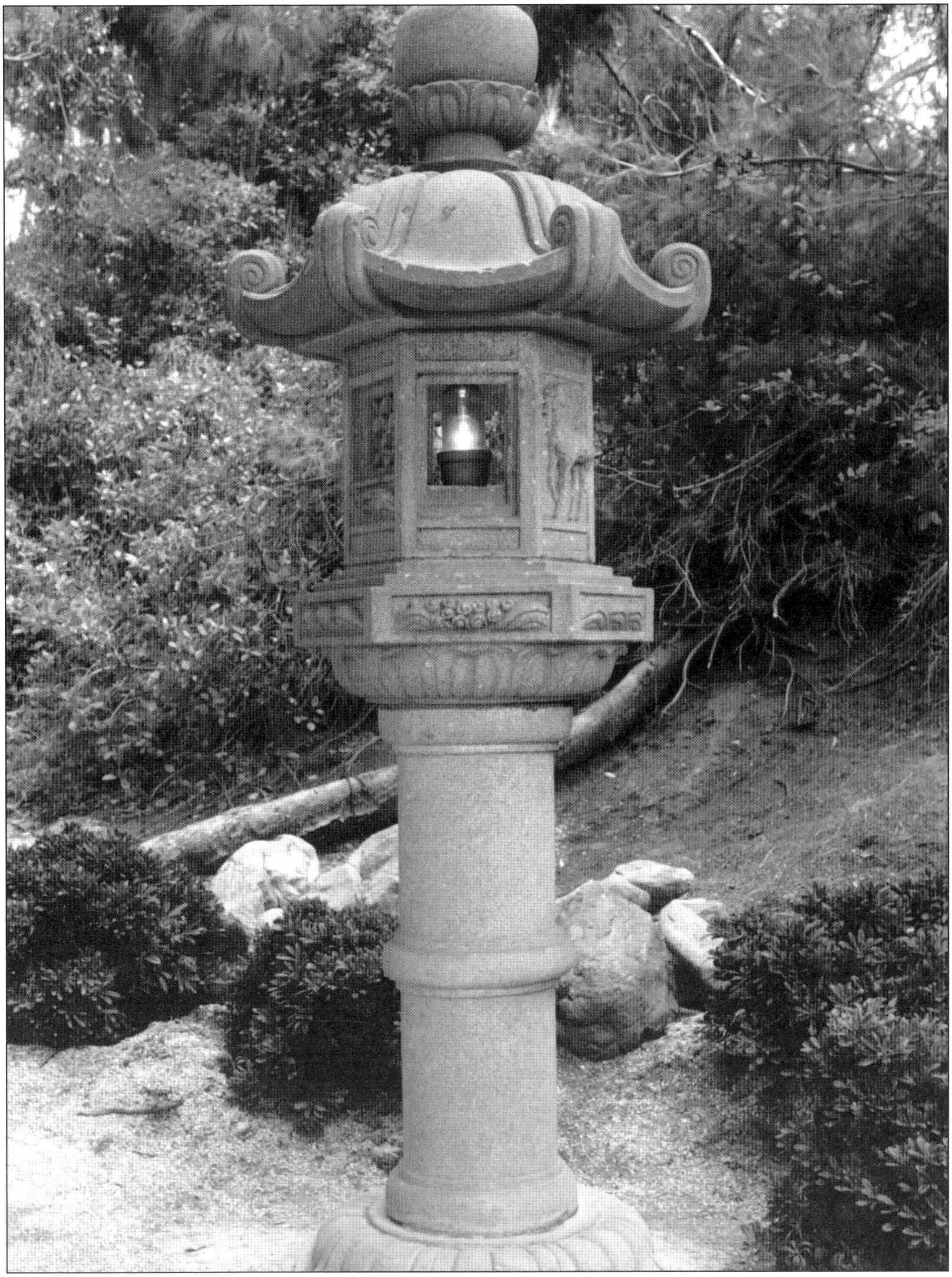

The Stone Lantern. Shipped from Japan in six pieces, the gift was placed on a hill adjacent to parking lot 37. The inscription on the back of the base reads, "To commemorate the opening of Dodger Stadium on April 9, 1962—Donated by Sotaro and Toku Suzuki, Guests." The lantern was the centerpiece for a Japanese garden that was maintained by local gardeners and contained two cherry blossom trees, river-rock paths, and pine trees cut in a Japanese style. One resident who was active in caring for the Japanese garden was Frank Ego, who made weekend visits to Dodger Stadium until the early 1990s.

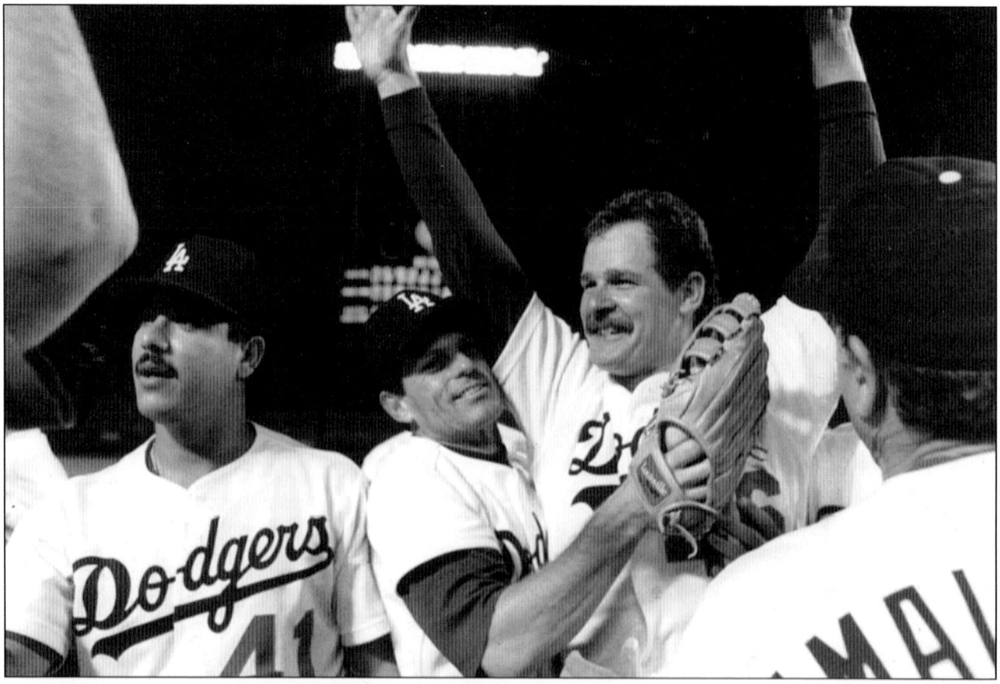

A Giant No-Hitter. Right-hander Kevin Gross authored the only no-hitter of his career on August 17, 1992 against the San Francisco Giants. The following season, Gross knocked San Francisco out of the playoffs with a 12-1 victory at Dodger Stadium on the final day of the regular season. The Giants needed a victory to force a one-game playoff with Atlanta in the National League West.

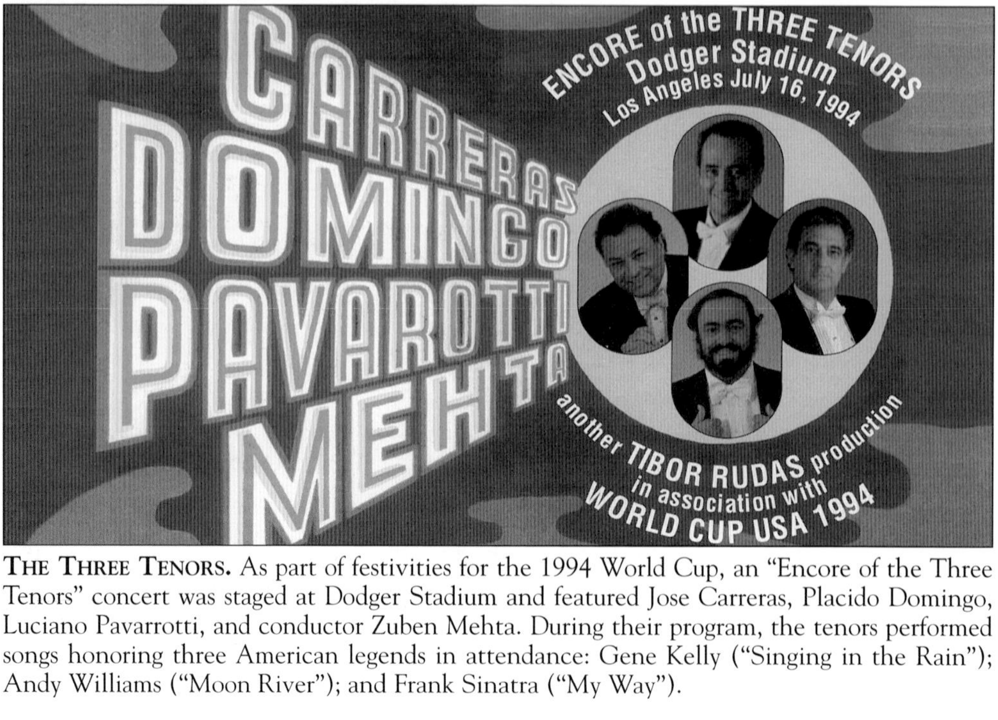

The Three Tenors. As part of festivities for the 1994 World Cup, an "Encore of the Three Tenors" concert was staged at Dodger Stadium and featured Jose Carreras, Placido Domingo, Luciano Pavarrotti, and conductor Zuben Mehta. During their program, the tenors performed songs honoring three American legends in attendance: Gene Kelly ("Singing in the Rain"); Andy Williams ("Moon River"); and Frank Sinatra ("My Way").

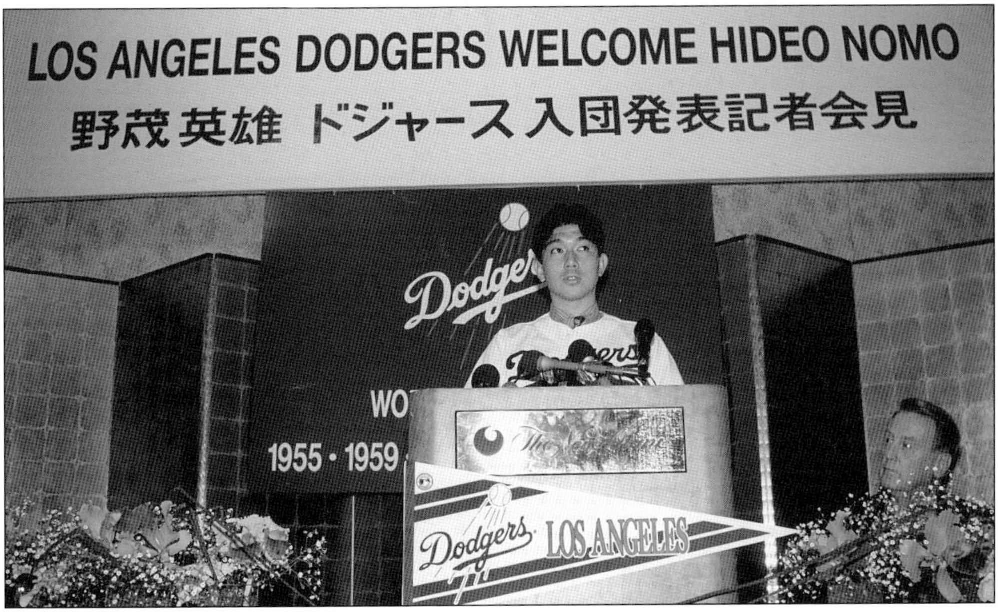

HIDEO NOMO. In 1994, Hideo Nomo became the first Japanese-born player to join a Major League team after playing professionally in Japan's Central or Pacific League. The previous Japanese player to appear in the majors was left-hander Masanori Murakami, who pitched for the San Francisco Giants from 1964 to 1965. The former Kintetsu Buffaloes star went 13-6 with a 2.54 ERA. Nomo set a Dodger rookie record with 236 strikeouts, including 16 against the Pittsburgh Pirates at Dodger Stadium on June 14. He became the first rookie pitcher to start an All-Star Game since the Dodgers' Fernando Valenzuela in 1981.

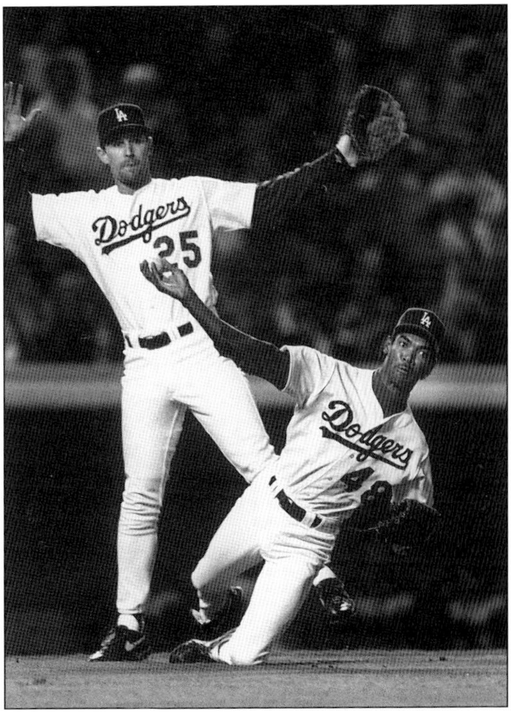

TOUGH PLAY. Pitcher Ramon Martinez slips while making a throw to first base as third baseman Tim Wallach looks on during a 1995 game at Dodger Stadium. Wallach, a Cal State Fullerton product, played for Los Angeles from 1993 to 1996. Martinez and Sandy Koufax are the only Dodger pitchers in history to record both a no-hitter and an 18-strikeout game. Koufax pitched three of his four no-hitters in Los Angeles, including the only perfect game in franchise history on September 9, 1965. Martinez authored his no-hitter against the Florida Marlins at Dodger Stadium on July 14, 1995.

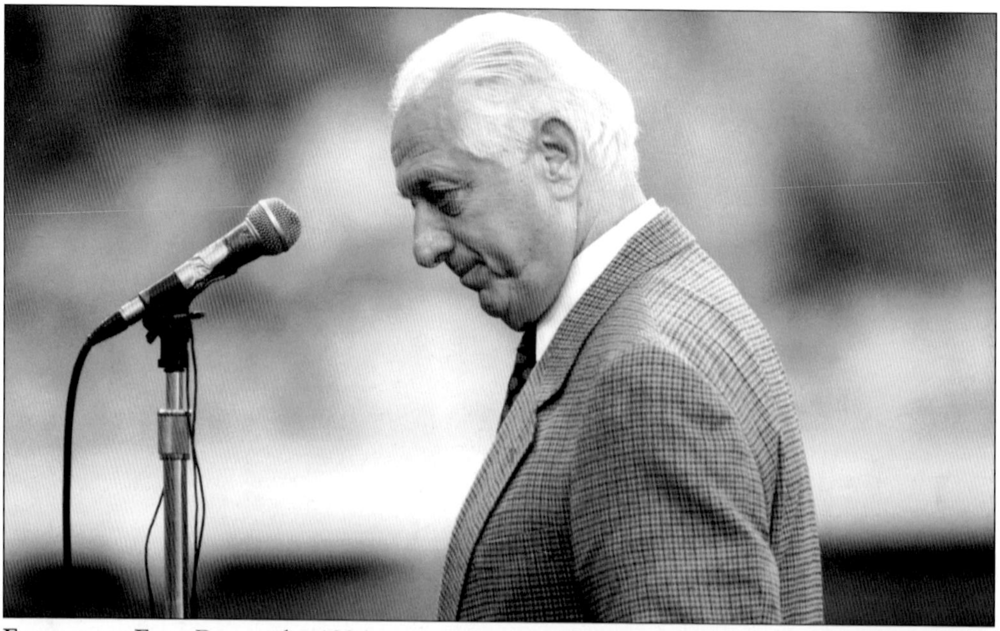

END OF AN ERA. During the 1996 season, Manager Tommy Lasorda was sidelined by a heart attack. Lasorda planned to return to the dugout that summer, but he opted to retire due to health concerns and became a Dodger vice president. After his announcement to the press on July 29, Lasorda later walked to a microphone behind home plate and bid farewell to the fans. He was elected to the Hall of Fame in 1997 after compiling 1,599 regular season victories and two World Series titles in 20 seasons.

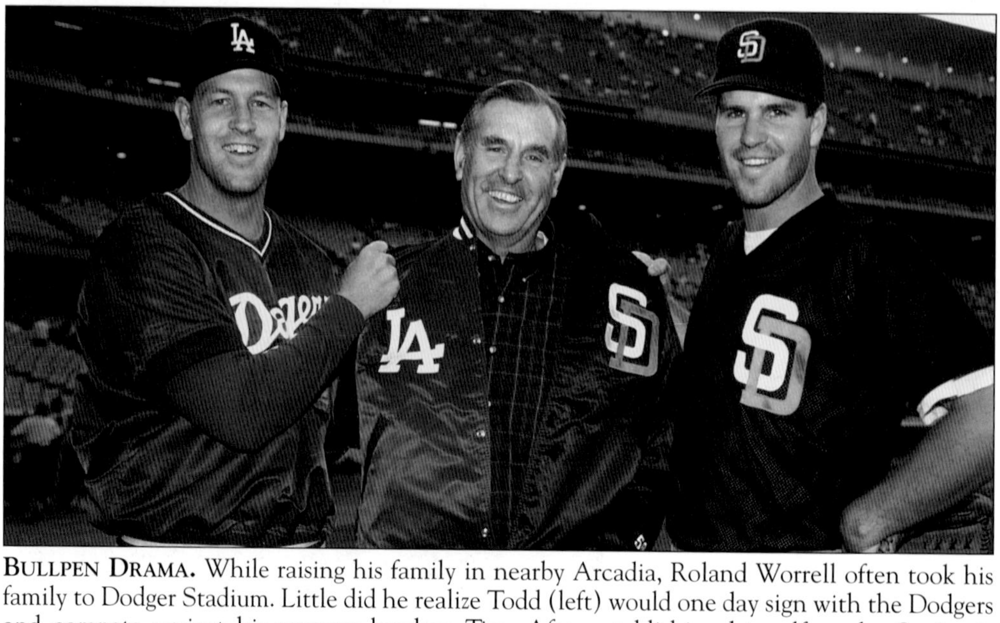

BULLPEN DRAMA. While raising his family in nearby Arcadia, Roland Worrell often took his family to Dodger Stadium. Little did he realize Todd (left) would one day sign with the Dodgers and compete against his younger brother, Tim. After establishing himself as the St. Louis Cardinals' all-time saves leader, Todd Worrell topped the Dodger chart by saving 127 games during his tenure with Los Angeles from 1993 to 1997. Tim Worrell broke into the majors with San Diego in 1993.

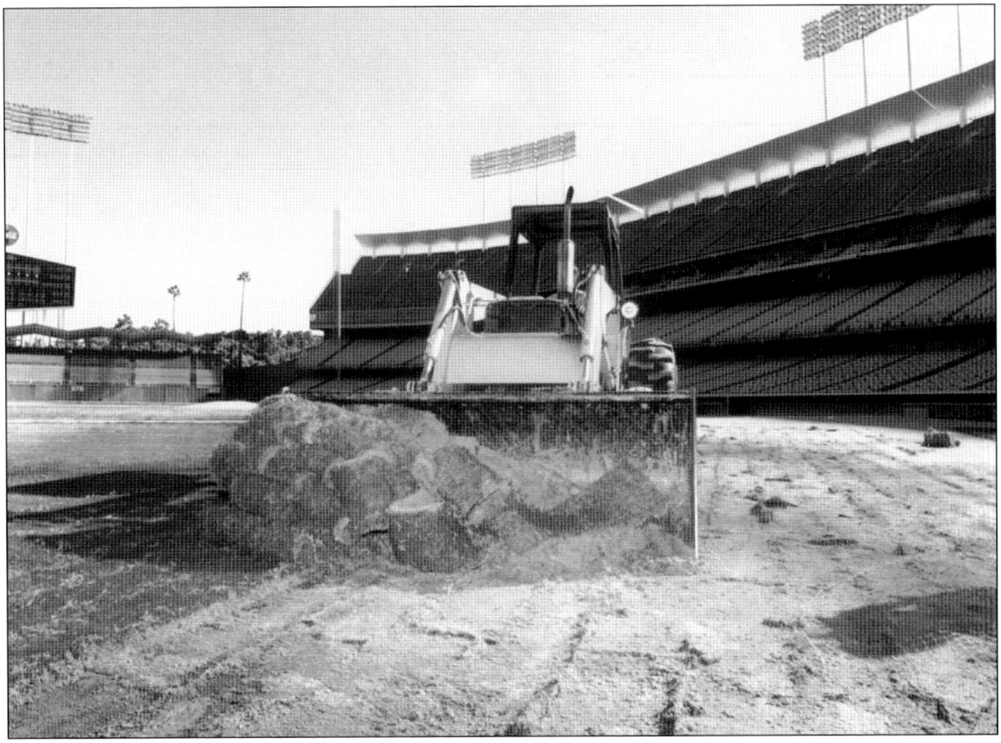

A New Field. Steve Garvey joins first baseman Eric Karros on the first day of construction following the 1995 season as the Dodger Stadium playing surface was replaced by a state-of-the-art grass field. Prescription Athletic Turf (PAT), created and installed by Cincinnati-based Motz Group, used the latest agronomic and engineering technology to manage field moisture through controlled drainage and irrigation. The 100,000 square feet of Bermuda grass is grown on pure sand, beneath which a vacuum chamber is laid over a water-tight plastic barrier that forcibly extracts water during heavy rains. New moisture gauges monitor the field's water level in coordination with a microprocessor that controls drainage functions. A computer controller has the ability to reverse the scenario and subirrigate when the sand's moisture reading drops below the optimal level.

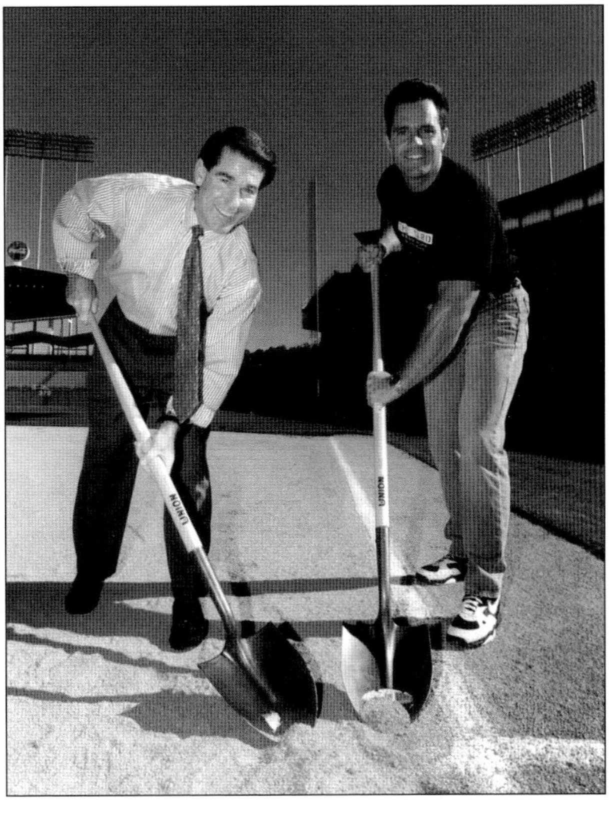

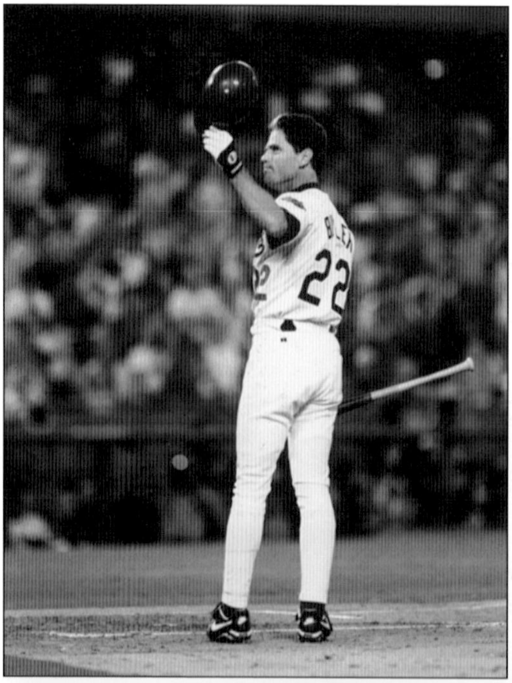

Butler Returns. During the 1996 season, a cancerous tumor was diagnosed in the tonsils of Dodger outfielder Brett Butler. On September 6, Butler received a standing ovation at Dodger Stadium in his first at-bat following his return from a six-week period of chemotherapy. Butler played with Los Angeles from 1991 to 1997 and compiled a lifetime .290 batting average in 2,213 games with the Braves, Indians, Giants, Dodgers, and Mets.

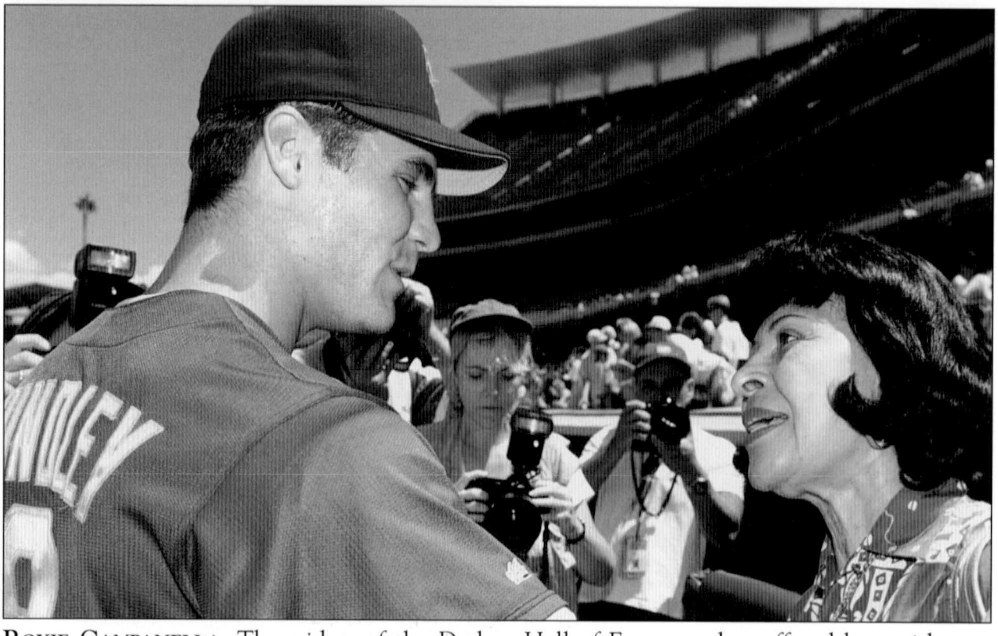

Roxie Campanella. The widow of the Dodger Hall of Fame catcher offered best wishes to New York Mets catcher Todd Hundley, who in the summer of 1996 was approaching Roy Campanella's single-season record for most home runs by a catcher, 40 in 1953. Hundley appreciated the gesture when the Mets visited Dodger Stadium in early September and later connected for No. 41 in New York against Atlanta's Greg McMichael to establish the record. Hundley would later have two different tenures with the Dodgers as a player. Roxie Campanella remained a fixture at Dodger Stadium after her husband's passing in 1993 and also serves as the director of the Roy Campanella Foundation.

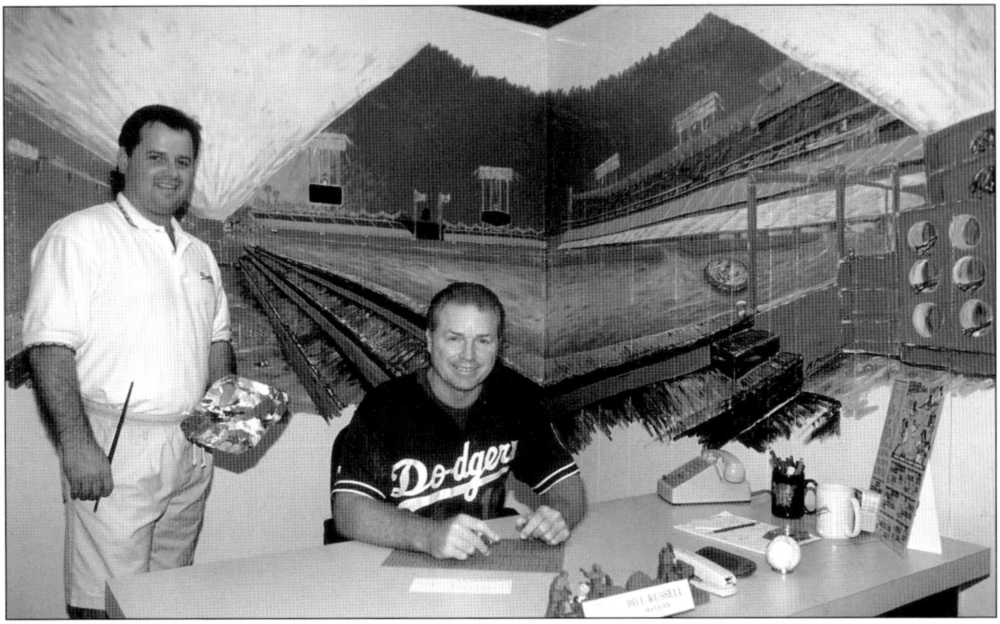

BRUSH WITH GLORY. When Dodger players accomplish certain milestones, clubhouse co-manager Mitch Poole is available to decorate the baseball with the details. The budding artist enjoyed a unique canvas when Dodger Manager Bill Russell invited Poole to paint a "view from the dugout" behind Russell's desk in his office. Russell managed the Dodgers from 1996 to 1998 and played in a Los Angeles record 2,181 games as an outfielder and shortstop from 1969 to 1986.

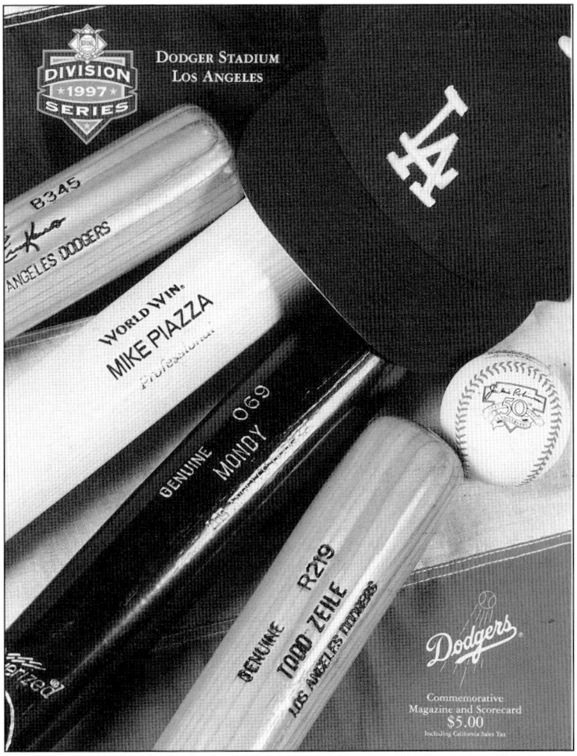

PHANTOM COVER. This was the planned cover of the Dodgers' 1997 Division Series playoff program. The bats salute Mike Piazza (40), Eric Karros (31), Todd Zeile (31), and Raul Mondesi (30) who became the second quartet in Los Angeles history to each hit 30 or home runs in one season. The Dodgers were knocked out of the National League West race on the final weekend of the season and finished two games behind San Francisco.

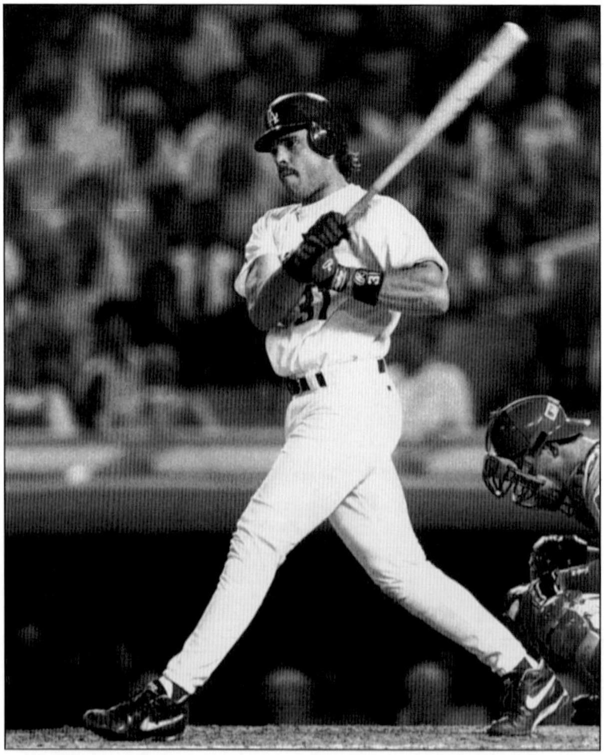

CATCHING HISTORY. A 62nd-round draft choice in 1988, Mike Piazza became a full-time catcher in the minor leagues and developed into one of the most prolific hitters in Dodger history. Piazza shattered single-season rookie records in 1993 with 35 home runs and 112 RBI. Piazza enjoyed his best season in 1997 with 40 home runs, 124 RBI, and a Los Angeles franchise-record .362 batting average. Piazza is the only Los Angeles player to hit a ball out of Dodger Stadium.

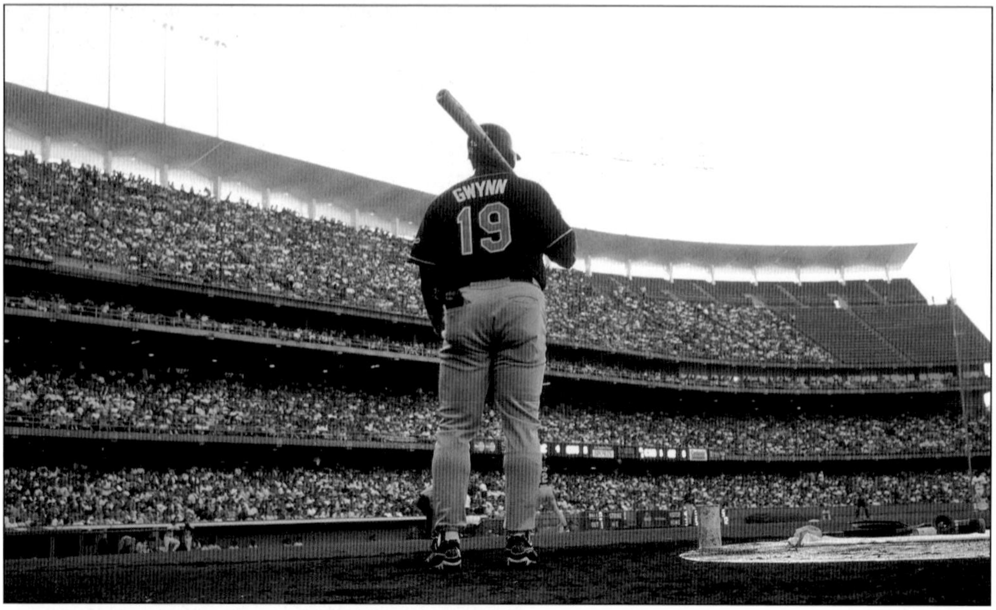

A GREAT OPPONENT. Tony Gwynn recorded 3,141 hits during his career with the San Diego Padres from 1982 to 2001. San Diego's lineups may have changed over the years during their rivalry with Los Angeles, but Gwynn's bat was always a challenge to Dodger pitching. Gwynn was a member of both San Diego World Series teams in 1984 and 1998. His brother Chris Gwynn was a former first-round selection by Los Angeles and he played in parts of seven seasons with the Dodgers and with his brother in San Diego in 1996.

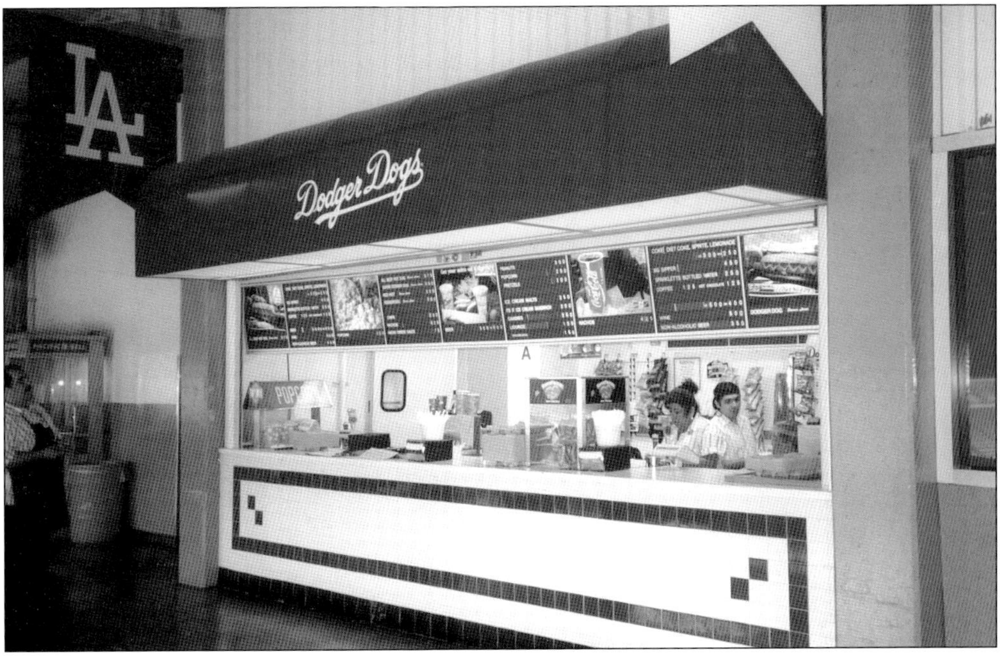

DON'T FORGET THE MUSTARD. The Dodgers sell an estimated 2 million Dodger Dogs per season and fans "slather" them with nearly 10,000 gallons of relish and more than 13,500 gallons of mustard.

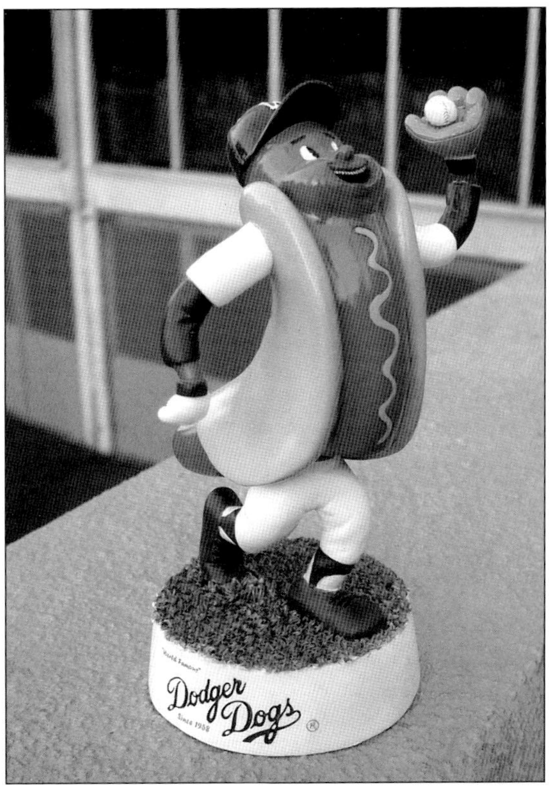

THE DODGER DOG. So famous, there is a "bobblehead" doll of the famous Dodger Stadium favorite. In 2002, the Universal CityWalk's food court added a "Dodger Dog" restaurant, featuring the classic 10-inch dog, the jumbo dog, and the spicy picante dog.

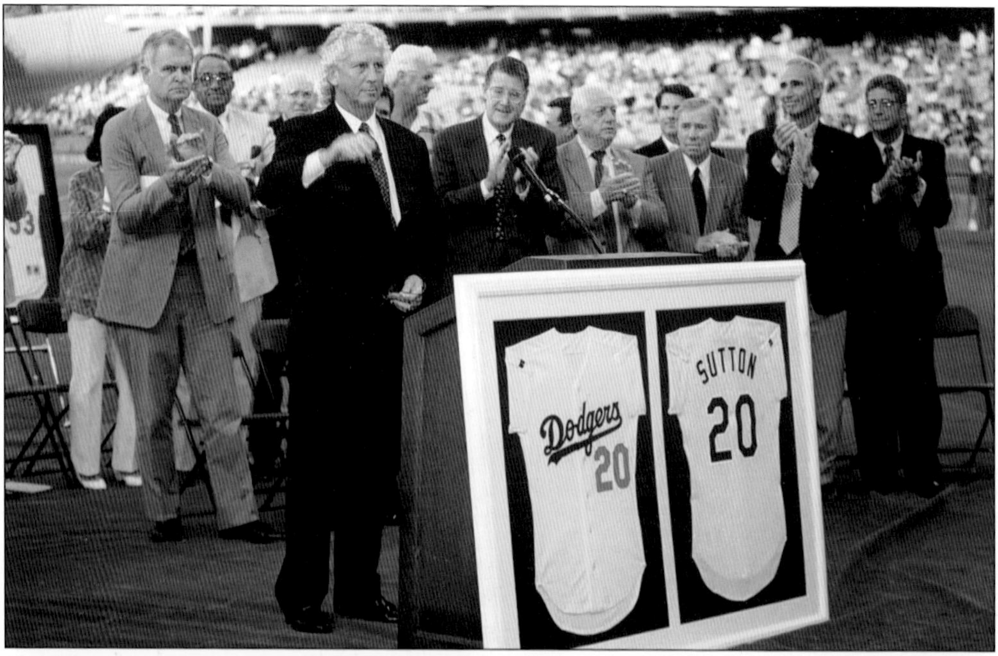

TOP HONOR. In 1998, the Dodgers retired the uniform No. 20 belonging to Hall of Famer Don Sutton, who posted a 324-256 career record over 23 seasons. Sutton, the Dodgers' all-time leader in wins (233), games pitched (550), innings pitched (3,814), strikeouts (2,696), and shutouts (52), was a four-time All-Star who appeared in three World Series. He won 21 games for Los Angeles in 1976 and led the National League with a 2.21 ERA in 1980.

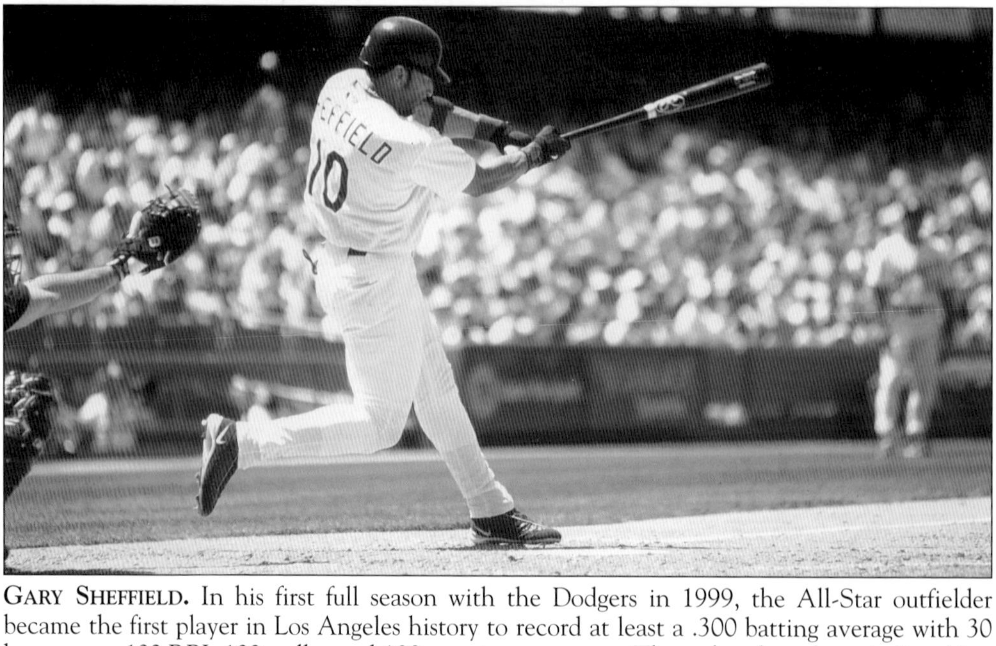

GARY SHEFFIELD. In his first full season with the Dodgers in 1999, the All-Star outfielder became the first player in Los Angeles history to record at least a .300 batting average with 30 home runs, 100 RBI, 100 walks, and 100 runs in one season. The only other player in Brooklyn history to accomplish the feat was Hall of Famer Duke Snider in 1955. Sheffield turned the trick again in 2000 and also set a single-season Los Angeles mark for slugging percentage (.643).

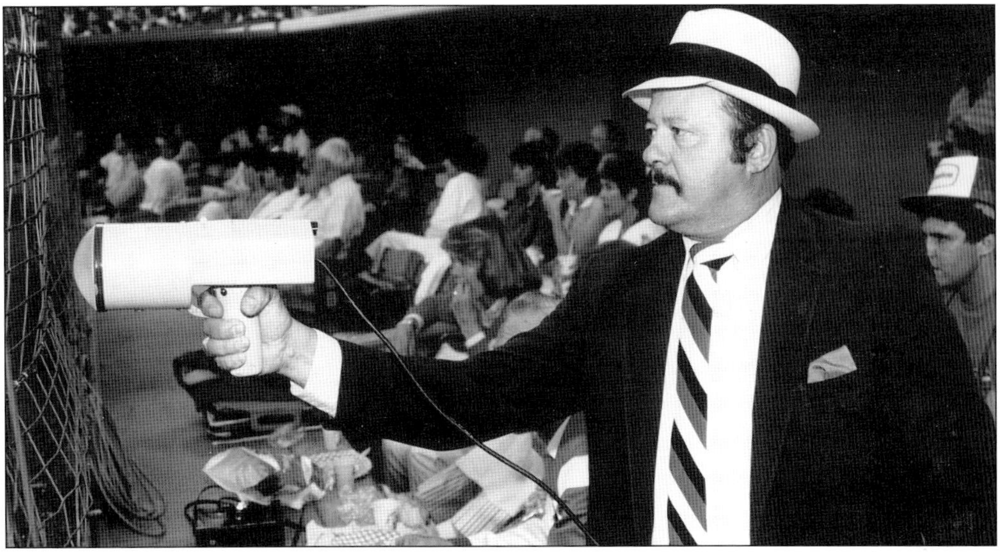

THE SCOUT. While playing in an adult league baseball game in East Los Angeles in 1977, Mexican League scout Mike Brito stepped to the plate with the bases loaded. The opposing team made a pitching change and brought in the third baseman, who fanned Brito on a full-count screwball. Brito immediately signed pitcher Bobby Castillo, whose success in Mexico led Brito to a full-time scouting job with the Dodgers. Castillo later taught the pitch to another prospect signed by Brito who struggled in the California League with a mediocre fastball and mastered his new pitch in just one week—left-hander Fernando Valenzuela.

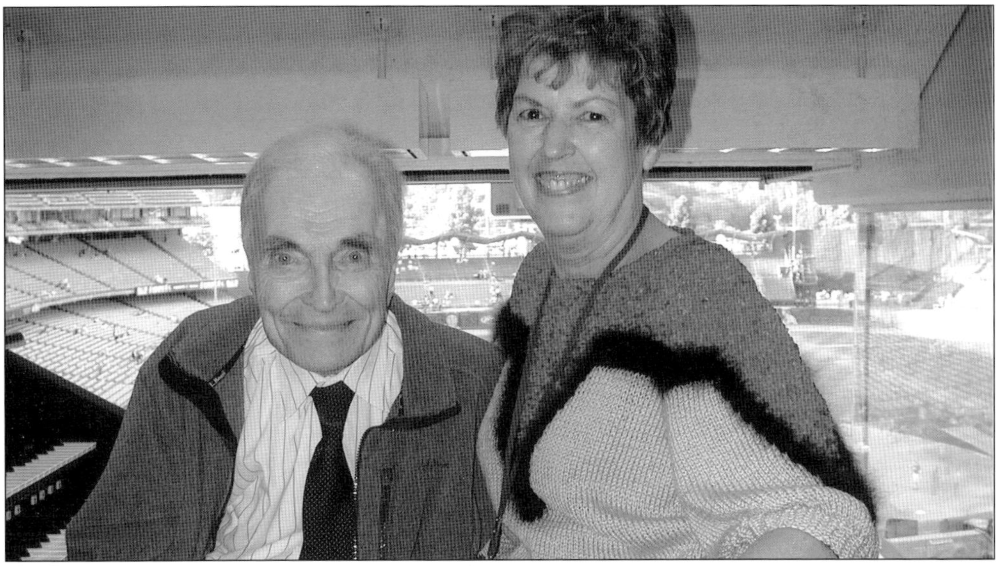

AT THE ORGAN. During the 2002 season, the original Dodger Stadium organist, Bob Mitchell, had a chance to play "Take Me Out to the Ballgame" as current organist Nancy Bea Hefley looked on. Mitchell in 1963 recorded a musical album titled *Baseball's Best*," which featured a large overhead Dodger Stadium photo on the album cover but was recorded in a Hollywood studio using a Wurlitzer Electric Organ model No. 4460. Hefley joined the Dodgers in 1988 and in 2003 became the first stadium organist to record a musical CD at the ballpark as microphones were placed along the perimeter of the field.

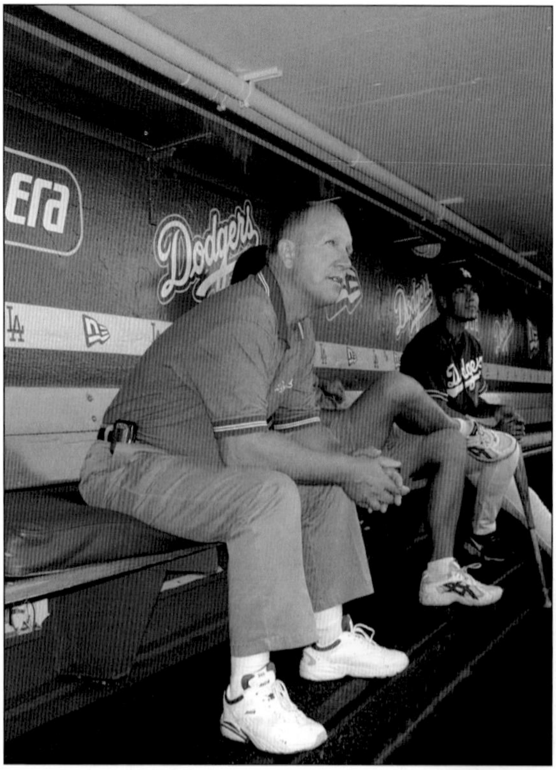

Keeper of the Grounds. Head groundkeeper Eric Hansen monitors the field during batting practice at Dodger Stadium. His crew's day began at 6:30 a.m. by mowing the lawn and eight workers stagger their hours to cover the field's maintenance. It takes roughly 60 to 90 minutes for the crew to "shut down" the field and make necessary repairs before leaving the ballpark.

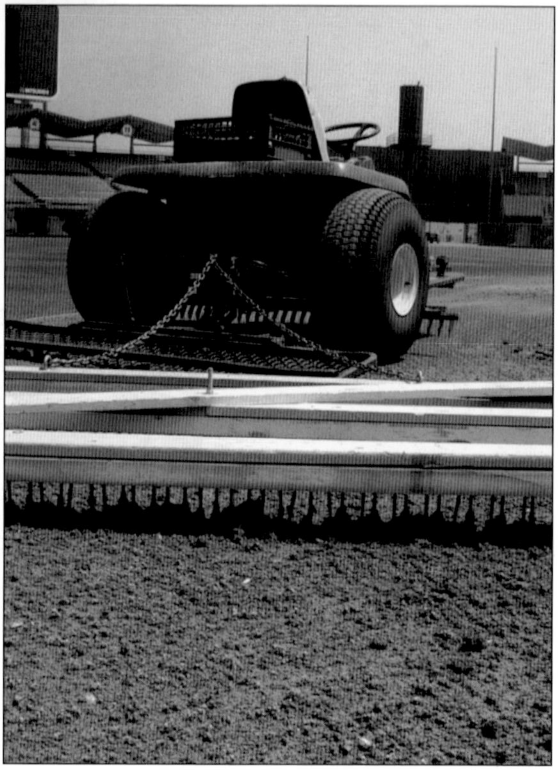

A Real Drag. Every morning during a homestand, the "nail drag" scarifies the infield dirt. When the team is out of town, the grounds crew continues a routine to keep the turf and dirt portions of the field on a consistent level.

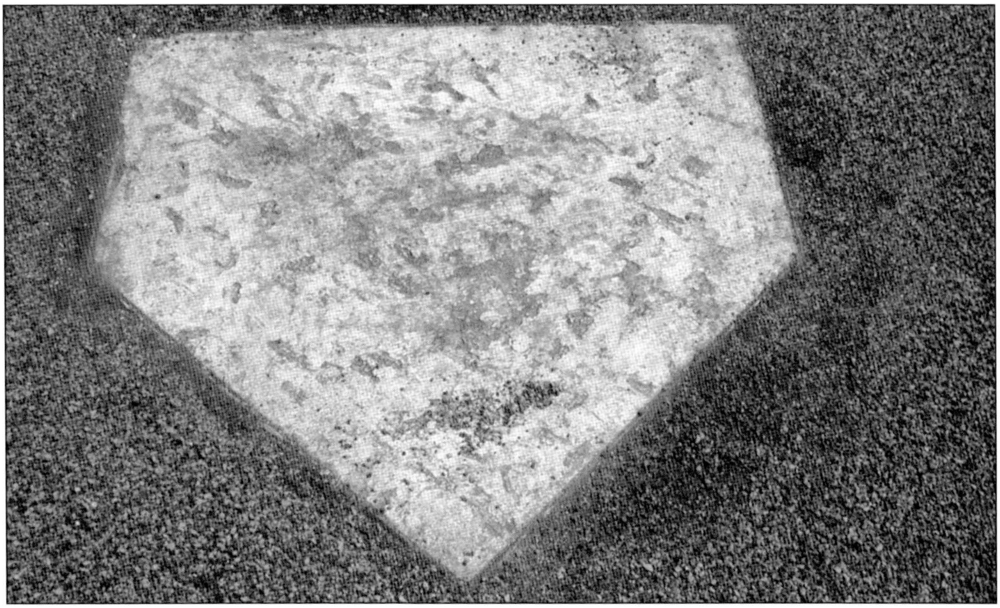

HOME SWEET HOME. A product called Stabalizer in front of home plate holds in moisture and binds the soil, not unlike glue. Groundskeeper Eric Hansen discovered the formula when mixing the material into the dirt and poured water on it. Originally intended to add more calcined clay, the Stabalizer trapped air pockets in front of home plate. "You could actually feel your feet going up and down and it felt like an air mattress when you walked on it," Hansen said. "Yet it bound so tight it wouldn't tear out on you. It was the strangest sensation I've ever felt. And we created it totally by accident."

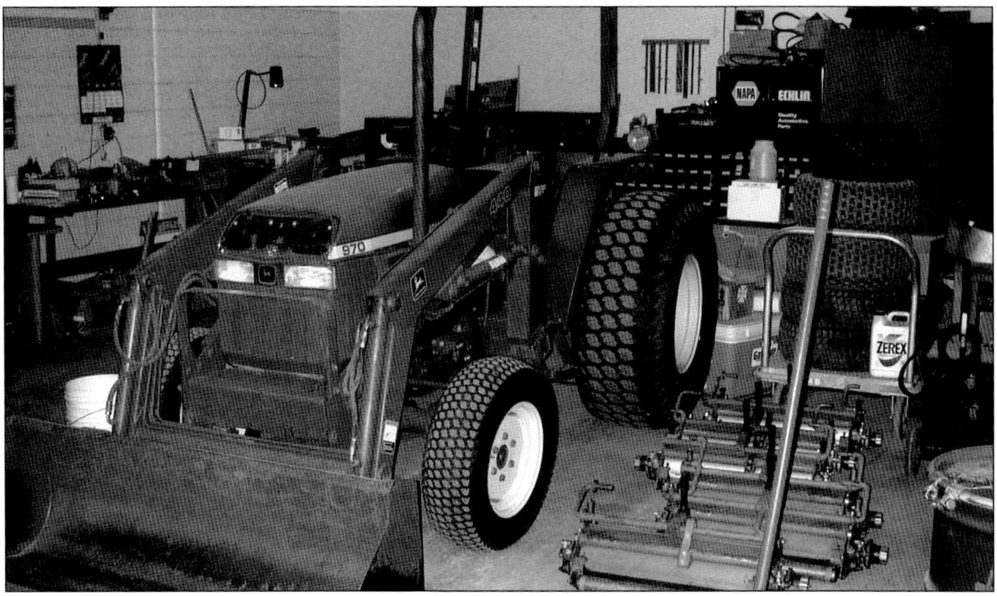

HIDDEN GARAGE. There is an equipment storage area beyond the Dodger bullpen area that is maintained by a full-time mechanic. This includes a virtual hardware store, home-and-garden accessories, and auto shop with everything from power tools and wheelbarrows to extra bases and tool chests.

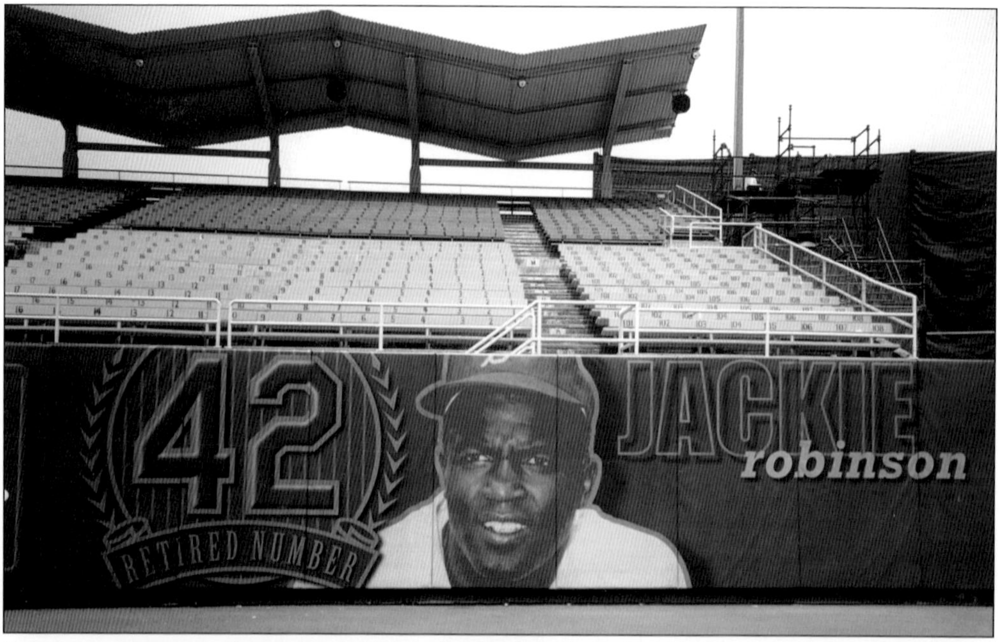

BALLPARK TRIBUTE. Beginning in 1998, the Dodgers have blended historical images along the outfield wall. This mural above the left field pavilion honors Jackie Robinson, the Hall of Fame infielder whose uniform No. 42 was retired by all major league teams on the 50th anniversary of his debut with the Dodgers in 1947.

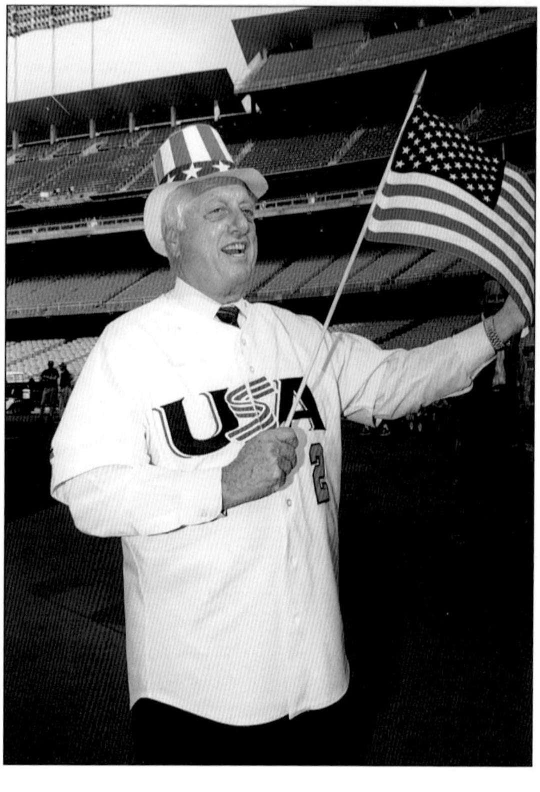

RED, WHITE, AND DODGER BLUE. After his Hall of Fame managerial career, Tommy Lasorda accepted a new challenge as the coach of the 2000 Olympic baseball team. He was introduced at Dodger Stadium during a press conference in 1999 and immediately showed his flag-waving enthusiasm. Team USA, which also featured former Dodgers Reggie Smith and Phil Regan on Lasorda's coaching staff, was considered an underdog and lost to Cuba in one of the early rounds of the tournament. But the USA came back and defeated Cuba, 4-0, in the championship game.

SIX

2000 and Beyond

During the 2002 season, the Dodgers celebrated their 40th anniversary. Attending Opening Day was Los Angeles Mayor James Hahn, the son of Los Angeles Supervisor Kenneth Hahn who as a youngster wore his Dodger uniform on the steps of City Hall on Opening Day 1958 when the Dodgers played their first game in Los Angeles.

"I think Dodger Stadium is a place that has really brought the entire city and Southern California together over the years," Hahn said. "It's a place of really fond memories for me, and I know for a lot of other people, too. Nobody has a bad time when they go to Dodger Stadium."

And standing alongside one another at home plate was a cross section of personalities who each had contributed to the Dodger Stadium legacy over the past four decades. They included current team officials, members of the O'Malley family, former city council member Rosalind Wyman, stadium painter Hector Mino, usher Antonio Flores, and the stadium's most famous food vendor. The daily enthusiasm of Roger "The Peanut Man" Owens around his Loge Level section eventually led to several appearances on *The Tonight Show* and an invitation to toss peanuts during the President Jimmy Carter's inaugural party in 1977.

"I've been selling peanuts at Dodger Stadium since Opening Day 1962," said Owens, who has thrown an estimated 2 million bags and whose biography is titled, *The Perfect Pitch*. "Dodger Stadium is a place I always enjoy and consider it a privilege to have a job where I meet so many wonderful people. It's a big part of my life. The ballpark is a happy place and it brings out the best in everyone. I look forward to each game because each game is never the same."

In 2002, the Dodgers added the retired numbers below the pavilion roofs, saluting Pee Wee Reese (1), Tommy Lasorda (2), Duke Snider (4), Jim Gilliam (19), Don Sutton (20), Walter Alston (24), Sandy Koufax (32), Roy Campanella (39), Jackie Robinson (42), and Don Drysdale (53). The Dodgers names of the past blended with the modern-day stars, embracing history and starting new traditions. Outfielder Shawn Green emerged as the most prolific left-handed power hitter in Los Angeles history. And at Dodger Stadium, he gave his batting gloves to kids in the stands following each home run "I was new to the Dodgers at the time and Vin Scully said on television, 'I wonder if this is something he always does?' It grew from there," Green said. "I thought it was a pretty good idea, so I started doing it. It's a great thing for me and I think it's nice for the kids. They love it and it's been good luck. I'm going to continue doing it."

During road trips as an Atlanta Braves broadcaster, Don Sutton always knows the visit to Los Angeles will be special, even watching the starting pitcher warm up in the bullpen like he did 533 times in a Dodger uniform, the first time at age 21 in 1966.

"There were so many great memories of ballgames here," Sutton said. "I get a charge out of seeing my picture on the wall along with those who have carved their niche in the history book.

There is something special about Dodger Stadium that is hard to explain to someone who hasn't spent time playing here. It's the ghost of Walter O'Malley. It's Walter Alston. It's Red Adams. It's Tommy Lasorda. There is just so much history of the game that you don't have to see the people to sense that they are still here. Even with all the 21st century changes, it is still Dodger Stadium."

Terry Seidler, Walter O'Malley's daughter, said some of her fondest memories include watching her mother, Kay, teach grandchildren how to score and her father explaining the infield fly rule to them. "My favorite sounds at Dodger Stadium will always be the 'Star-Spangled Banner,' followed by 'Play Ball' and hearing the voices of Dodger broadcasters on hundreds of transistor radios throughout Dodger Stadium as they tell their interesting behind-the-scenes stories," she said. "As for the senses of taste and smell, what could be more enticing than Farmer John Dodger Dogs! Lastly, the sense of touch—nothing is sweeter than getting a hug of appreciation carrying a sleepy child to the car after the last out knowing that a few hours together at a Dodger game will be a memory treasured forever by both of us."

In October 2003, Peter O'Malley held a reception at the Stadium Club. But instead of the usual folding chairs and table decorations, there were banks of computer terminals. For the 100th anniversary of Walter O'Malley's birth, his family unveiled walteromalley.com—a website commemorating his words, works, and achievements. The site included a complete biography, historical documents, and multimedia sections for the man ranked by *The Sporting News* as the 11th Most Powerful Person in sports over the last century.

The podium and stage was positioned toward the back of the room, and as O'Malley spoke as the press conference, he was surrounded by spectacular bay windows. To his right, a series of smaller windows along the lower-floor dining area overlooked the manicured playing field. To his left, the oversized window looked like a whale's aquarium, engulfing the mountains, hills, and vegetation beyond the blue horizon. O'Malley didn't need words to describe the pride of his father's ballpark. No matter which angle, the views looked like a stack of neatly arranged postcards, ready to drop in a mailbox with a tourist's description. "I remember, the last year of his life, I would drive him to Dodger Stadium every day," Peter O'Malley said of his father, who died in 1979. "Some mornings, it would be foggy, other mornings it would be clear. But every morning, Dodger Stadium was shining."

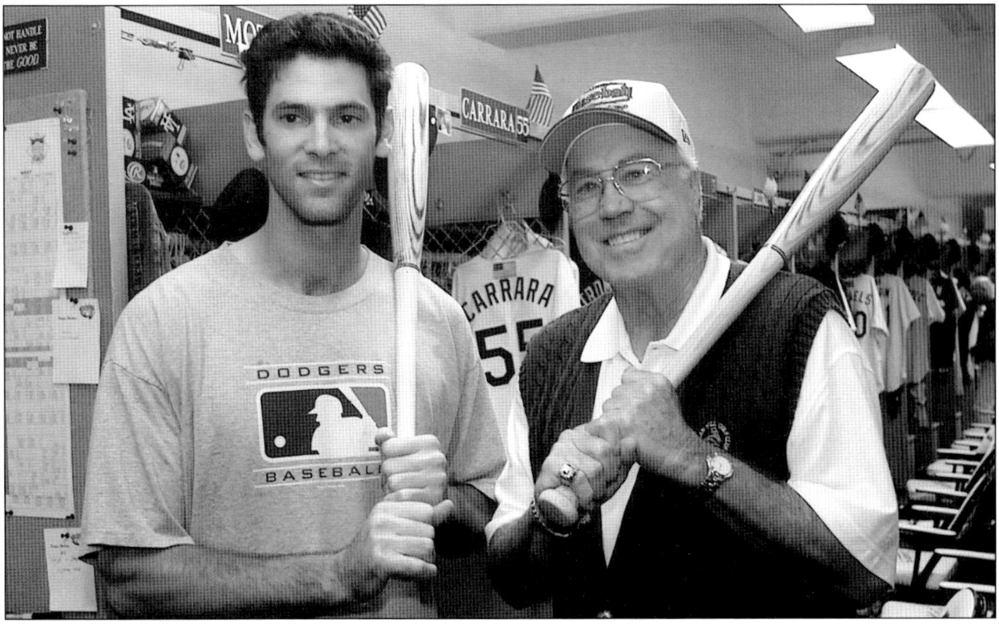

THE LEFTIES. Outfielder Shawn Green joined the Dodgers in 2000 and became one of the most prolific left-handed power hitters of all time. Green set a single-season mark with 49 home runs in 2001 and his 42 round-trippers in 2002 gave him 91 home runs, the most over a two-year period in Dodger, surpassing the 85 home runs by Brooklyn's Duke Snider in 1955 and 1956. Green also started a unique routine at Dodger Stadium by tossing his batting gloves to a youngster into the crowd on his way to the dugout following a home run. In 2003, Green set a Dodger-single season mark with 49 doubles, eclipsing the mark of 47 by Wes Parker in 1970.

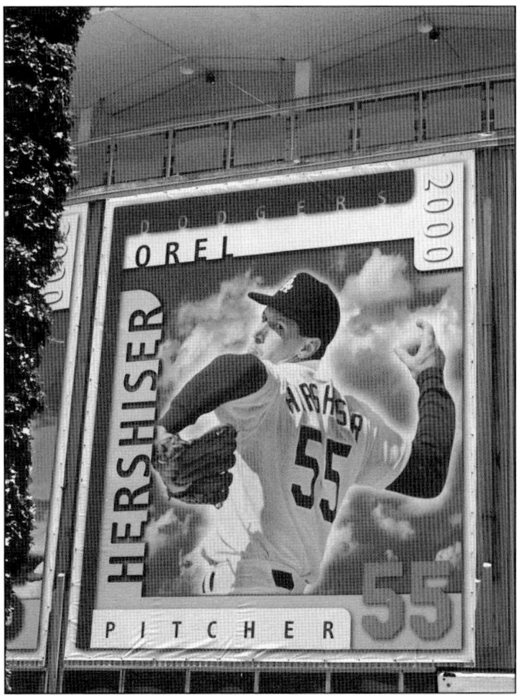

THE FINAL SEASON. Orel Hershiser returned to the Dodgers at age 43 in 2000 and became the oldest Dodger to start a home opener and the second-oldest pitcher to start an Opening Day at Dodger Stadium (the Mets' Warren Spahn was 44 when he beat the Dodgers and Claude Osteen, 3-2, on April 20, 1965). Hershiser defeated the Cincinnati Reds, 8-1, his 135th victory as a Dodger and the final triumph of his career.

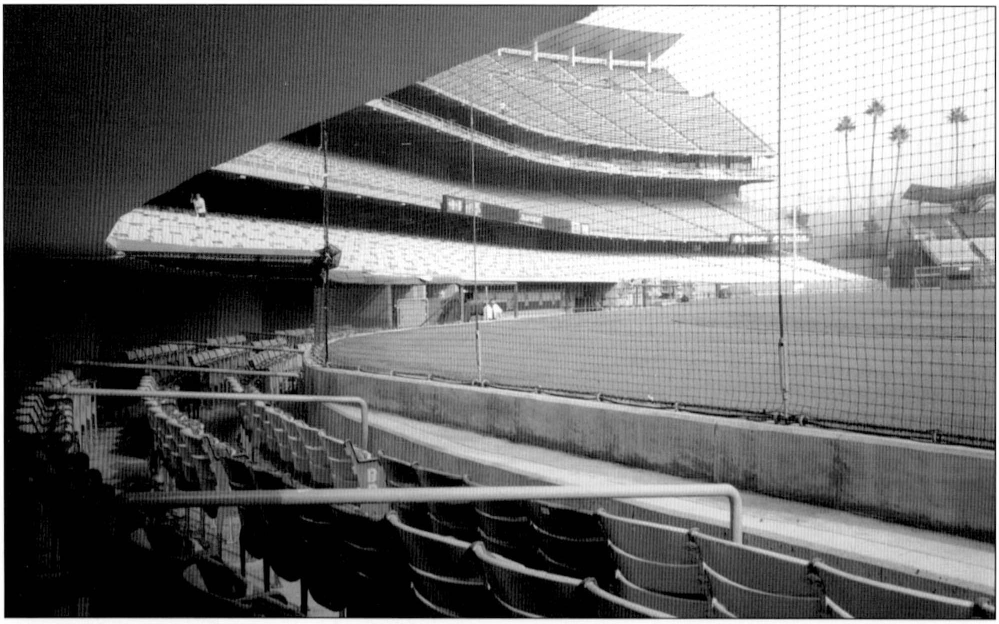

The Dugout Seats. The original dugout seats were replaced following the 1999 season as construction soon began on the Dugout Club, part of a program of investment and limited renovation of Dodger Stadium. Former Los Angeles Mayor Norris Poulson, one of the main political supporters of the Dodgers' move to the West Coast and who threw out the ceremonial first pitch on Opening Day 1958, watched the first game at the new ballpark from the dugout seats on April 10, 1962.

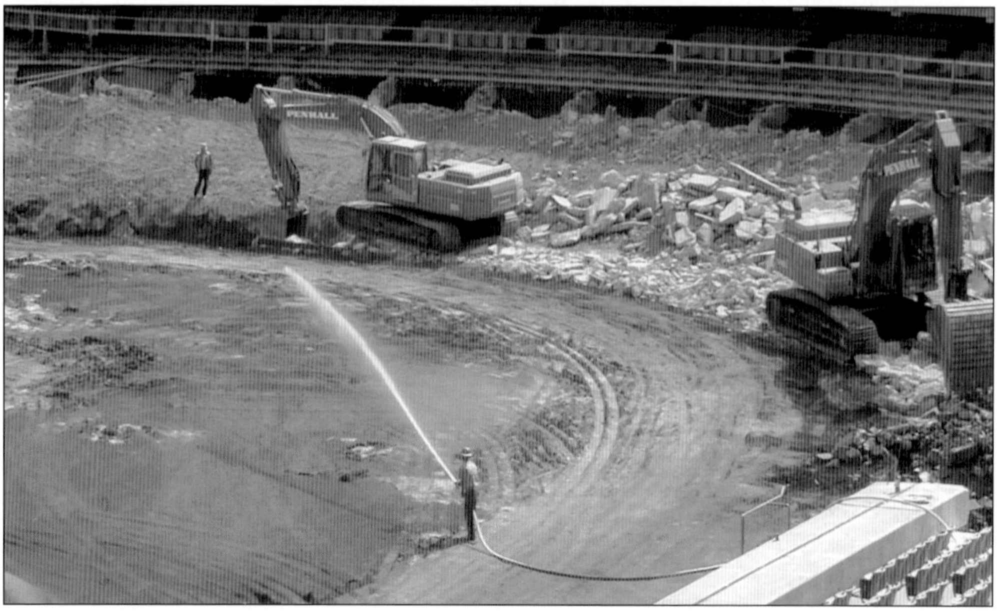

Construction. This is the view during the Dodger Stadium renovation project, which began following the 1999 season. The Dodgers added new field level seats down the foul lines beyond the dugouts and a new expanded dugout section with an adjacent club area. In addition, suites were added on the Club Level.

A New View. The Dugout Club boasted "The Best Seats in Baseball" with some locations actually closer to home plate than the pitcher's mound. Patrons in this section also enjoy access to a private club, pre-game buffet, and complimentary in-seat food service.

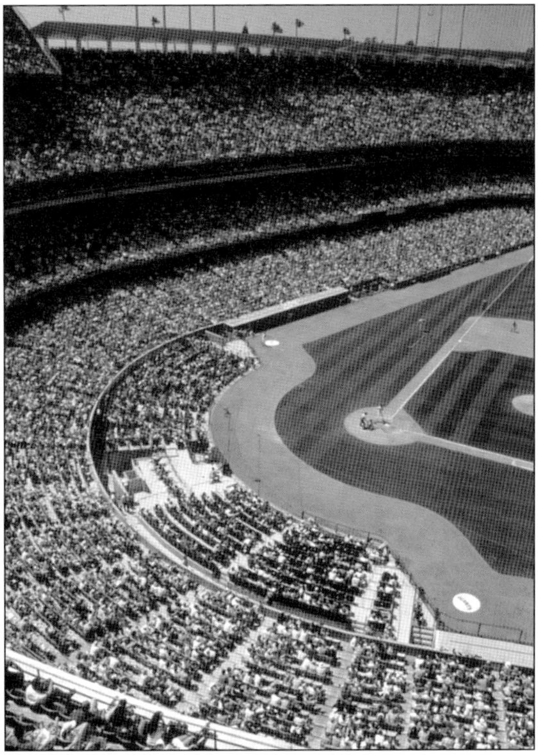

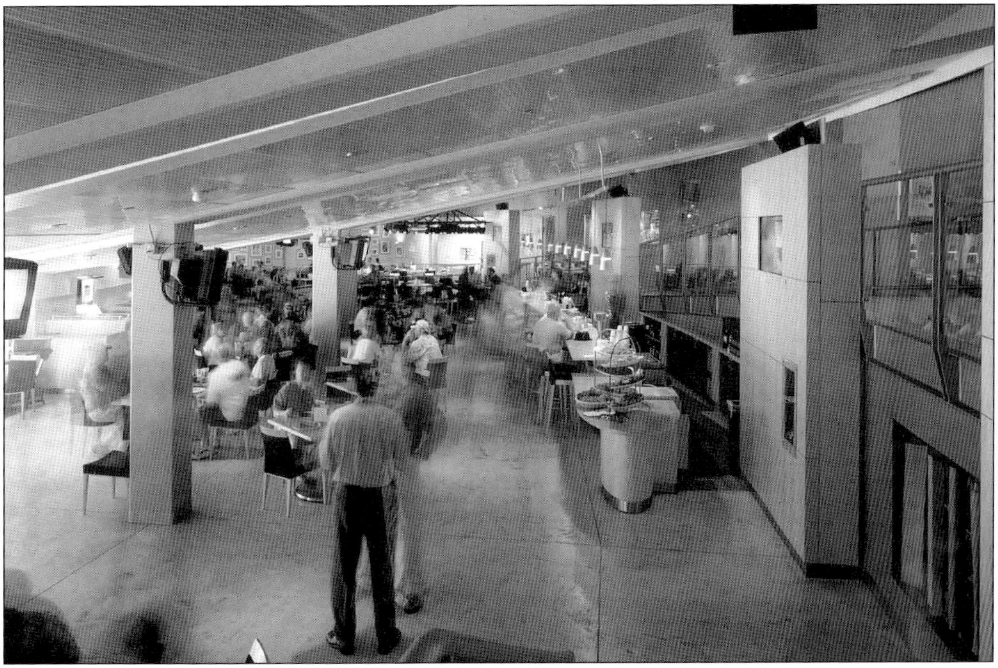

The Dugout Club. The interior of the Dugout Club features a wide variety of television monitors and seating areas, along with displays of Dodger memorabilia and photos along the walls and in display cases. Other uses for the Dugout Club include press conferences, the taping of television programs, and other special events.

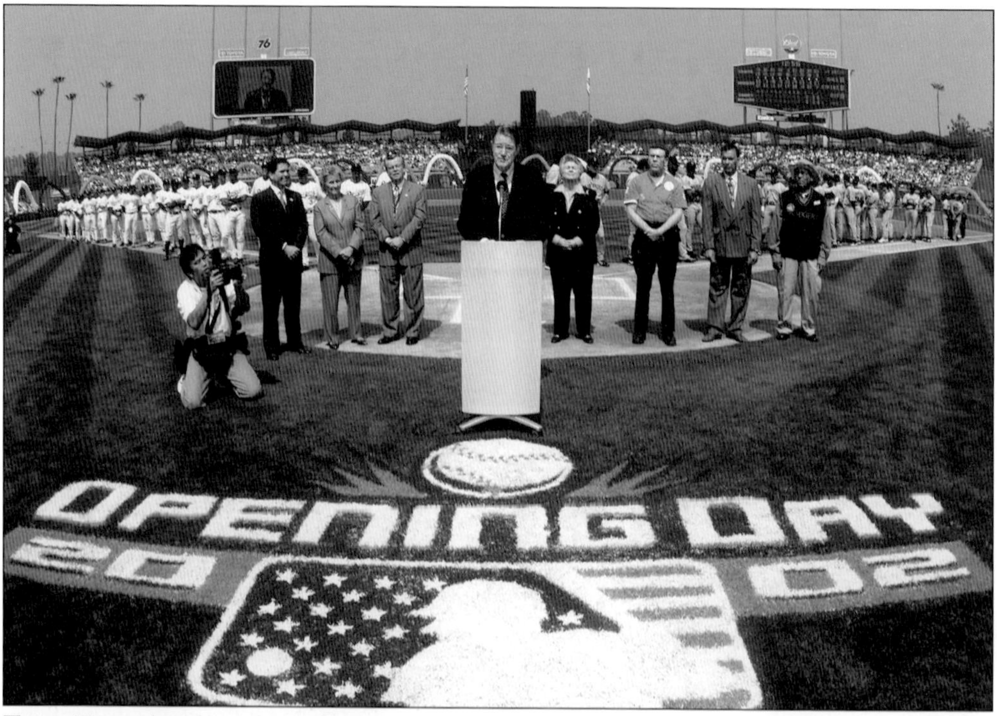

THE 40TH ANNIVERSARY. Former team president Peter O'Malley was one of many dignitaries on hand for Opening Day 2002. Along with baseball officials and stadium employees, former players from the 1962 team in attendance included Johnny Podres, Maury Wills, Larry Burright, and Duke Snider.

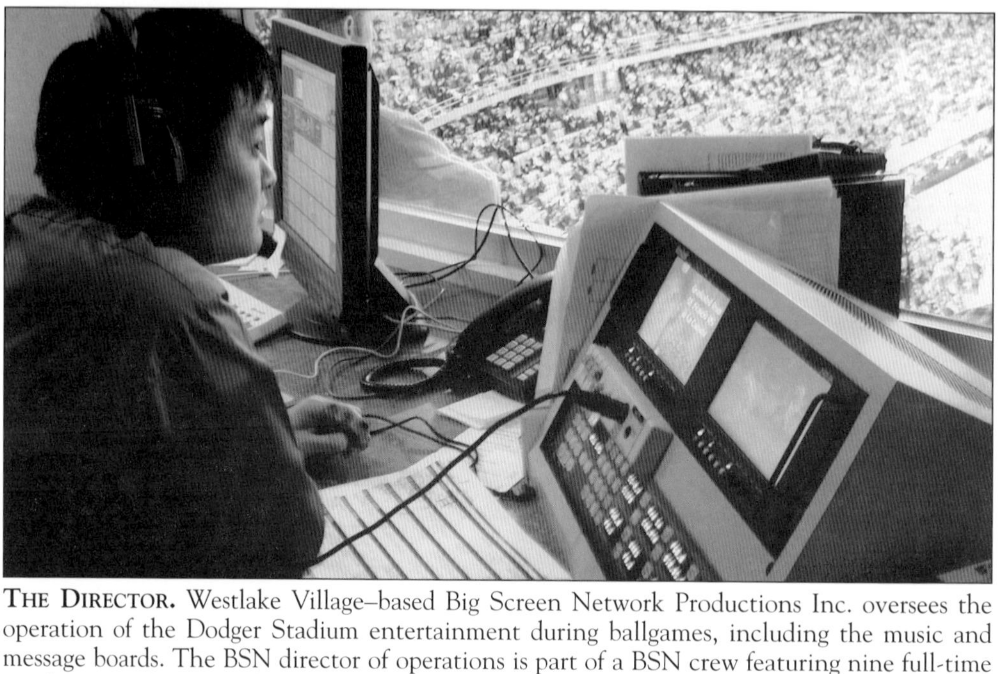

THE DIRECTOR. Westlake Village–based Big Screen Network Productions Inc. oversees the operation of the Dodger Stadium entertainment during ballgames, including the music and message boards. The BSN director of operations is part of a BSN crew featuring nine full-time employees and a crew of 22 on game days.

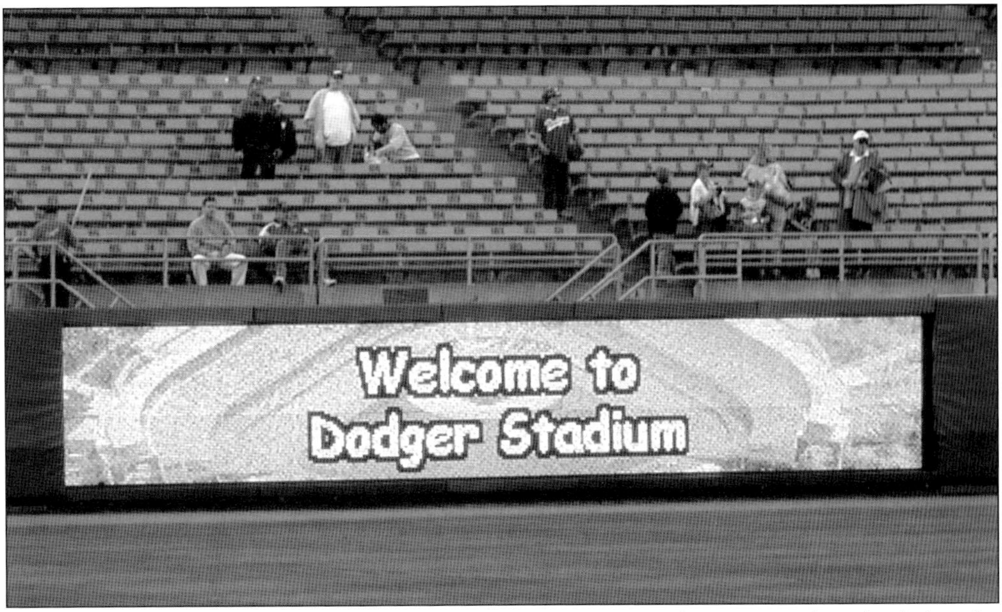

Outfield Scoreboards. While the DodgerVision screen and main scoreboard inhabit the same physical structures as in years past, two new scoreboards were installed into the outfield walls prior to the 2003 season. The out-of-town scoreboards were constructed with input from players like Dodger outfielder Shawn Green in terms of how to cover the scoreboard and make it safe for the players. Green suggested a plastic-coated chain-link.

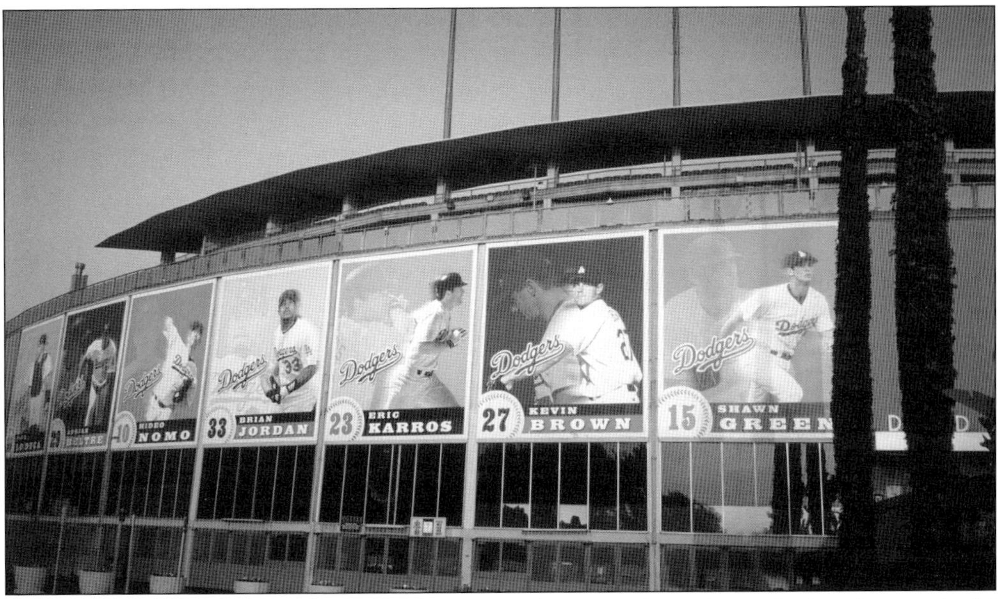

Window Dressing. A collection of giant-sized images have been displayed on colorful banners and murals throughout Dodger Stadium since 1998. "It's kind of neat, driving to the stadium and seeing a big picture of yourself," first baseman Eric Karros said in 2002. "It's a nice way to promote the players. The Dodgers started doing it a few years ago and now you see other teams doing it. I don't know who first came up with the idea, but I think it adds a bit of character to the stadium."

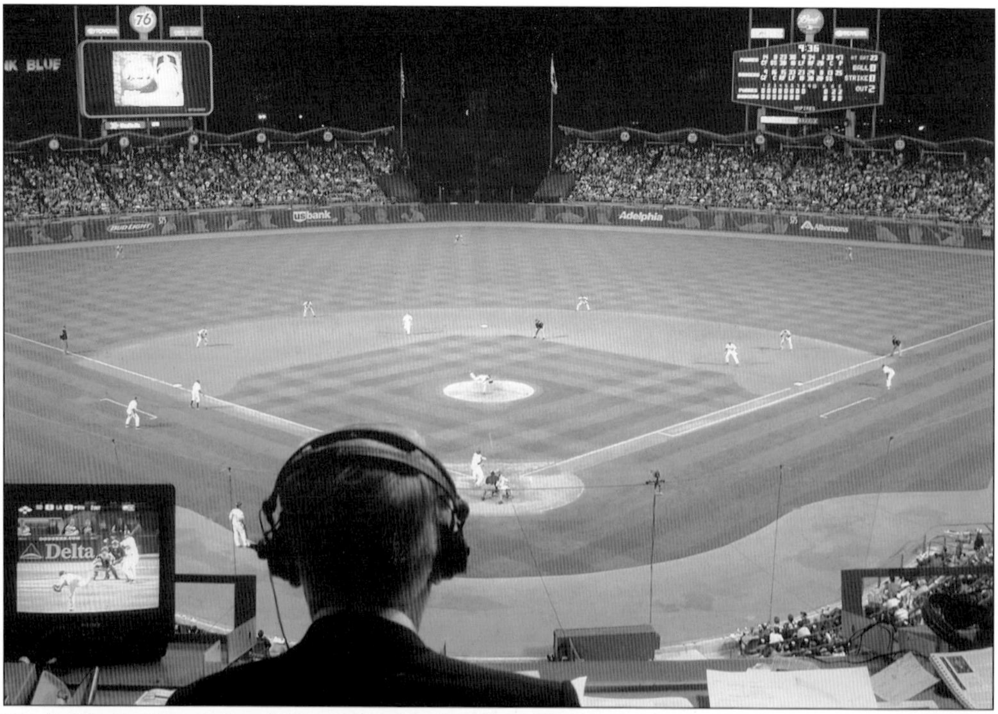

VIN'S VIEW. This is the perspective of Hall of Fame broadcaster Vin Scully, who has chronicled Dodger baseball games since 1950. In his early days at Ebbets Field, Scully used binoculars and monitored a hand-operated scoreboard. His current workplace is a busy television booth with a floor producer, camera operator, and statistician in the background.

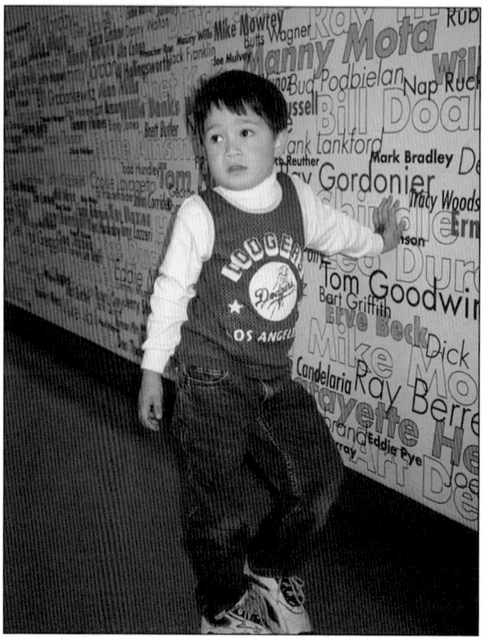

THE PLAYER WALL. Along one of the walls of the corridor leading from the elevator to the Dugout Club is a timeline of Dodger history beginning in the 1880s. The other wall features the names of every Dodger who had played for either Brooklyn or Los Angeles in the 19th and 20th centuries. This young Dodger fan leans against the name of Bill Shindle, who played for the Brooklyn Dodgers from 1894 to 1898.

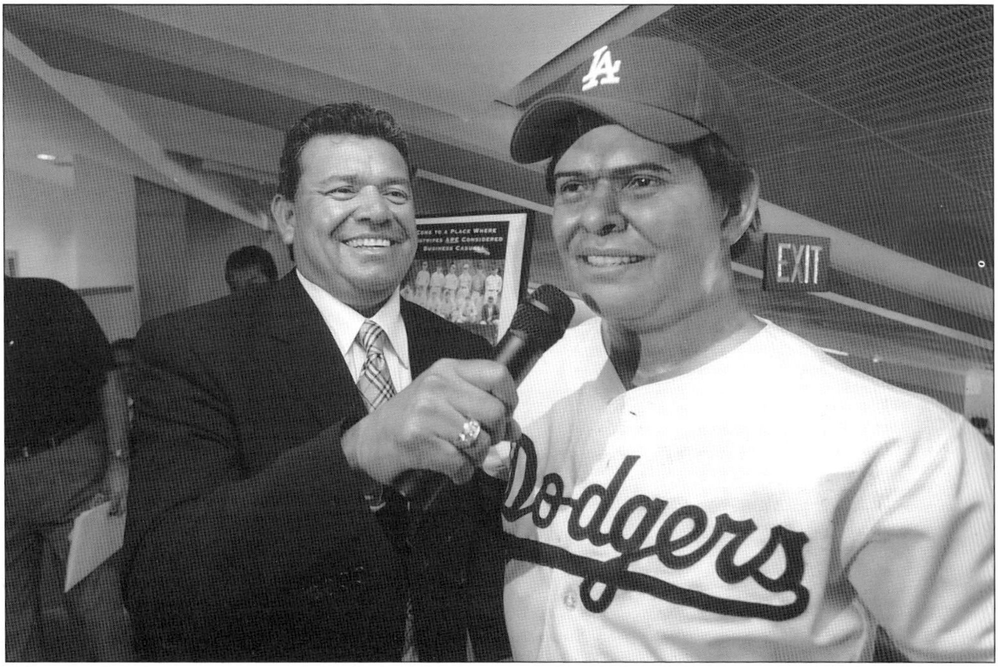

Trading Faces. Fernando Valenzuela returned to the Dodgers as a broadcaster in 2003. After his press conference at the Dugout Club, Valenzuela spotted his statue created during his career as a player in Los Angeles from 1980 to 1990. The popular pitcher joined the Spanish-language broadcasting team with Hall of Famer Jaime Jarrin and Pepe Yniguez.

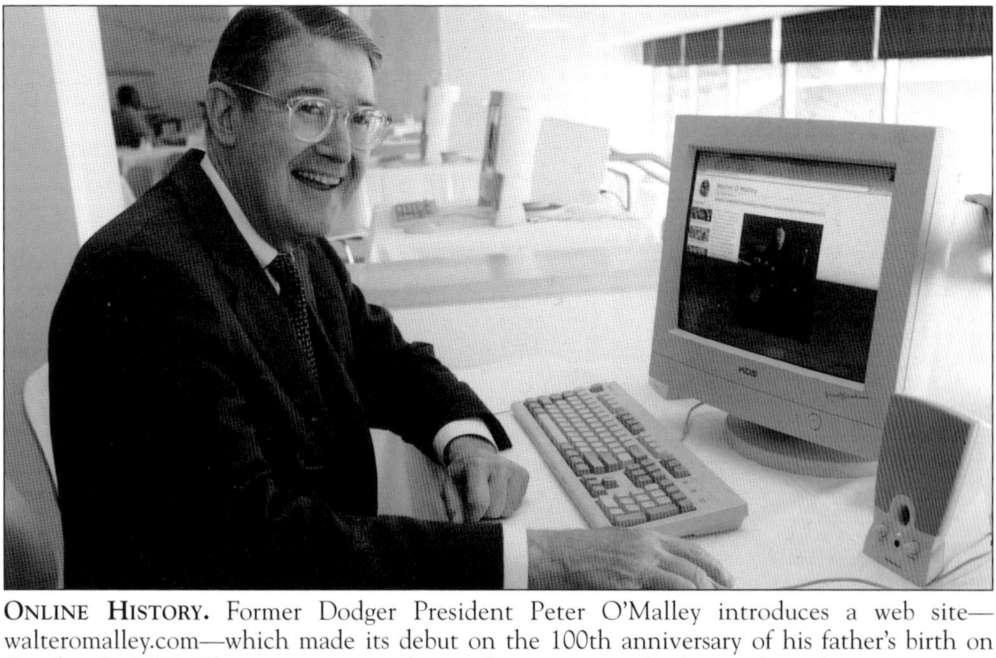

Online History. Former Dodger President Peter O'Malley introduces a web site—walteromalley.com—which made its debut on the 100th anniversary of his father's birth on October 9, 2003. The site contains photos, documents, and other multimedia pertaining to O'Malley's works and achievements. The launch party was held at the Stadium Club, where Walter O'Malley watched part of the first game in Dodger Stadium history on April 10, 1962.

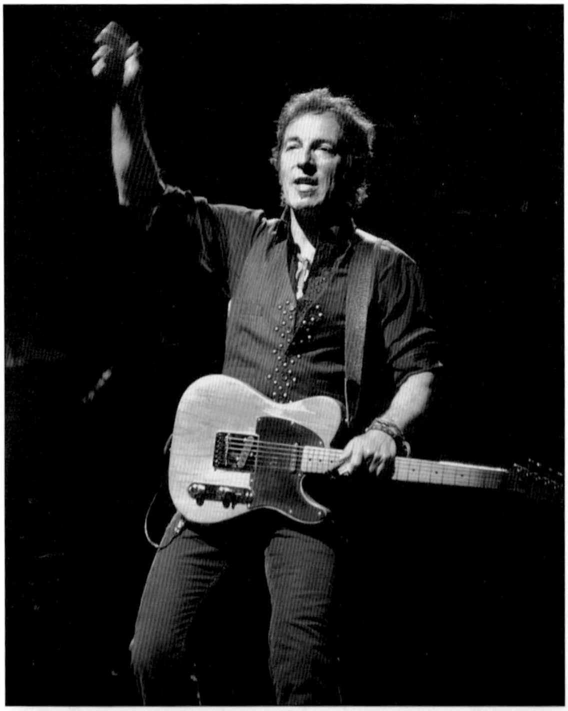

The Boss. When Bruce Springsteen performed at Dodger Stadium on August 17, 2003, the Dodgers played a day game at Chicago's Wrigley Field in which Ozzy Osbourne and his wife, Sharon, sang "Take Me Out to the Ballgame" during the seventh inning stretch. The Dodgers won the game and arrived back in Los Angeles with enough time for several players to drive to the stadium for the remainder of Springsteen's concert.

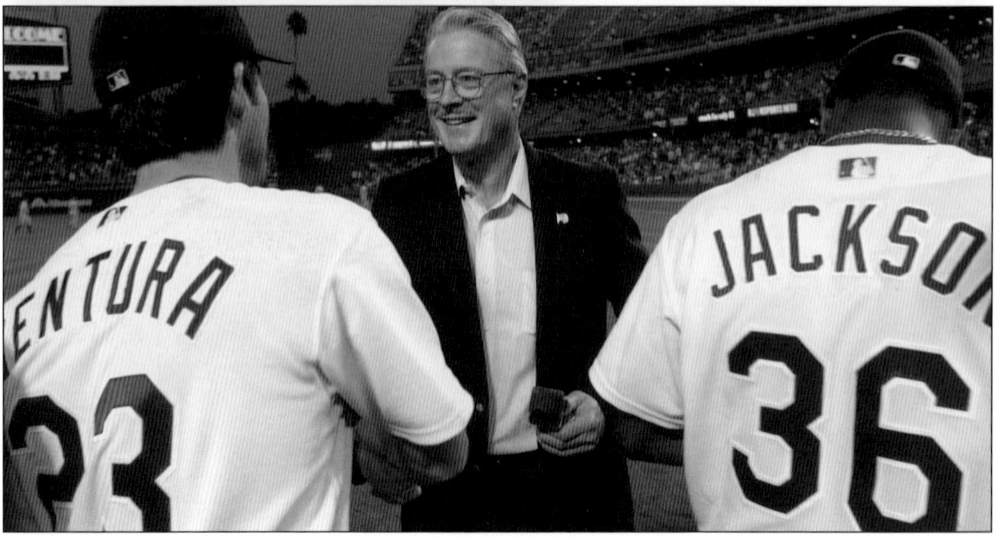

The Return. As a blue-chip minor league prospect, outfielder Roy Gleason was promoted to the Dodgers for the final month of their 1963 championship season. He appeared in eight games, seven as a pinch runner. In his only major league at-bat on September 28, Gleason stroked a pinch-hit double off Phillies' left-hander Dennis Bennett. Gleason returned to the minor leagues and later became the only player with major league experience to be drafted into Vietnam military service. On September 20, 2003, Gleason was invited to throw out the ceremonial first pitch before the Dodgers-Giants game. The Dodgers and Manager Jim Tracy then emerged from the dugout and presented Gleason with a 1963 championship ring. The soldier who received a Purple Heart, a Bronze Star, and 14 overall military honors took his place alongside the Dodgers for the national anthem.

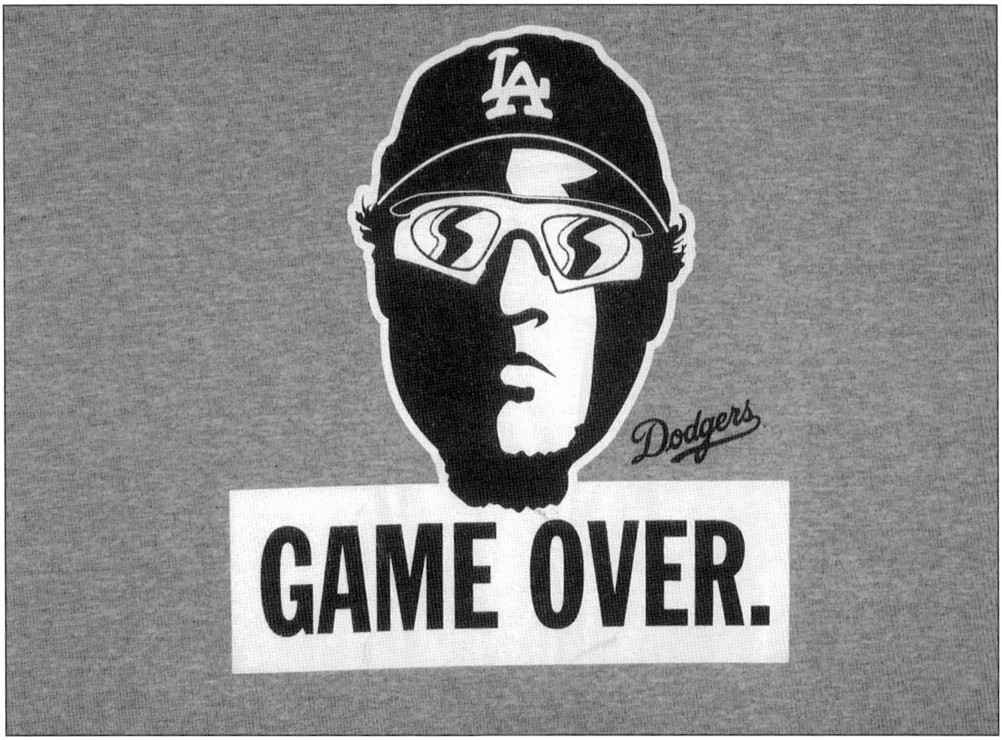

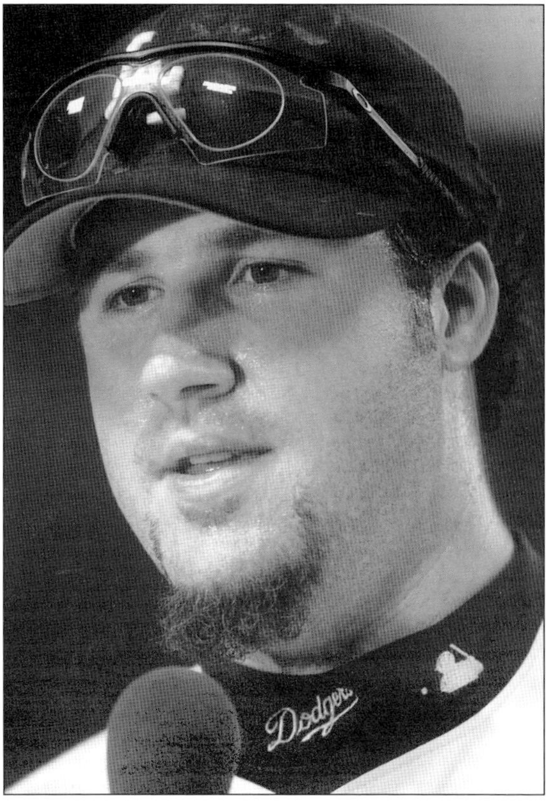

The Perfect Season. During Eric Gagne's overnight success as a closer in 2002, Ross Yoshida and Rob Basom of the Dodger Merchandise Department tinkered with the idea of producing Gagne T-shirts for the players in the clubhouse. Their "GAME OVER" logo with Gagne's goggles and goatee captured the spirit of Dodger Stadium's late-inning marquee star and eventually became a fashion staple in Southern California. After saving 52 games in 56 chances in 2002, Gagne was perfect in his encore. The Quebec native and former hockey player converted all 55 save opportunities in 2003 and extended his major league record to 63 consecutive saves. Gagne became the seventh Dodger to win the Cy Young Award, joining Don Newcombe (1956), Don Drysdale (1962), Sandy Koufax, (1963, 1965, 1966), Mike Marshall (1974), Fernando Valenzuela (1981), and Orel Hershiser (1988).

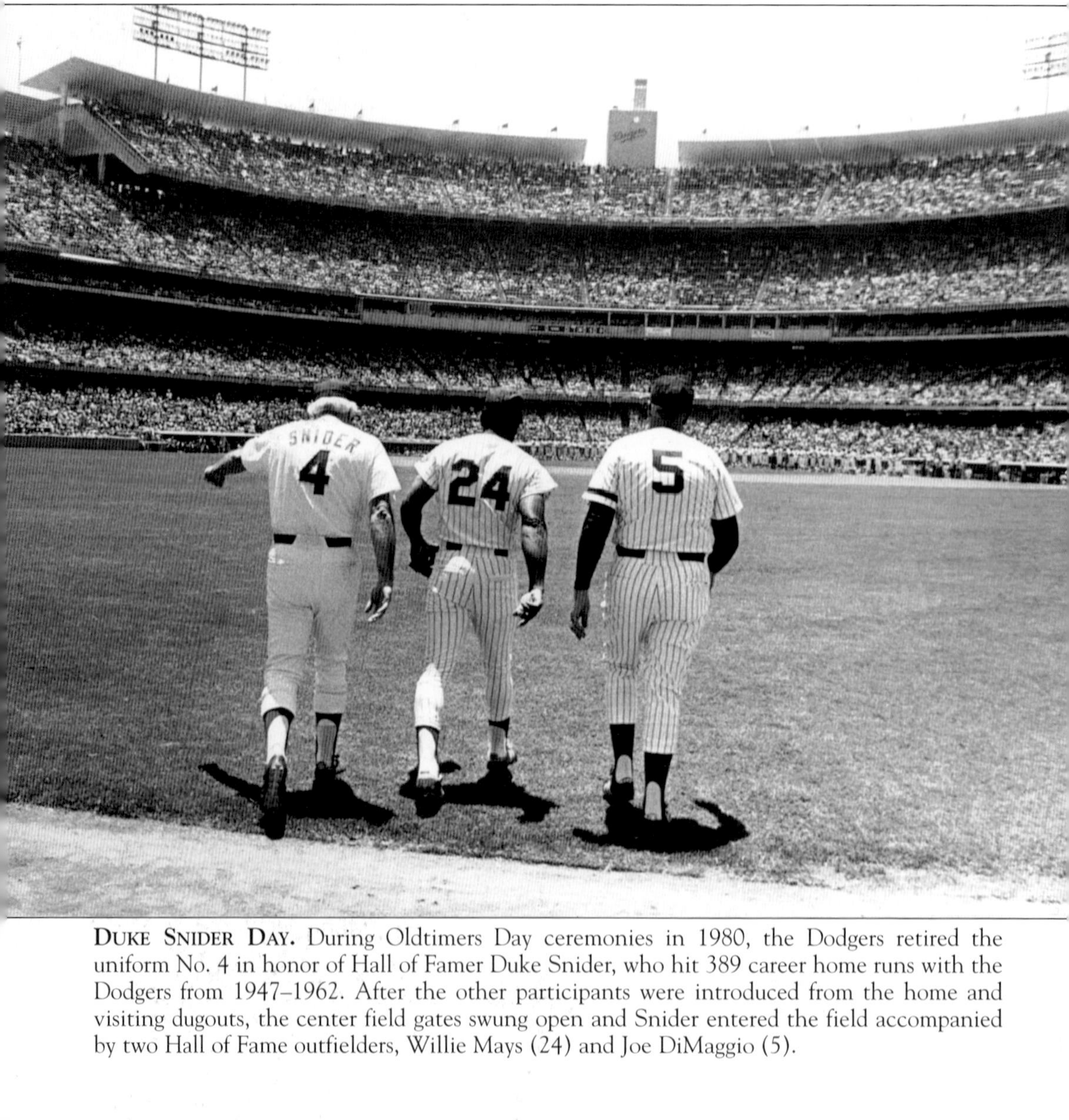

DUKE SNIDER DAY. During Oldtimers Day ceremonies in 1980, the Dodgers retired the uniform No. 4 in honor of Hall of Famer Duke Snider, who hit 389 career home runs with the Dodgers from 1947–1962. After the other participants were introduced from the home and visiting dugouts, the center field gates swung open and Snider entered the field accompanied by two Hall of Fame outfielders, Willie Mays (24) and Joe DiMaggio (5).